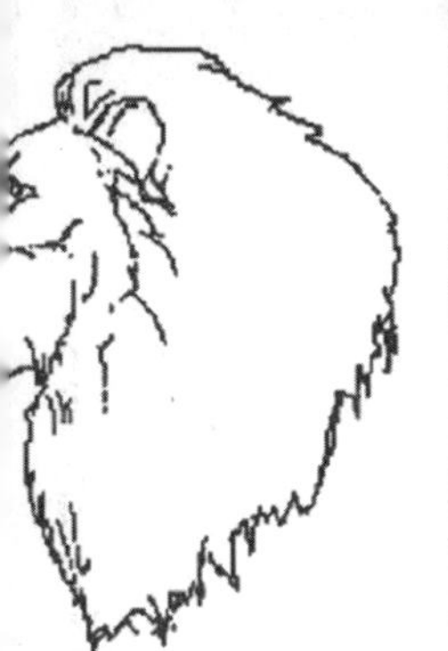

The Safari Club & Restaurant

Nafka Lounge

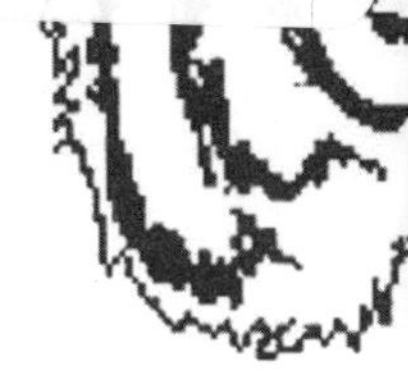

18 And Over - Night Shows
Free Parking Available In Rear
925 5th St., NW
(Between Massachusettes Ave. & K St., NW)
For Info Call 371-9275

WEDNESDAY July 12th
Ladies Happy Hour With
EXPRESS
MALE DANCERS
Complimentary Buffet
Starts At 5:00PM

ALL AGE SHOWS

Starts At 2:00 PM

SATURDAY
Hardcore/Punk

July 8th ....Crucial Youth/Screaming Weasels
Two-faced Judy
July 15th ..Instead/Wind Of Change/Admiral
July 22nd .American Standard/Solution
July 29th ..Insecticide

SUNDAY
Thrash/Speed Metal

July 9th ....Solitude/Skeleton/Medussa
July 16th ..Toxic Shock/Medussa/Oblivion
July 23rd ..Dead Issue Records Party
Undead/Images/Sticks & Stones/Dream Smas
July 30th ..Necrosus/Iron Christ/Lynx

JULY

July 4th ....Junkyard Band with special guest
July 5th ....Lucy Brown/Cadaver/Zen Parade
July 6th ....Saddle Tramp/Psycho Girls

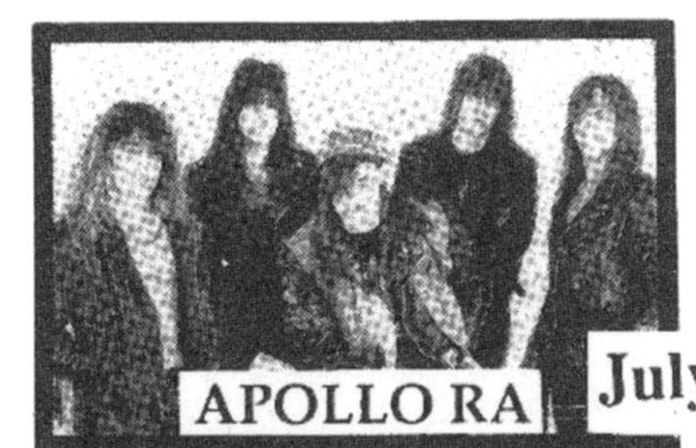

July 24th

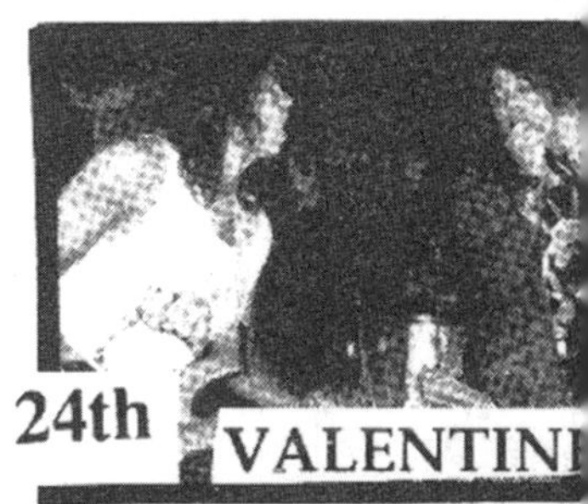

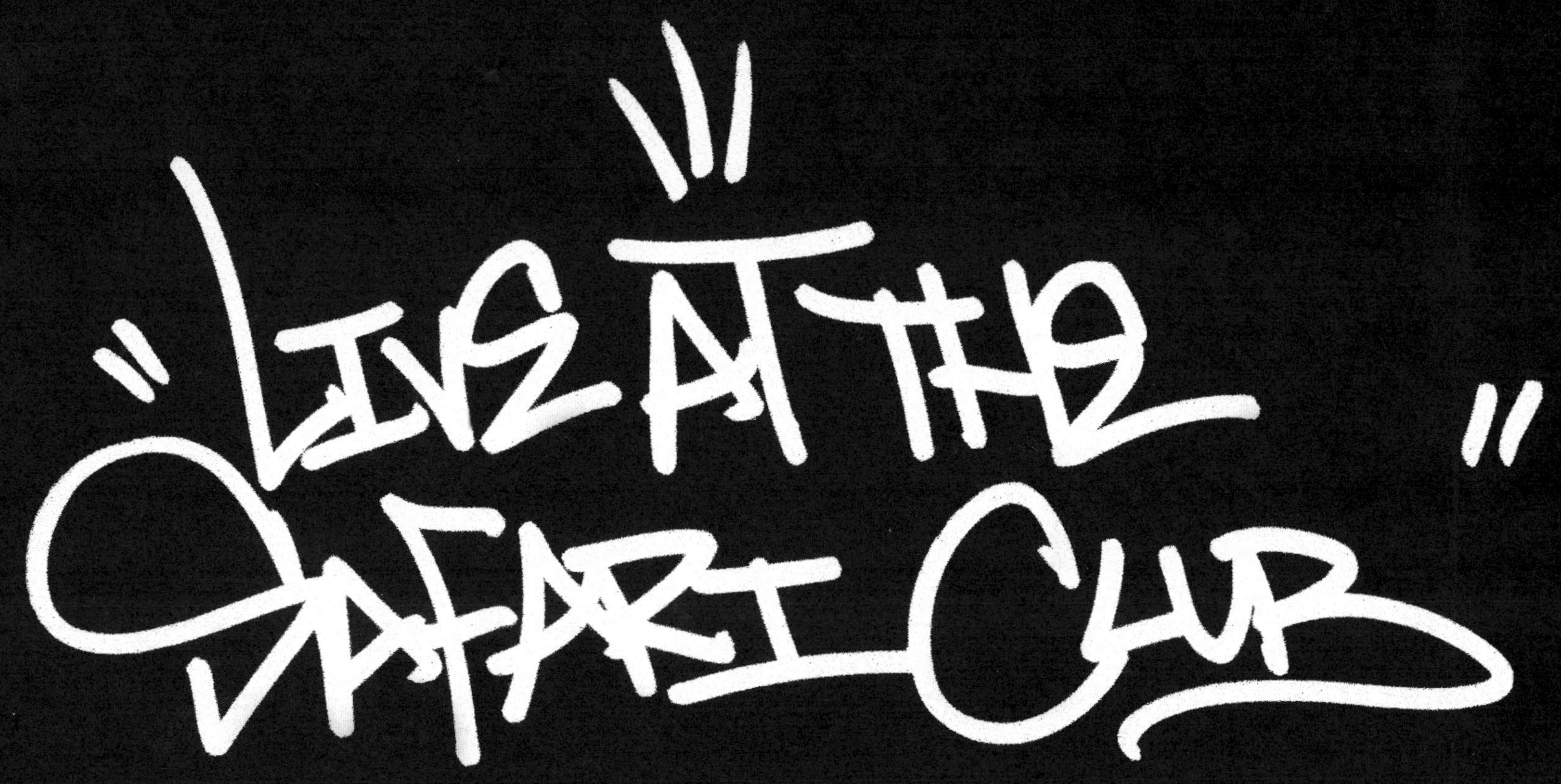

A History of harDCore Punk in the Nation's Capital: 1988–1998

SHAWNA KENNEY *with* **RICH DOLINGER**

foreword by A. C. Thompson

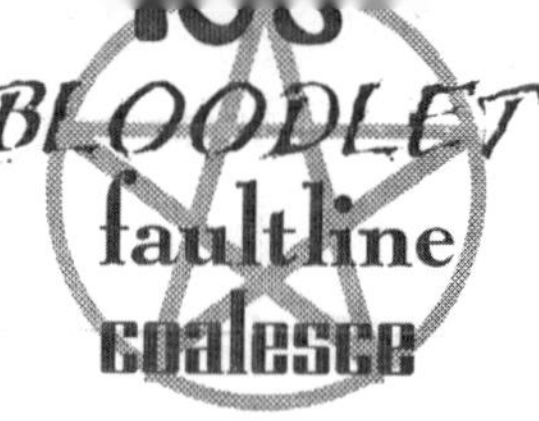

AT THE CHAMBER OF SOUND
925 5th st nw dc gallery pl metro
contact jon at 301-239-1685
martin at 202-393-5336
look for safe parking across from the club
Wednesday aug. 2nd @ 5pm..

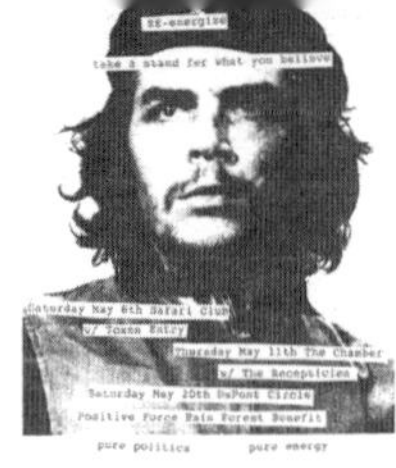

AGENT 86

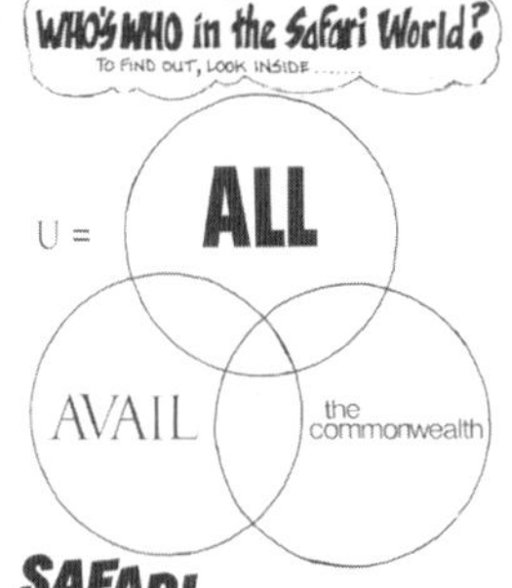

CLUB
28
ALTER NATIVES
BURMA JAM

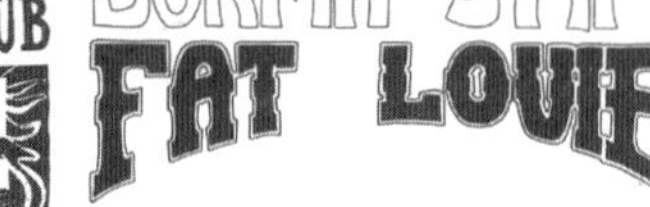

Immoral

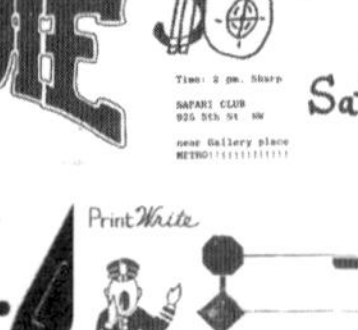

YEAH, BUDDY! IT'S:
ECONOCHRIST
WITH 3, COUNT 'EM, 3 BITCHIN' BANDS!!!
Transilience
the Pee-Tanks
&
YOUTH with HAIR
AT: the SAFARI CLUB 5th & K st. N.W.
JULY 23, 1990 (MONDAY)
6:00 p.m.
BRING $
NOTE NEW DATE

FLUX
OUTCROWD

HOWLIN' LIKE THE DOG THAT GUARDS HELL!
FUN JUNKIES
FRI OCT 28
ADMIT IT... YOU'RE FRIGHTENED
SAFARI CLUB

No Scene Zine Presents:
Pig band! Boom band!
Big band! Broom band!
My poor mouth can't
say that. No, sir.
My poor mouth is
much too slow, sir.
Well then . . .
bring your mouth this way.
I'll find it something
it can say.
at the Safari Club
MAY 27 at 2:00 PM
$6 dude!
GORILLA BISCUITS (FROM N.Y.C.)
with
OUTCROWD
and
Discipline

SAT. MAR. 4
no scene zine presents:
IMMORAL DISCIPLINE.
ABRA-CADAVERS
&
L.D. KIDS
$6
AT
THE SAFARI CLUB
925 5th ST. NW
(BETWEEN MASS. AVE. & K St.-- close to GALLERY PLACE METRO)
2 PM

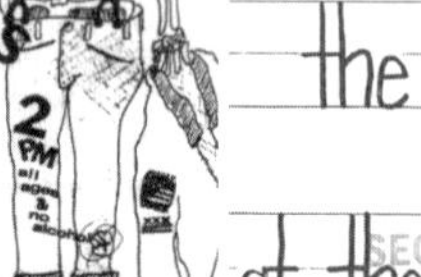

SCRA
and
the Pla
at the

KING FACE
(D.C.)
FOUNDATION
(Reston, VA)
STICKS and STONES
(New Jersey)

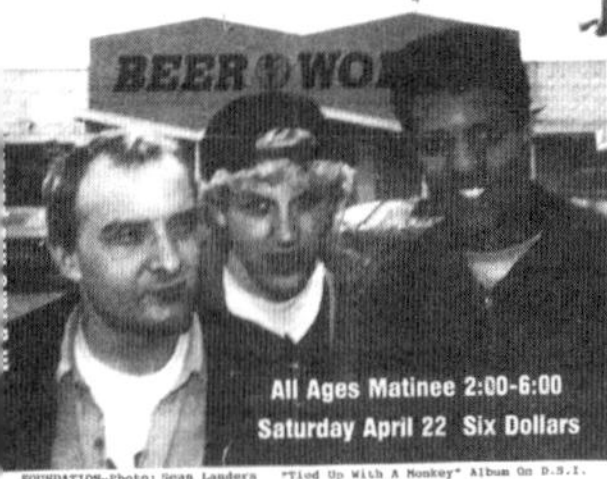

THE SAFARI CLUB

(D.C.)
FOUNDATION
(Reston, VA)
STICKS and STONES
(New Jersey)

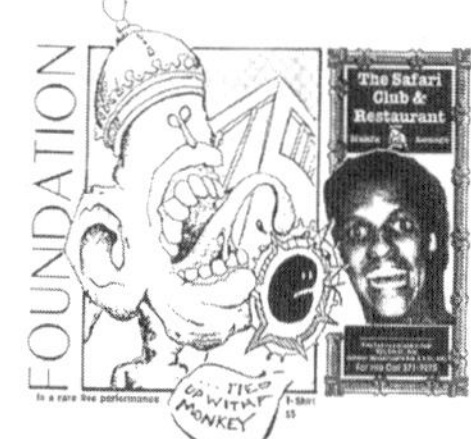

All Ages Matinee 2:00-6:00
Saturday April 22 Six Dollars

CLOCKWORK FANZINE PRESENTS:
THE MAJOR CONNECTION
IN YOUR FACE (NY)
RELEASE (NJ)
STOMP (ROCKVILLE, MD)
AVAIL (RESTON, VA)
LOVE SLUG (?)
SAFARI CLUB
WASHINGTON, D.C.
MAY 26, 1990
SATURDAY 1 PM
$5.00 925 5TH ST

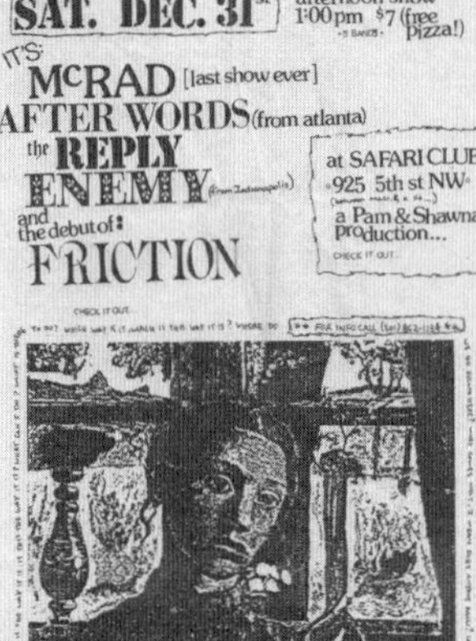

No Scene Zine Presents:

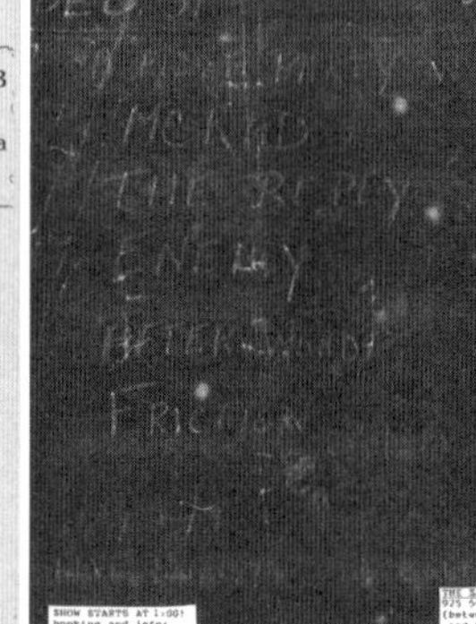

No Scene Zine Presents

REGGAE FEST
The Safari Club & Restaurant
Nakfa Lounge
Safari Club & Restaurant
Nakfa Lounge
presents
Wammie Nominees
MACABEE & ENGLISHMAN
Live in Concert with Special Guest
CIRCUS MIND
Friday, May 12, 1989
10:00 p.m.
The Safari Club & Restaurant
925 5th Street, N.W., Washington, D.C.
For directions/information, call the Club at 371-9275

SAFARI CLUB

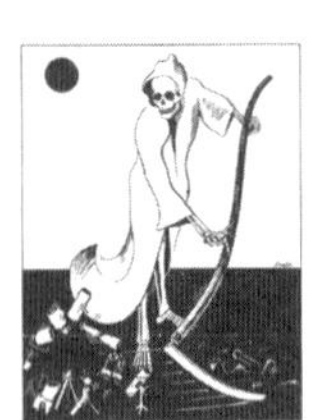

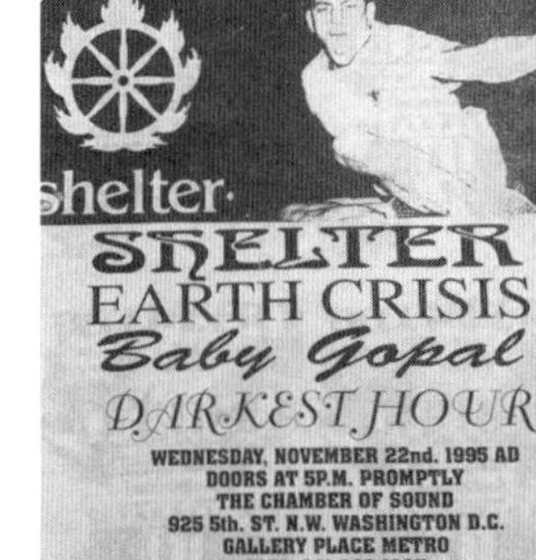

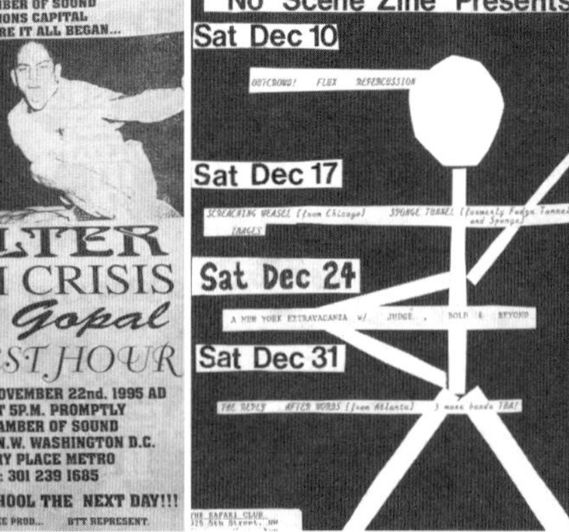

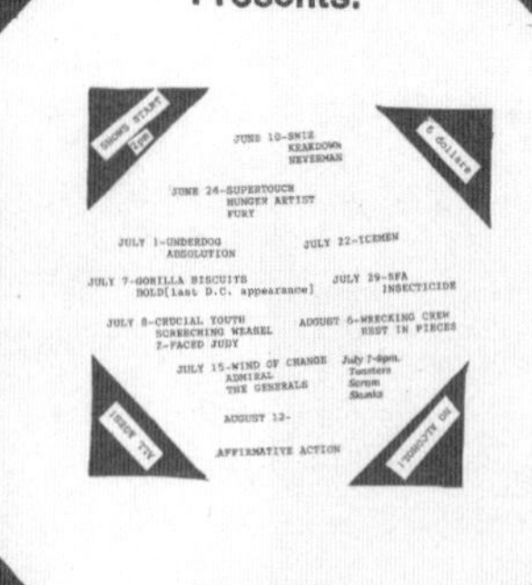

No Scene Zine Presents:
S H O W S

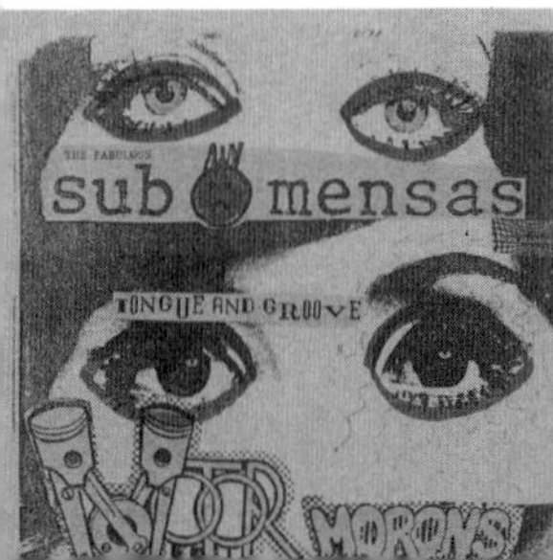

cornerstone productions present:

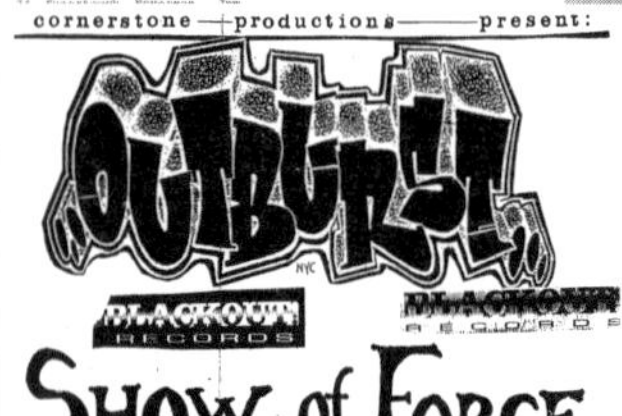

SHOW of FORCE
EDGEWISE

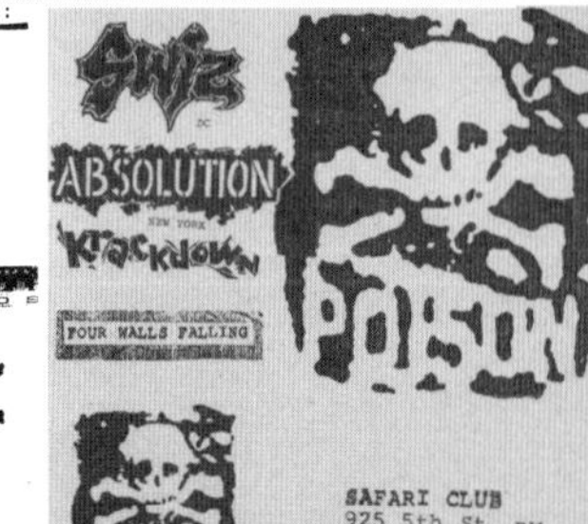

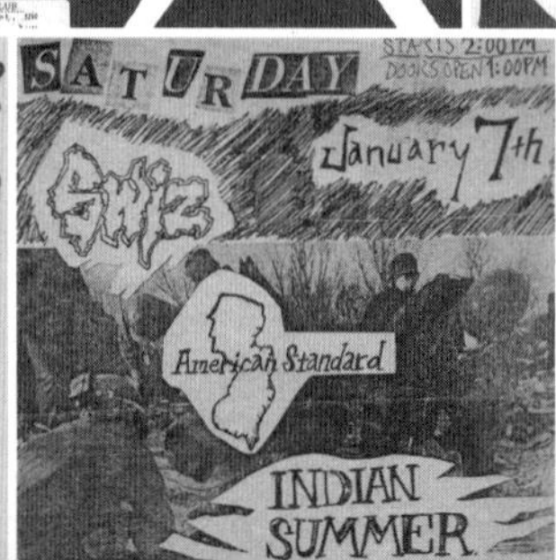

SWIZ

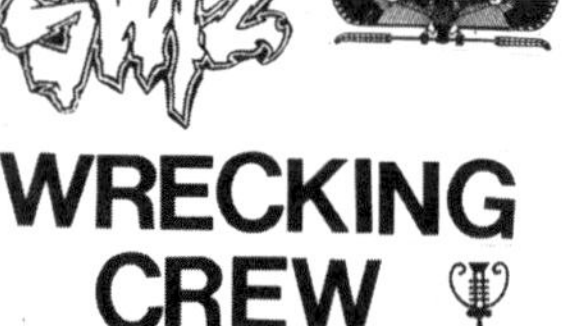

three o'clock
KRACK

WHAT WOULD YOU GIVE FOR

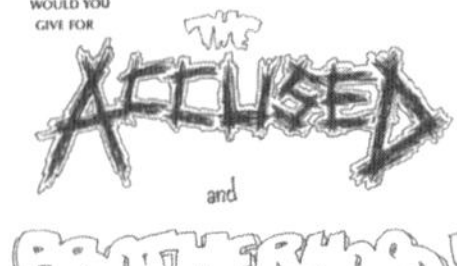

(from Seattle)
Tuesday
May 23rd
6 dollars?

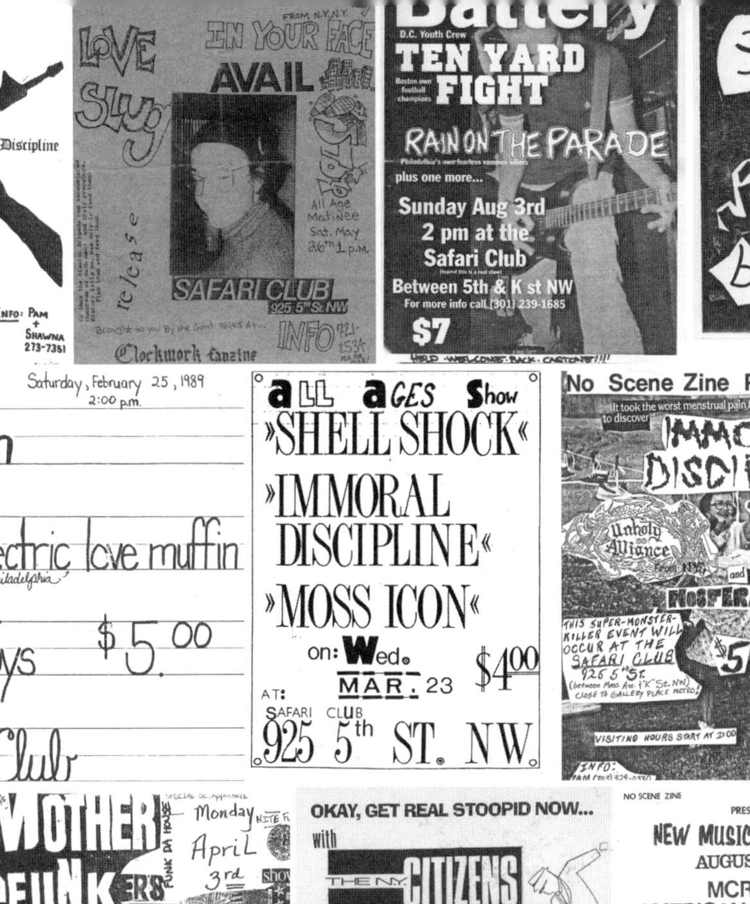
Discipline
Info: Pam + Shawna 273-7351
Love Slug
In Your Face
Avail
release
All Age Matinee
Safari Club
925 5th St NW
Clockwork fanzine
Battery
D.C. Youth Crew
Ten Yard Fight
Rain on the Parade
plus one more...
Sunday Aug 3rd
2 pm at the Safari Club
Between 5th & K st NW
For more info call (301) 239-1685
$7
Bold
Jan. 28
Judge
Beyond
$7
Born Against
Dunamis
Just Cause
Out of Bounds
8-Bark
Six bands for $6
Appearing at the Safari Club 925 5th St N.W. near Gallery Place Metro doors open at 1:00 pm
August 12th
Saturday, February 25, 1989
2:00 p.m.
Electric love muffin
Philadelphia
$5.00
Club
All Ages Show
»Shell Shock«
»Immoral Discipline«
»Moss Icon«
on: Wed. Mar. 23
$4.00
At: Safari Club
925 5th St. NW
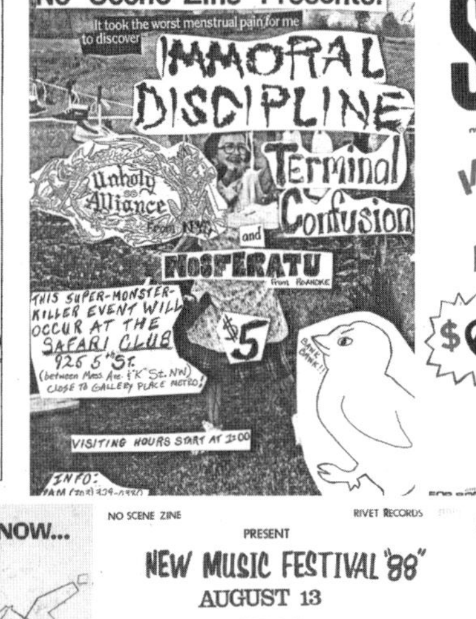
No Scene Zine Presents:
Immoral Discipline
Terminal Confusion
Unholy Alliance
Nosferatu
$5
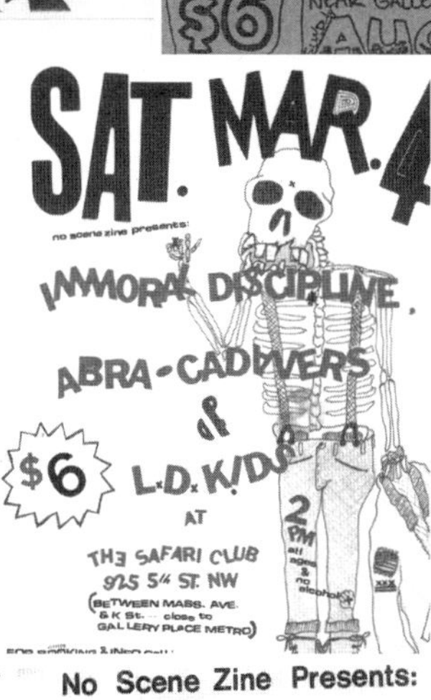
Sat. Mar. 4
Immoral Discipline
Abra-Cadavers
&
L.D.K/D
$6
At The Safari Club
925 5th St. NW
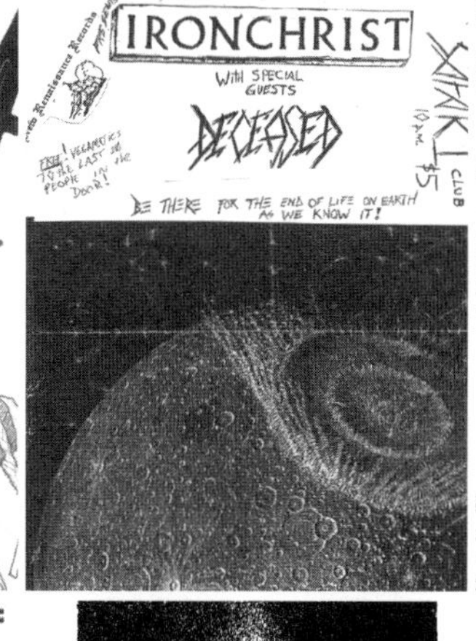
Ironchrist
Deceased

Crucial Youth
6 buckaroos.
Saturday July 8th
Screeching Weasel
at the Safari Club
2-Faced Judy

King Fac
-and-
Outcrowd!
Tuesday 29
1987
Back Alley Cafe
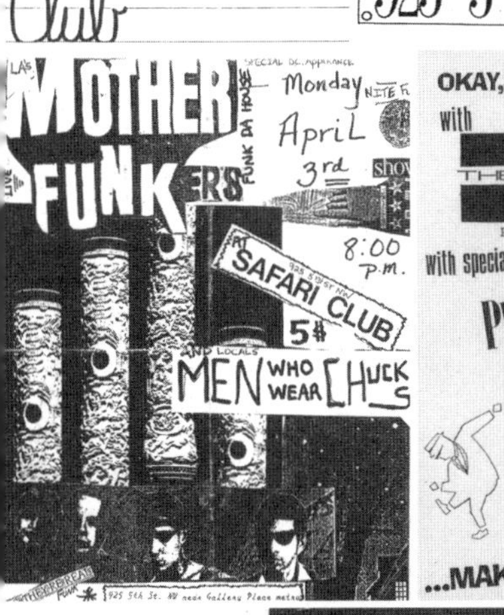
Mother Funkers
Monday April 3rd
8:00 p.m.
Safari Club
5th
Men Who Wear Chucks
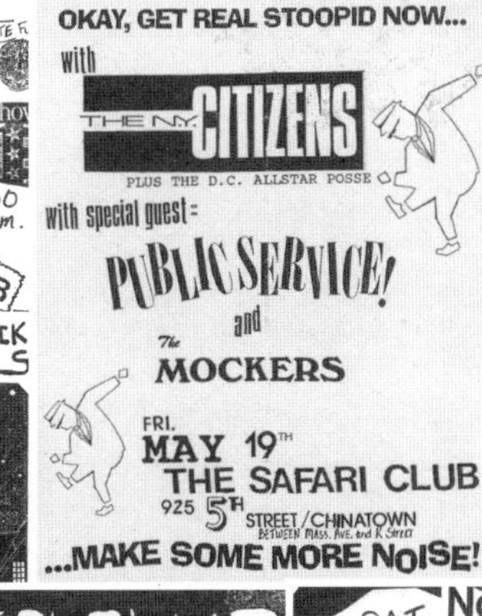
Okay, get real stoopid now...
with The N.Y. Citizens
plus the D.C. Allstar Posse
with special guest:
Public Service!
and
The Mockers
Fri. May 19th
The Safari Club
925 5th Street/Chinatown
...Make some more noise!

New Music Festival '88
August 13
MCRAD
American Standard
Outcrowd
Electric Love Muffin
Trained Attack Dogs
Images
Moss Icon
The Criminally Insane
Burndoggers
Great Mills Ampitheater
Lexington Park, MD
2-12
$5
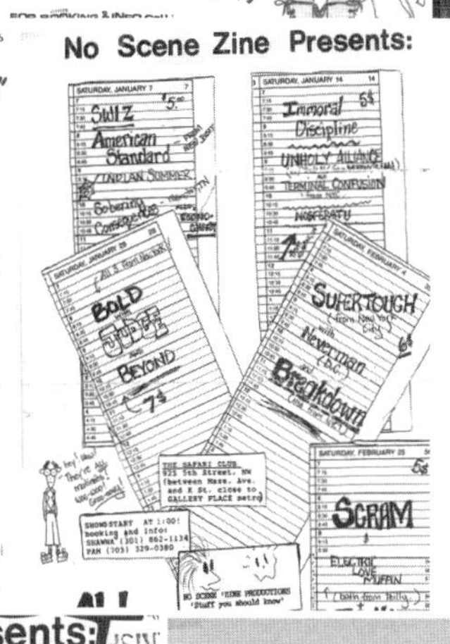
No Scene Zine Presents:
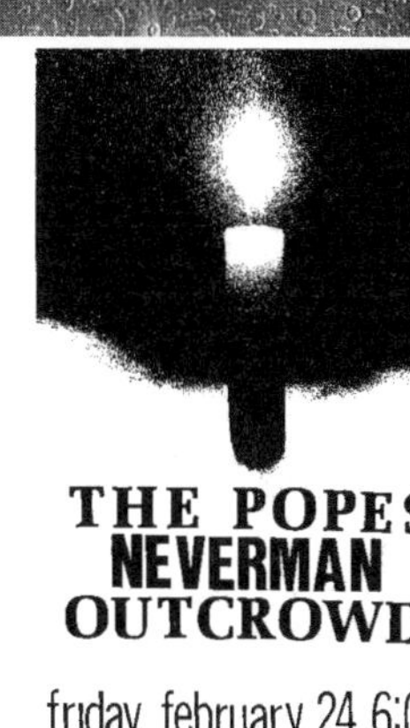
The Popes
Neverman
Outcrowd
friday. february 24. 6:00.
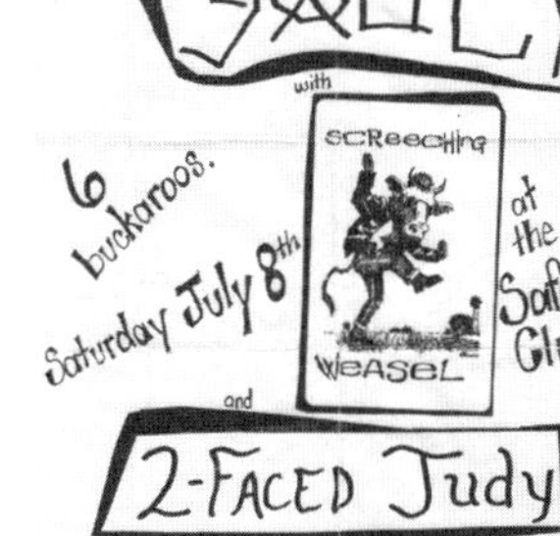
Crucial Youth
6 buckaroos.
Saturday July 8th
at the Safari Club
2-Faced Judy
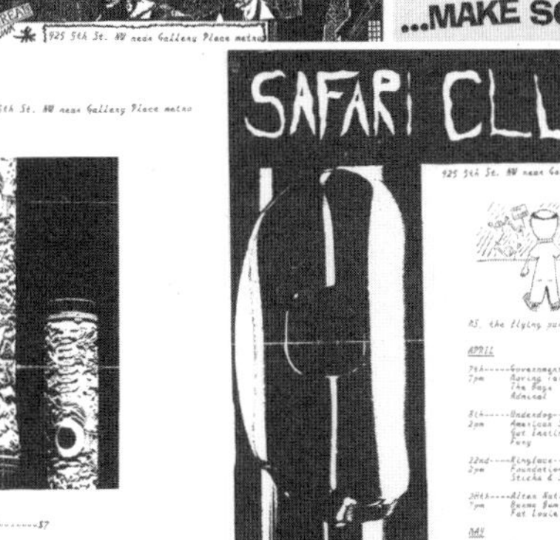
Safari Club
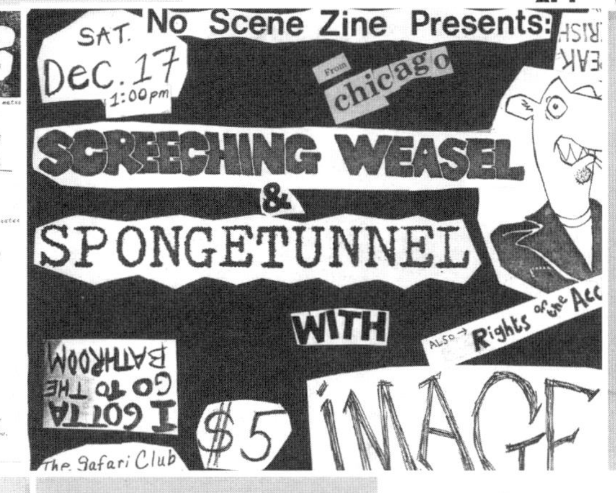
No Scene Zine Presents:
Sat. Dec. 17
1:00 pm
From chicago
Screeching Weasel
&
Spongetunnel
with
Images
$5
The Safari Club
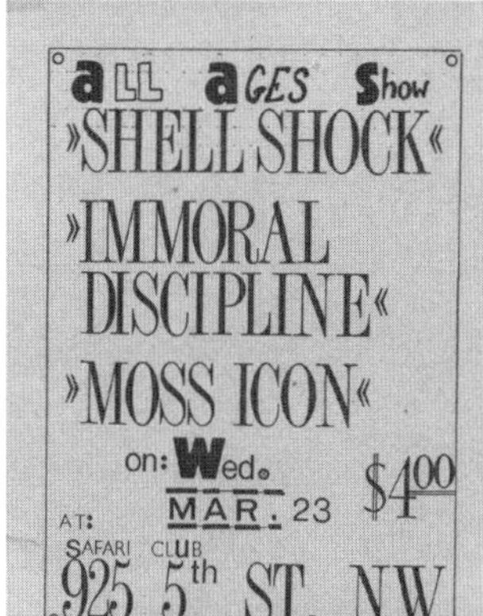
All Ages Show
»Shell Shock«
»Immoral Discipline«
»Moss Icon«
on: Wed. Mar. 23
$4.00
At: Safari Club
925 5th St. NW
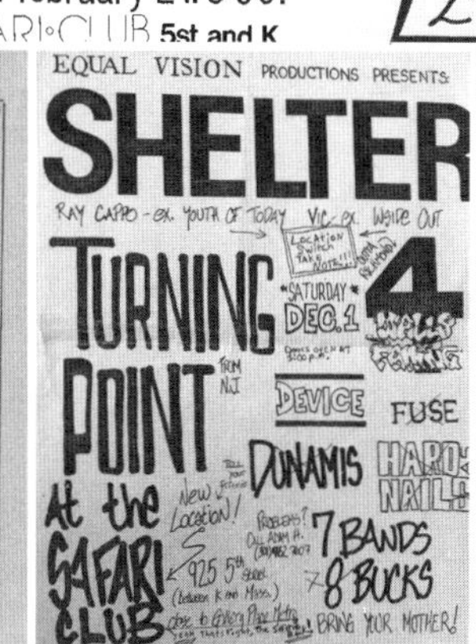
Equal Vision Productions presents:
Shelter
Turning Point
4
Dunamis
Device
Fuse
At the Safari Club
7 Bands 8 Bucks
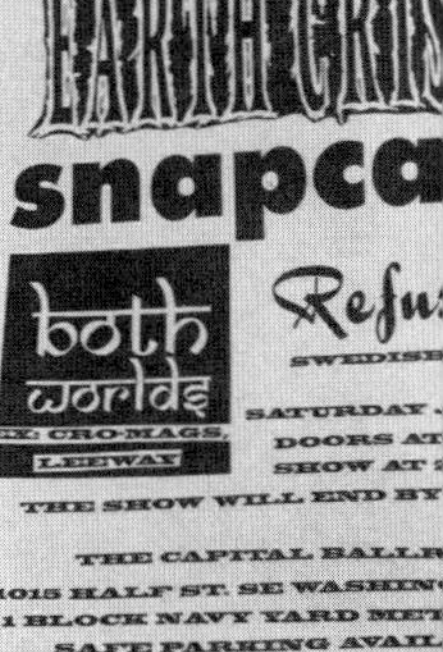
Earth Crisis
snapcase
both worlds
The Capital Ballroom
$7.00 Dollars
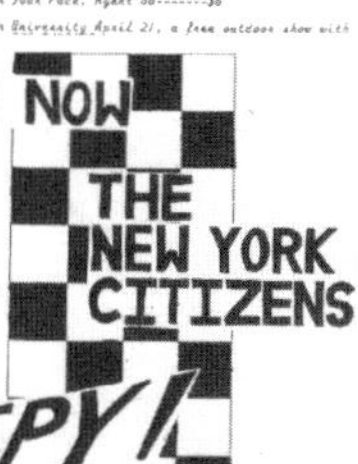
The New York Citizens
The Townsmen
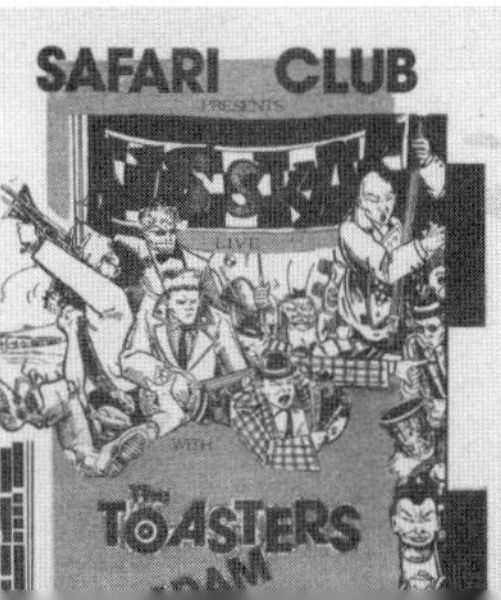
Safari Club
The Toasters
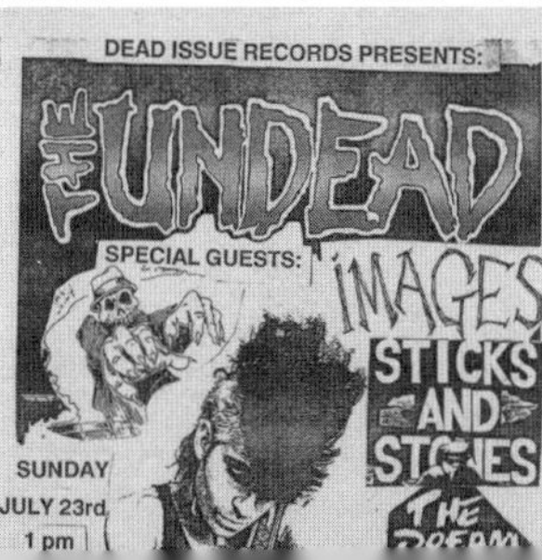
Dead Issue Records presents:
The Undead
Special Guests:
Images
Sticks and Stones
Sunday
July 23rd
1 pm
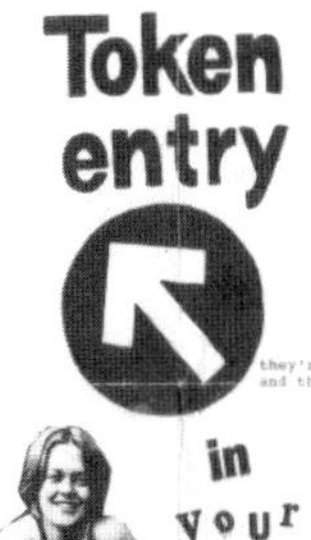
Token entry
in your
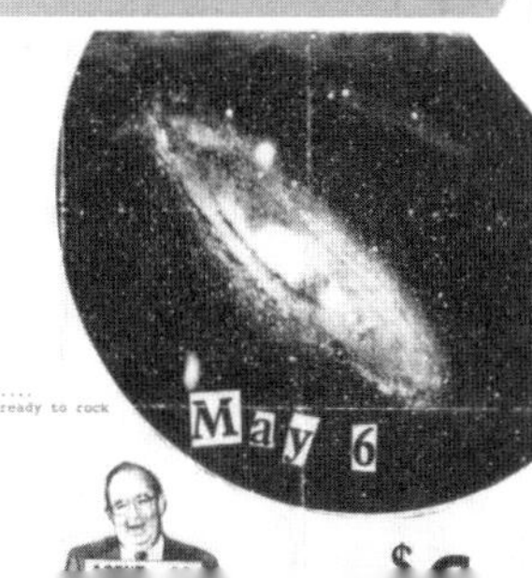
May 6
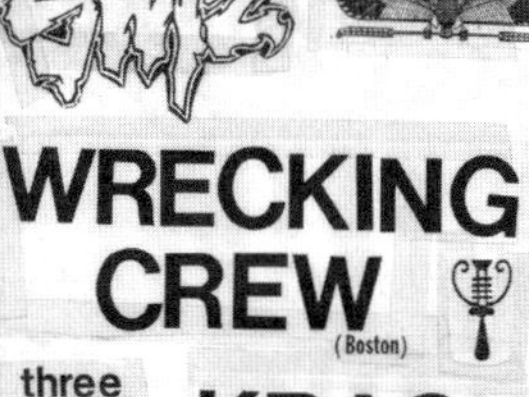
Swiz
Wrecking Crew
(Boston)
three o'clock
Krack
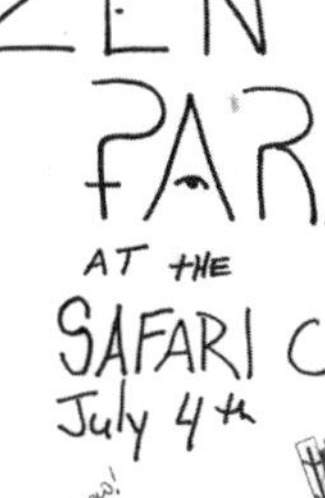
Zen
At the Safari
July 4th

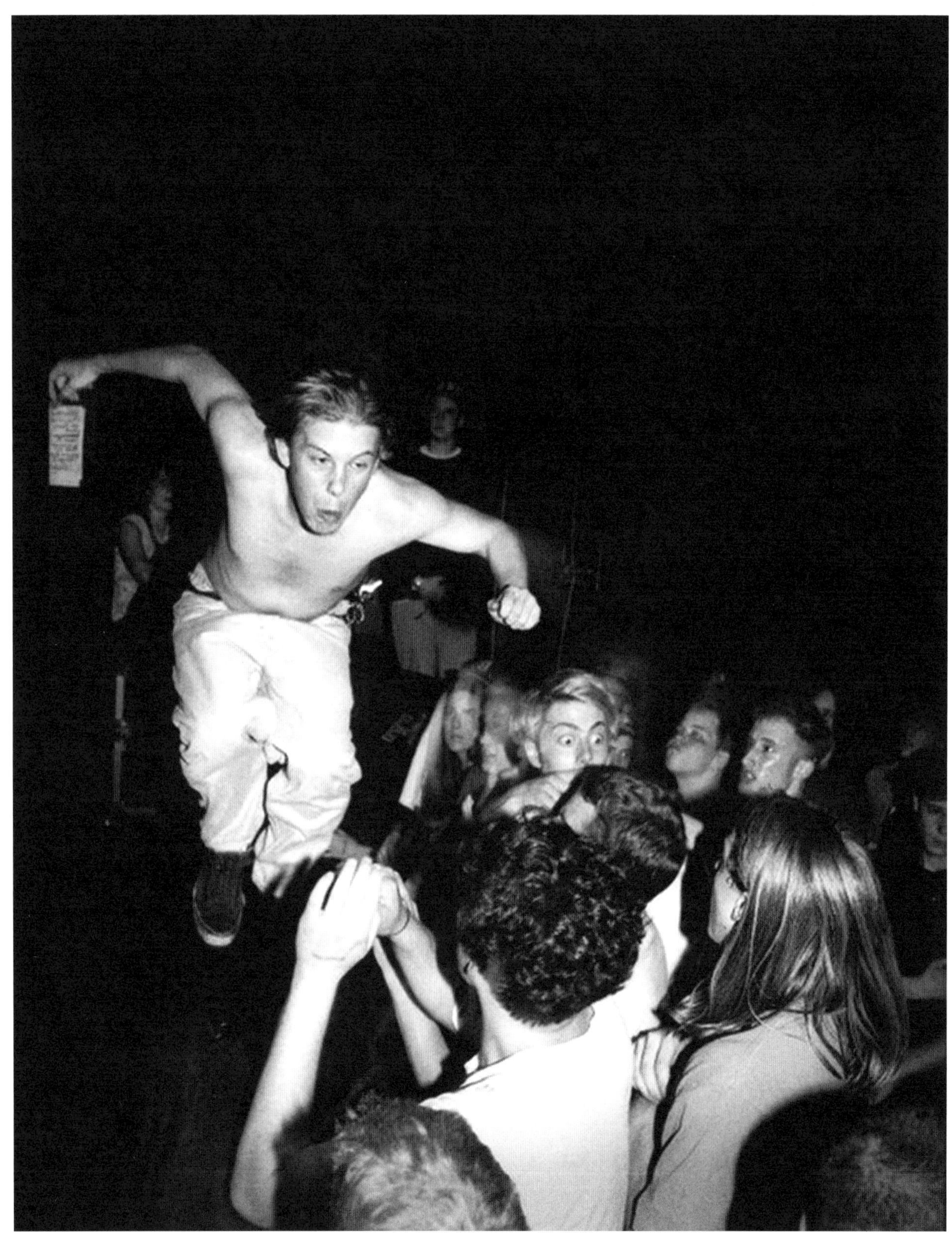

Rob Swartz, ready to stage dive. Photo by John Galbraith.

Foreword

So:

There was a time, back in the second half of the twentieth century, when capital fled American cities, nesting instead in bland suburban office parks and gated clusters of identical mini-mansions. The urban centers began a long slide into disrepair and decrepitude. City governments atrophied. Weeds sprang up from fissured sidewalks and crater-pocked streets. Buildings emptied. Some remained vacant, ghostly. Some collapsed into ruin.

Many landlords found new tenants with far less money to move in. Such was the story of the Safari Club.

Music, art, dance, sex, radical politics, and uncategorized weirdness flourished in these spaces. This was a sort of feral culture, promoted by word of mouth and xeroxed flyers taped to walls or wheat-pasted on light poles.

It was outlaw culture. Municipal codes of all varieties were often disregarded. If the cops or the city inspectors showed up, it was a bad fucking sign.

These places were absolutely vital to those of us drawn to the margins, who felt alienated by the dominant forces at work in American society. At the Safari Club, and all the other places of its ilk, we found art and music and words and people we understood. Many of us shuffled through life feeling pretty much dead inside; at the Safari Club we felt absolutely and truly alive.

There was no Internet back then. Well, actually there was, but it was only being used by a very select group of super-nerds. We were outcasts and underdogs seeking human connection and that meant moving our bodies to a physical location where members of our tribe congregated. We weren't tethered to minicomputers/phones that allowed us to blab and text incessantly. If we wanted to talk to our coconspirators we generally had to find them in the flesh. For us, life occurred in the material world with all of its three-dimensional complexities, not the phony digital sphere.

Not everything that occurred at places like the Safari Club was lovely. There were brawls and sometimes worse. Some underground nightclubs became marketplaces for hard, shitty drugs, though I really don't remember that being the case at the Safari Club.

Today, many years later, I sort of appreciate the grimy stuff from that time period. Yeah, it was fucking crazy at times. But that chaos could be invigorating. There was a sense that anything could happen at any second and you had to be prepared for it. It was unscripted. In short, it felt very very different from this moment.

During the past two decades, money has flooded back into cities like DC. Prosperity has returned, bringing with it the death of many hallowed underground cultural institutions. The spaces that once hosted fringe happenings have been transformed into posh businesses catering to well-paid keyboard jockeys and monoculture chain stores aimed at everyone else.

I have lived for many years in California. When I return to DC now, I'm gripped by a sense of vertigo. I feel wobbly. I have trouble finding my way around because most of the landmarks I used to navigate through the city during the eighties and early nineties, the Safari Club days, are gone. Much of the town has been rendered utterly unrecognizable by the influx of capital. Honestly, I pretty much hate it.

It's the same story in many other places.

Still, I have no doubt that alienated young people will continue to seek one another out. They will develop new subcultures on top of the bones of the subcultures that came before. They will continue to give the finger to the mainstream.

Right on.

—Adam "A. C." Thompson

December 2016

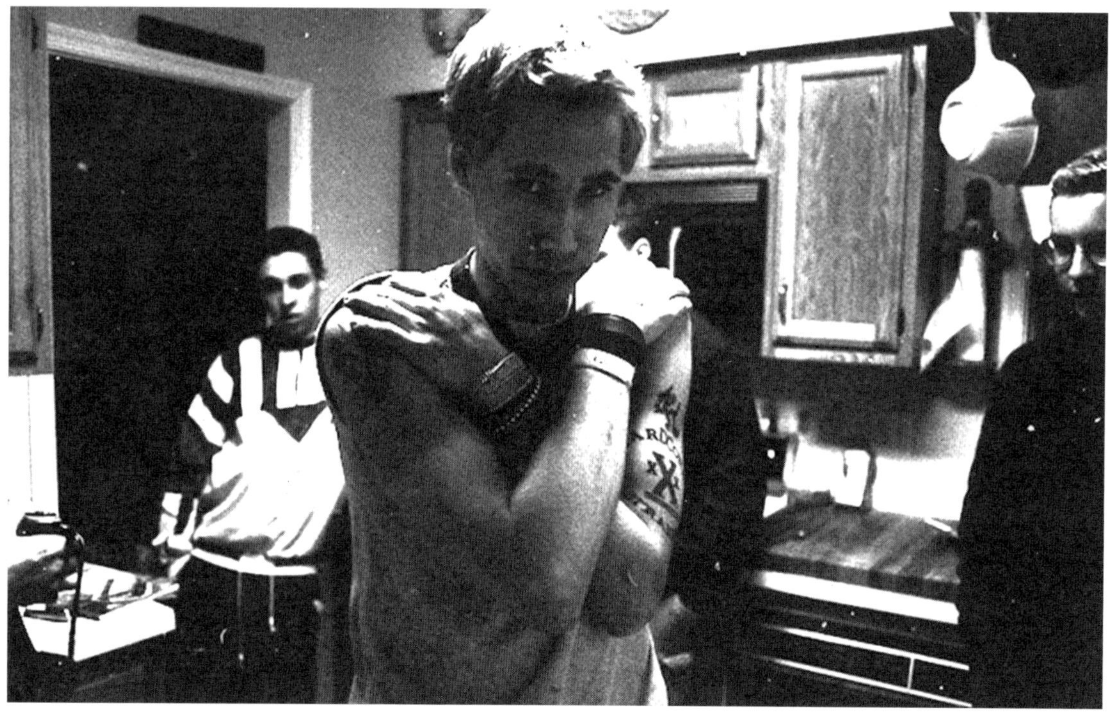

A. C. Thompson, 1988. Photo by Joe Wongananda.

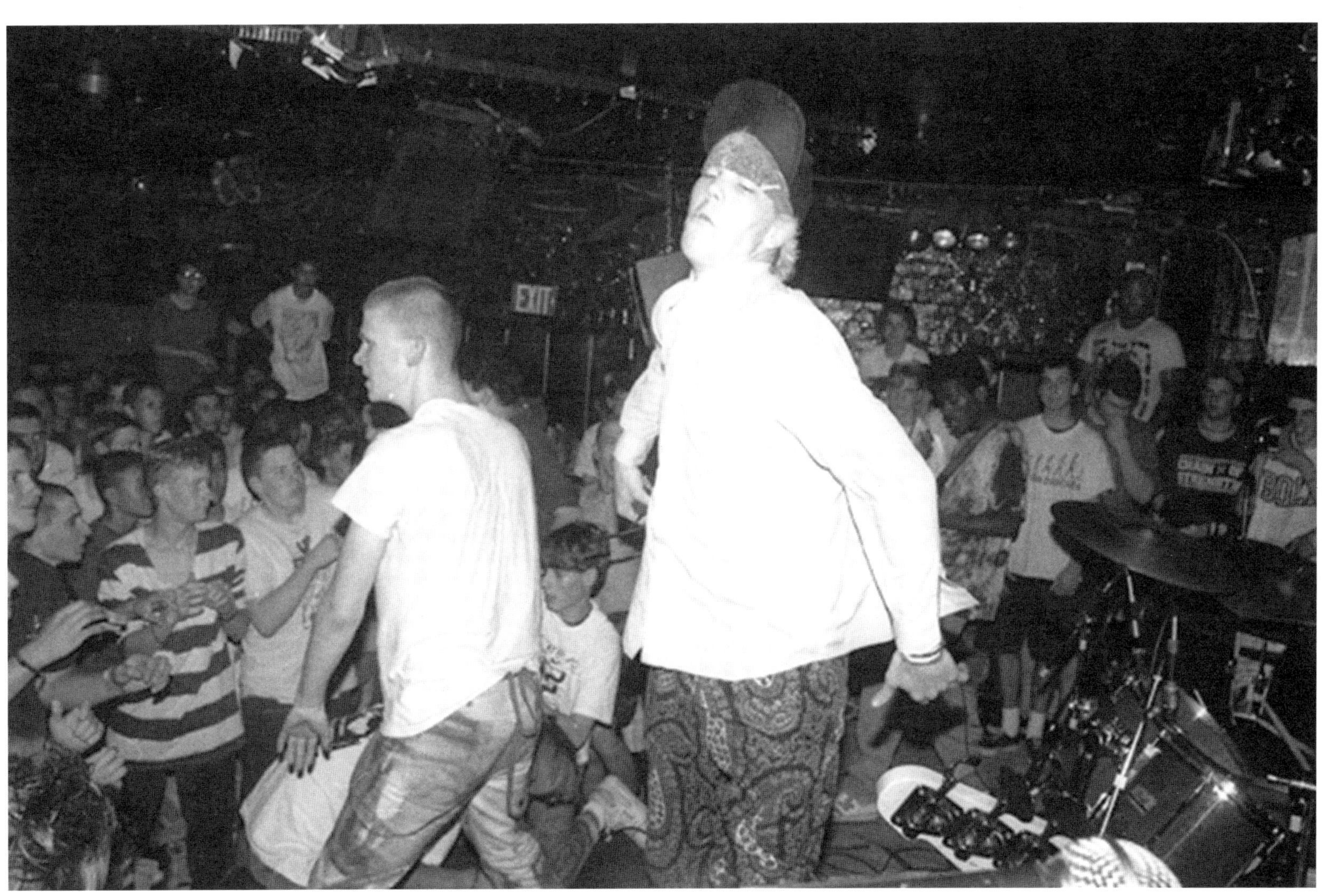

Token Entry, 1989. Photo by Joe Wongananda.

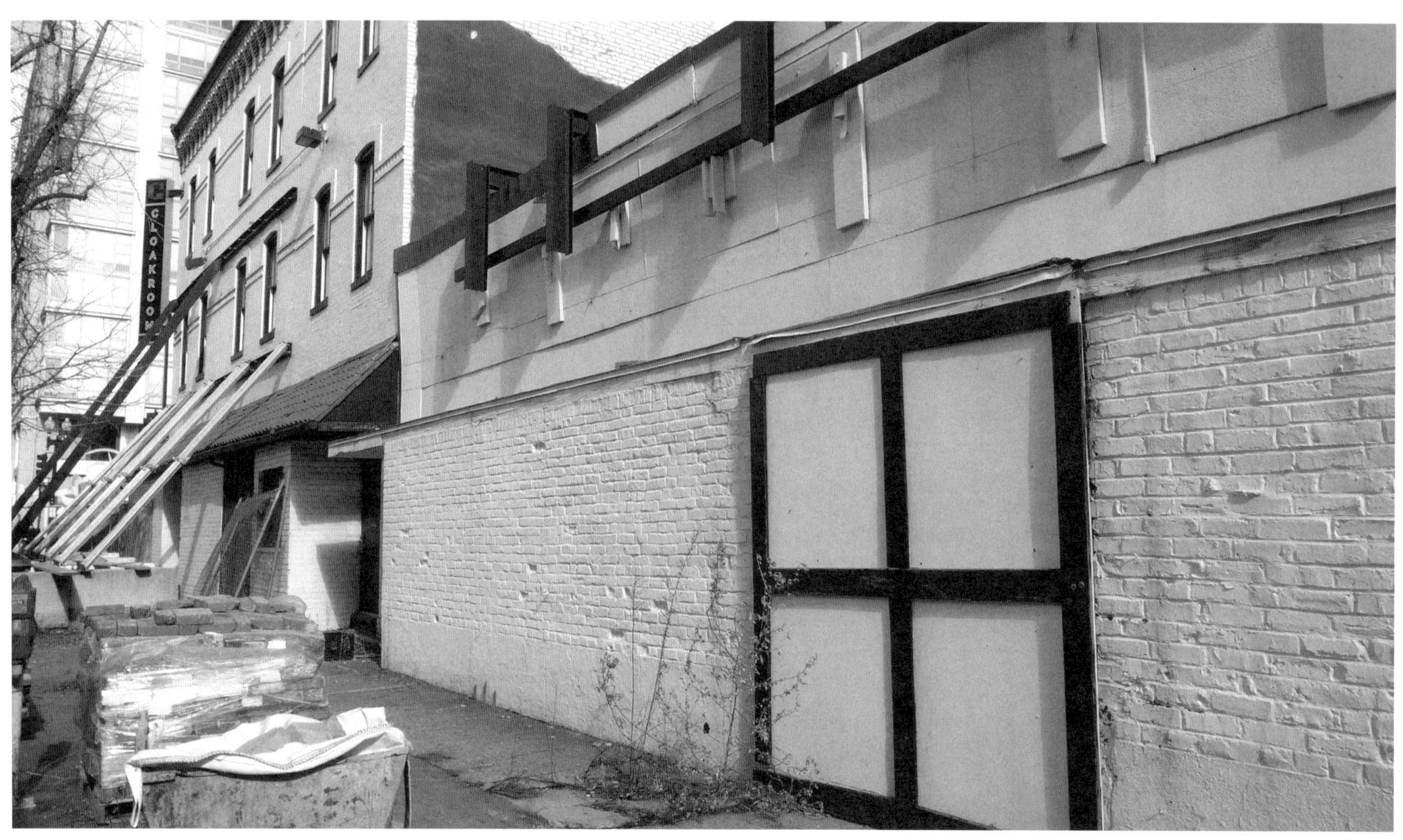

Safari Club building (925 Fifth St., NW) under construction, 2016. Photo by Eric Hochberg.

LIVE AT THE SAFARI CLUB: An Oral History of harDCore, 1988–1998

Introduction

We'll be the first to say there was nothing special about the building. It was basically four walls painted black. It was the scene swirling around inside, the people who played and experienced music there, that brought it to life.

A building is just a body, a structure made to hold whatever its inhabitants can imagine. Washington, DC is full of well-known marble buildings—school field trip destinations, monuments to heroes, and memorials of history. Beyond the manicured lawns and massive white monuments, behind the Capital building and well below the international spotlight, lies the "real DC." Its local inhabitants put the city on the punk rock map with the birth of Dischord Records in 1980. The fiercely independent label that began as a vehicle for Minor Threat became the home of many more influential punk and hardcore bands, launching a scene that spawned the likes of the Bad Brains, Henry Rollins, Dave Grohl, Dag Nasty, the Meatmen, and Bikini Kill, just to name a few.

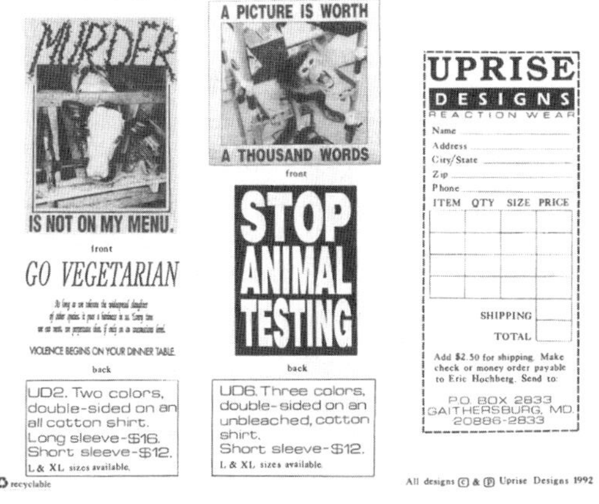

Eighties-era ephemera from the collection of Eric Hochberg.

The early days of DC's music scene have been well-documented, with most stories ending in the mid-eighties, depending on what book you read or which documentary you watch. Our question is this: if punk died in '85, what the hell was it that we were doing? Plenty happened after Washington, DC's Revolution Summer. When the first generation of punks started making different music, a second and third wave of youth culture rose up, putting on their own shows, forming bands, record labels, and lifelong connections. This is that story, told by the people who lived it.

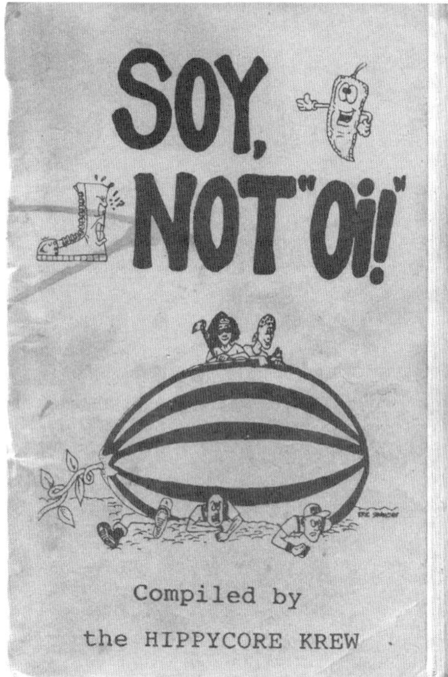

The building we know as the Safari Club wasn't much to look at—a square, one-story windowless joint, where bands loaded in through an upward-rolling metal grate in the front. The inside was solid black with a low wooden stage in front of a square wooden dance floor, complete with a disco ball hanging from the ceiling. Two bars sat in the back, a full professional kitchen beyond a set of swinging doors (they served Ethiopian food there on weekdays), and two semifunctional bathrooms. The most notable thing about the club's appearance was the presence of five or so life-size African animals scattered throughout the space. The stuffed (not taxidermied) zebra, gorilla, giraffe, etc., obviously part of the safari motif, had definitely seen better days. A tattered leopard-skin print served as a backdrop to the stage. On weeknights, the place was as hopping as an Eritrean dance club. Random promoters occasionally booked rock or metal acts there. Weekend nights were reserved for go-go groups (DC's indigenous pre–hip-hop funk), with Junkyard Band being the house band in the late eighties. But the sound system was decent and the owners had no clue about punk rock or hardcore, so it seemed the perfect place to put on a show.

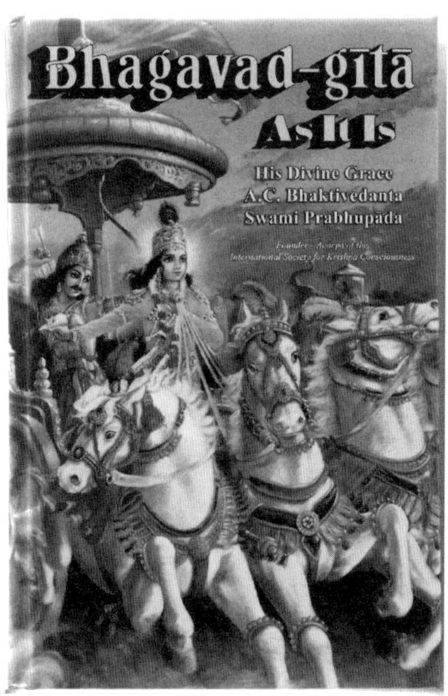

Way before it became a musical melting pot, the structure (which stretched from 925 to 929 Fifth Street, NW) served as a corned beef distributor. It was built in 1947 by Directors Distributing as one of four commercial buildings designed for meat sales and distribution in the Mount Vernon market

Cookbook and journal from the collection of Rich Dolinger.

district. A light imprint reading *Director's Corned Beef* can be seen on the front to this day. Records show neighbors 917–919 Fifth Street as the site of the first animal rights protest in DC and the second in PETA's history. PETA founder Ingrid Newkirk recalls discovering the appalling conditions of the store's chickens while inspecting as chief of Zoonotic Disease Control for the DC Department of Public Health. In her off hours, she'd formed PETA and arranged for her new organization to hold a protest outside the place. This was 1980. "That was such news that the next day everyone read it in the *Post*, it was on all the radio stations, no one could believe anyone would stick up for chickens," she said. "I was on the elevator in the District Building and people were talking about it."

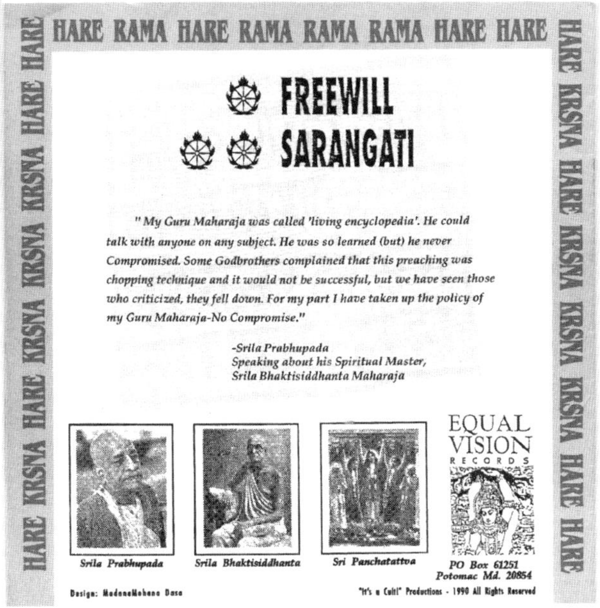

By the late eighties, DC was dubbed the "murder capital of the world," University of Maryland basketball star Len Bias died of a cocaine-related overdose, and DC Mayor Marion Barry had been caught on tape smoking crack with a prostitute. The Chinatown neighborhood where the Safari Club stood housed many homeless people, crack dealers, prostitutes, boarded-up row houses, and a few grimy bars. Still, teenagers gathered here every Sunday afternoon to youth-crew, stage-dive, fight, sing, and sweat together, week after week, for nearly ten years. Krishnacore and PETA brought an interest in vegetarianism to the scene, so many of Safari Club's bands were voicing concern for animal and human rights in a building that once made corned beef, right next to an old chicken market, deep in the hidden corners of our nation's capital.

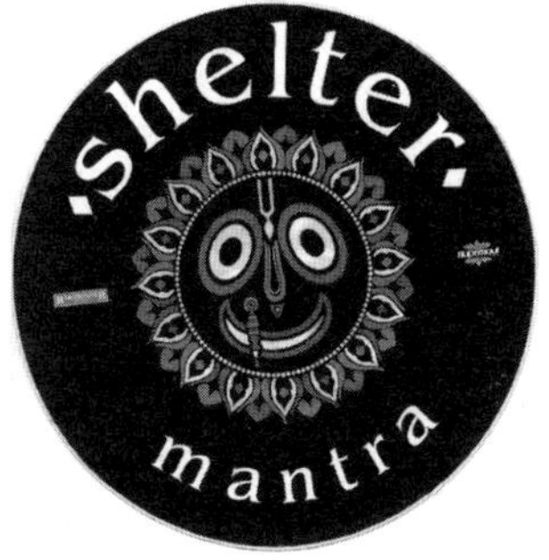

What remains of the building now is a crumbling façade. There are no supporting interior walls. The roof is gone. A tree pushes up between bricks that once held a dance floor. Broken mirrored glass lays scattered near the front door. Part of the low wooden stage remains. This shell of a sanctuary sits around the corner from a modern building housing a coffee shop and a restaurant advertising "gourmet sandwiches." It is blocks from where legendary arts venue DC Space once stood—a space that is now a Starbucks. The lot is listed with a real estate firm for $7 million. DC's Historic Preservation Office is interested in "maintaining the façade," admitting there's "little more than that left," and predicts its new owner "will construct a much taller building behind [it]." Despite its decayed appearance, its date of origin and locale qualify it as part of the Mount Vernon Triangle Historic District of DC (as determined by the US Department of Interior's National

Eighties-era ephemera from the collection of Eric Hochberg.

Park Service). The *Washington Business Journal* recently mentioned it as a spot of "urban blight" that's caught the eye of corporate hotel developers.

Someone will swoop in to make it match the rest of the neighborhood. Landscapes change—natural ones shaped by time and weather, cities by revitalization and gentrification, whatever you choose to call it. This space was important to the underground culture of our city. It was what we made it. It is more than a structure. Our hope is that this book serves as a document of an era, a feeling, and a scene that meant so much to so many.

Most of us were teenagers when the events in this story took place. Some of us have families, serious careers, teenagers of our own. We see one another now—grayer, fatter, maybe mellower. Names escape us and memories fade. Some of us are dead. This is for those who have dragged boxes of flyers and photos around over the years, for those who sold their records or never did, for anyone who has ever tried to explain what these years meant.

Memory is a tricky animal, so we chose to offer a collective version of the story. This book is a footnote in the worldwide conversation about punk, hardcore, and music that was once counterculture. It's not perfect. It's not just our point of view. It's a lot of voices coming together. This book is our song.

—Rich Dolinger and Shawna Kenney

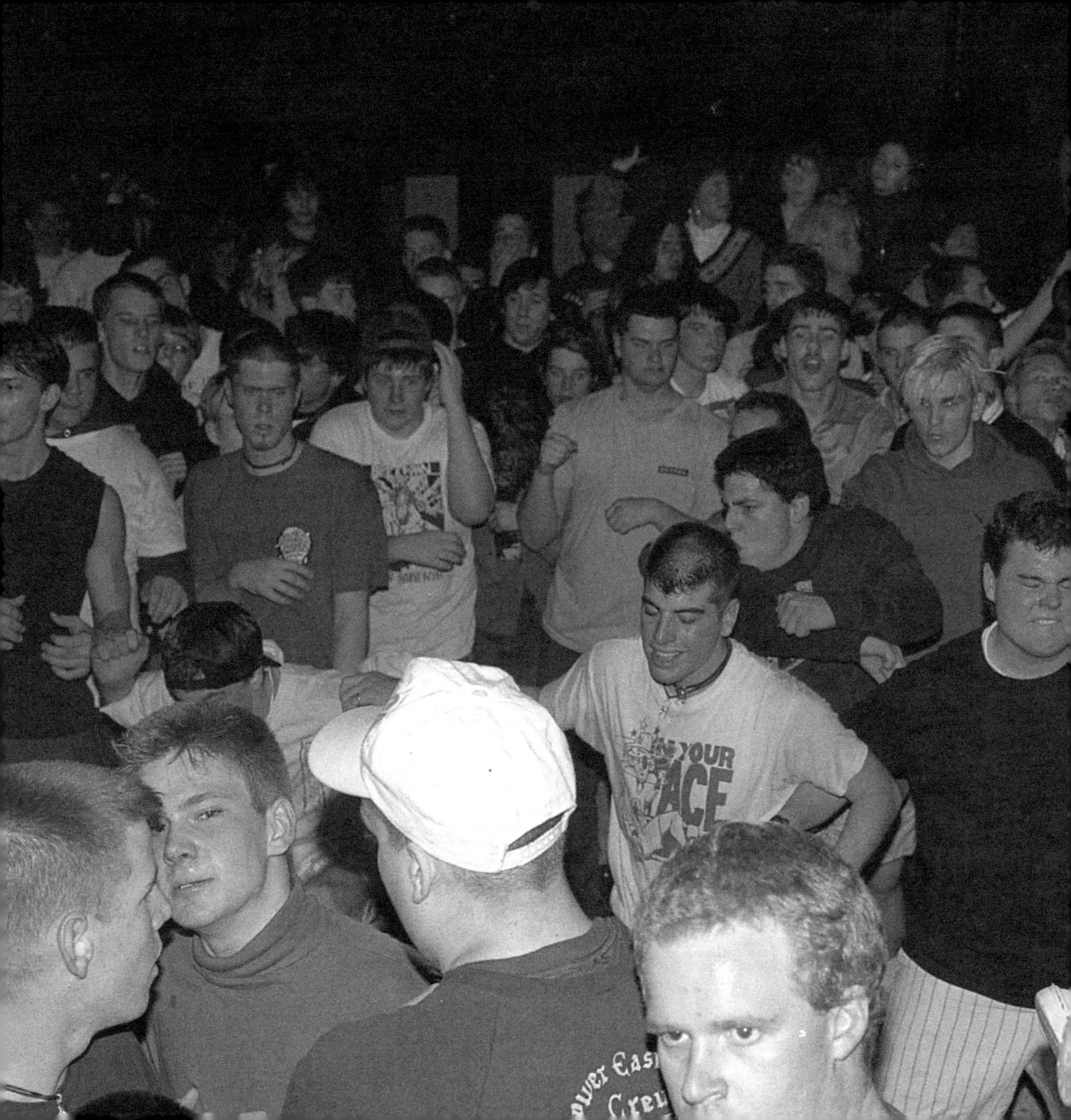
YOUR

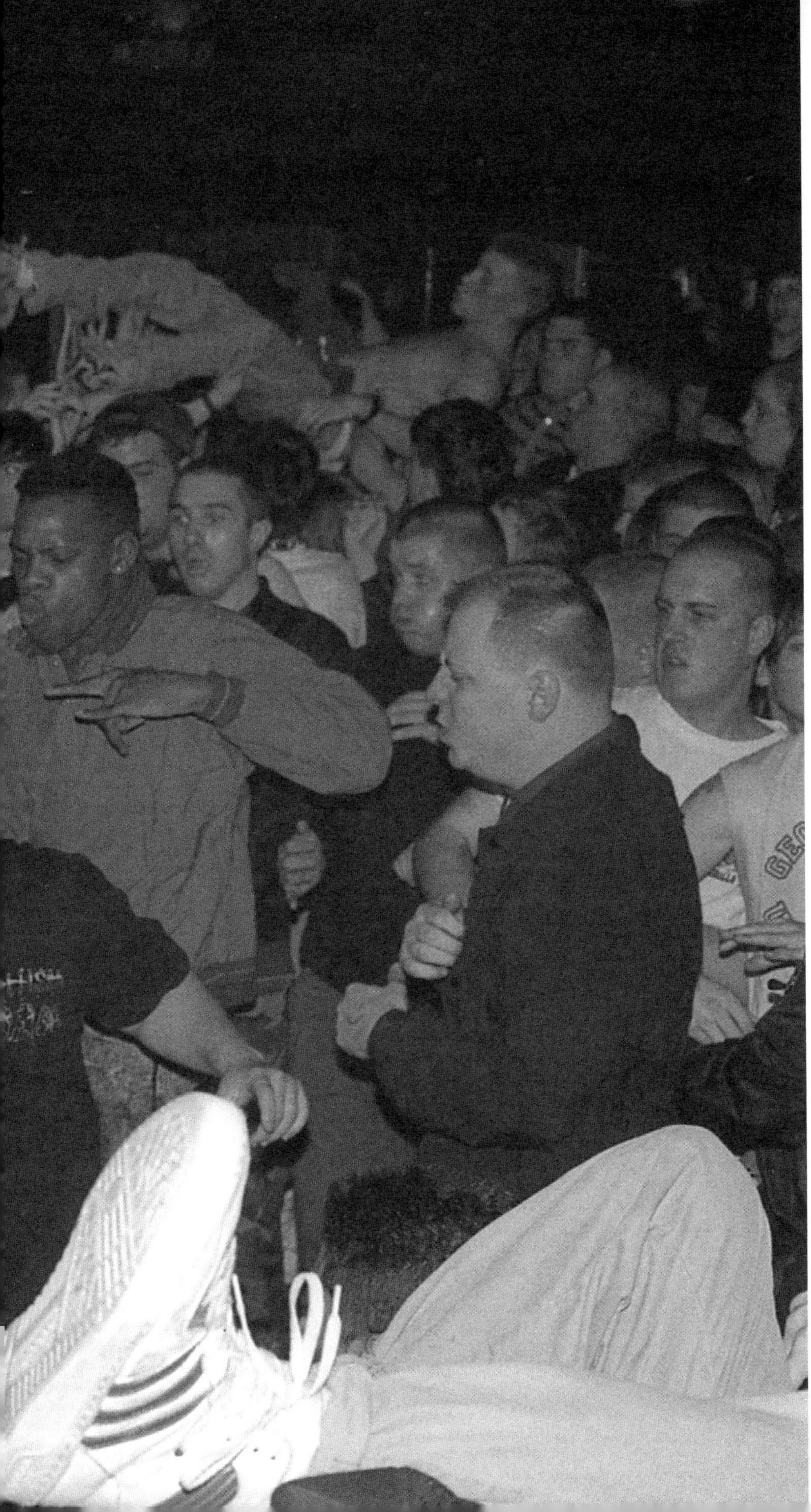

Safari Club was the first steady matinée situation, perfect for that crowd. You could tell kids had almost been waiting for that.
—Ken Olden

Crowd at Krakdown show, March 2, 1989.
Photo by Joe Wongananda.

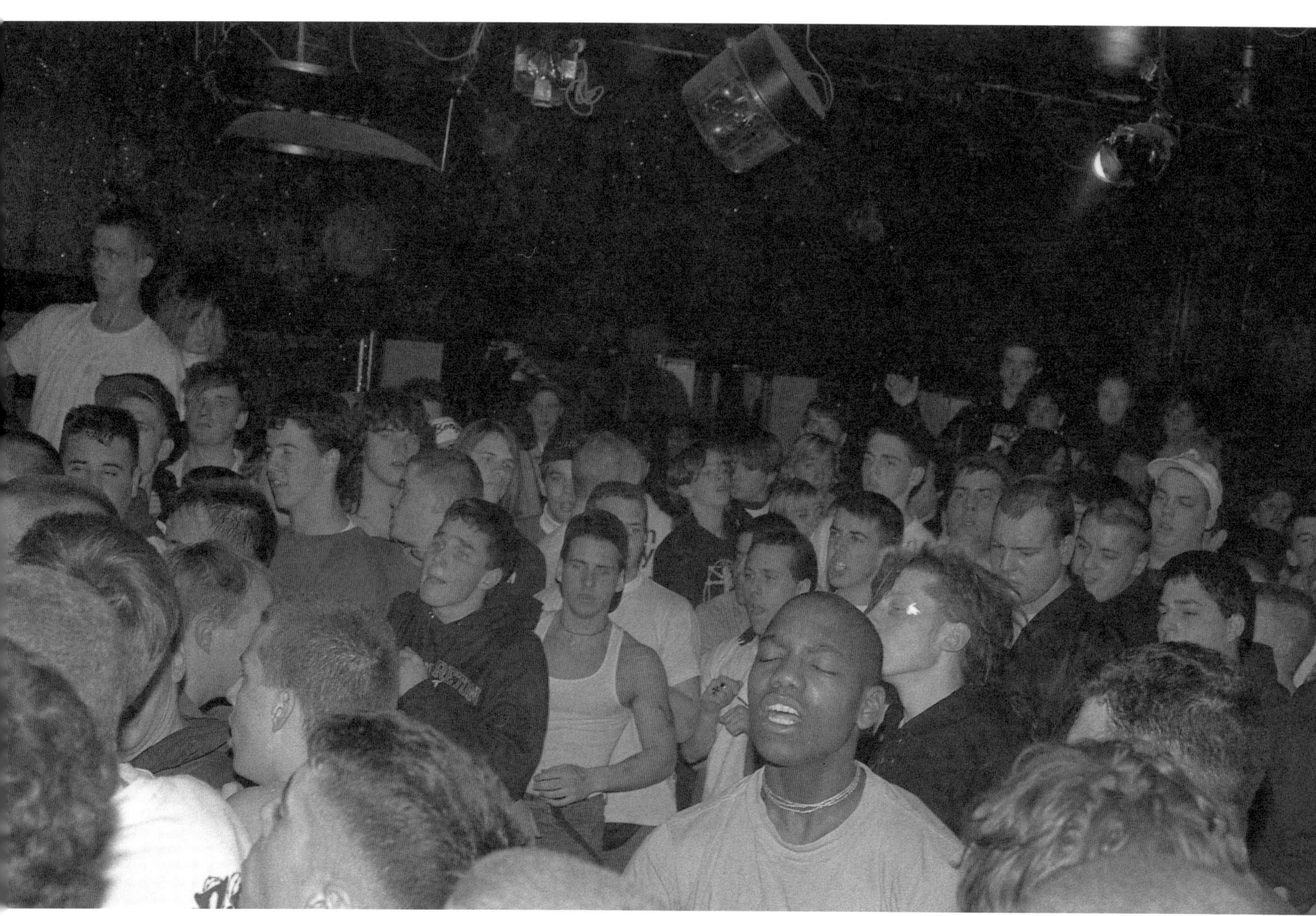

Crowd at Krakdown show, March 2, 1989. Photo by Joe Wongananda.

CHAPTER 1: BEHIND THE SCENE

1988–1990

SHAWNA KENNEY: I grew up in southern Maryland, graduated from high school in 1987, and moved to upstate New York for a few months. When I came back, Toby Morse (who I had gone to high school with) introduced me to Pam, this cool punk girl who had moved from St. Louis. She and I moved to Fairfax and we made our *No Scene Zine* together and shows seemed like a natural extension of that. We started looking around for places to have all-ages matinées. We wanted something like what CBGB had going on. We talked to the 9:30 Club, but they said they weren't interested in opening up in the middle of the day for shows where they couldn't sell alcohol.

PAM GENDELL: Shawna was dating this guy from Indian Summer. One morning, she told me the guy had abandoned her in Chinatown at some random bar—and never came back! I was appalled! But Shawna didn't seem too bothered by it. In fact, she was really excited about the fact that the African guys she met there said they would open up at lunchtime and let us book matinées on the weekends.

SHAWNA KENNEY: Before we did matinées there, Safari was known as kind of a shady place. I was dating the guitar player from Indian Summer and they were supposed to play with Swiz one night at the Safari. When we got there, the club said something about paying the soundman in order to play. I think Indian Summer was trying to decide what to do.

Phone Numbers Frequently Used

NAME AND ADDRESS | TELEPHONE

WALTER - N.Y. / ARTHUR (718) 932-5974
GORDON -
SAFARI CLUB 925 5th St., N.W.
"ENEMY" (Indianapolis) - CHRIS
BILL DOLAN (FLUX, & AMERICAN STANDARD)
John Porcelly - JUDGE - Tom /BOLD/Beyond
CAROL SCHUTZBANK (Philly.)
★ PAM
BRAD SIGAL (NOMADIC UNDERGROUND)
ADAM
ALEX MORRIS (Unholy Alliance)
SHAWN B.
JOE G. (SUPERTOUCH)
SPOKEN WORD - Amer. Machine
Mike ~ AGENT 86
TOBY
RON COLEMAN Clockwork Talent
ALL

SHAWNA
No Scene "ZINE"
(703) 273-7351

Nov. 19th, 1988 IMAGES, PARASITE, The PLASTIC TOYS 69
Nov. 26th GORILLA BISCUITS, SWIZ, Lucy Brown 398
Dec. 10th OUTCROWD, FLUX, REPERCUSSION 64
Dec. 17th IMAGES, SPONGE TUNNEL, SCREECHING WEASEL 72
Dec. 31 McRAD, THE REPLY, AFTER WORDS, ENEMY, FRICTION 145
Jan. 7th SWIZ, AMERICAN STANDARD, INDIAN SUMMER, ECONOCHRIST + Sobering Conquerors 215
Jan. 14th IMMORAL DISCIPLINE, UNHOLY ALLIANCE, TERMINAL CONFUSION, NOSFERATU 250
Jan. 28 BOLD, BEYOND, FED UP 410
Feb. 4 SUPERTOUCH, BLIND AMBITION, NEVERMAN 171
Feb. 18th SICK OF IT ALL, RAW DEAL, IMAGES 289
Feb. 24th OUTCROWD, THE POPES, NEVERMAN 21
Feb. 25th IGNITION, SCRAM, ELECTRIC LOVE MUFFIN, PLASTIC TOYS 19
March 4th IMMORAL D., ABRA CADAVERS, L.D. KIDS 187
March 11th SWIZ, ABSOLUTION, KRAKDOWN, 4 WALLS FALLING 310
March 18th PSYCHO, PARASITE, DWARVES, MOPAGANS 24
March 25th INSTED, VISION, UP FRONT, 183
April 1 L.D. Kids, INDESTROY, DECEASED 83
April 8 UNDERDOG, AMERICAN STANDARD, GUT INSTINCT, FURY

STEVE FRANCIS: Swiz arrived and joined in the discussion. After some internal squabbling, they let it be known they were disappointed with the lack of people in attendance and would refuse to pay up front. They put on a magician's hat and performed their greatest disappearing act. We were left with a decision. Play or go home. We were a band still trying to establish ourselves. We chose to stay and play. We had fun playing. The crowd was minimal. Merely a handful of people. I think some of them were actually part of the waitstaff. The chain of events of that night did alter the future. That night's show would become the catalyst for what would usher in a new era at the Safari Club—those popular hardcore matinée shows that were a mainstay for many years after.

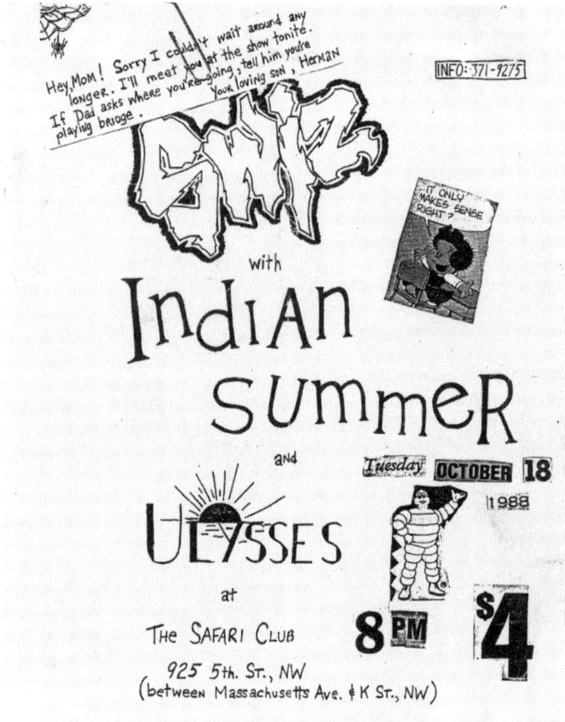

JOHN DUGAN: Most of my memories of Safari Club were around it being one of my band Indian Summer's first gigs in the city. I remember the first night we played there being very strange, somewhat scary, and not that well attended (or promoted) except for some high school friends—one of whom asked me to her prom. And perhaps the other band canceled? It's a bit fuzzy, but I doubt we would have "paid to play" anywhere. I was sixteen. I just wanted to play some shows.

SHAWNA KENNEY: Swiz took off and the members of IS scattered—I thought they were going to go home and get some equipment they'd forgotten. I was left there alone with no ride back to Northern Virginia, so I sat there all night drinking Cokes and talking to the club owner (Haile Daniels) and the bartender. I was only eighteen. I asked them what they did on the weekends and whether I could book some "rock shows." The owner ended up having one of his cabbies drive me home at 3:00 a.m. and wouldn't take any money.

PAM GENDELL: I think I was out all night and came home the next day to Shawna all excited to tell me that we had a place to do shows.

JOHN DUGAN: The niche they filled booking Safari Club matinées was an important one as a lot of the hardcore-style punk of that era was shut out of the city clubs like the 9:30.

PAM GENDELL: Our first line-up was Parasite, the Plastic Toys, and Images—local bands we knew. There were about seventy people there. The agreement with the club at first was to split the door fifty/fifty, we pay the bands out of our half. But that was always changing—later they wanted us to pay sound, then security—but we fired security and said we could do it ourselves. Then they tried demanding sixty/forty when the shows got bigger.

After putting our phone number in MRR, our answering machine was constantly full of messages from bands from all over wanting to play.
—Shawna Kenney

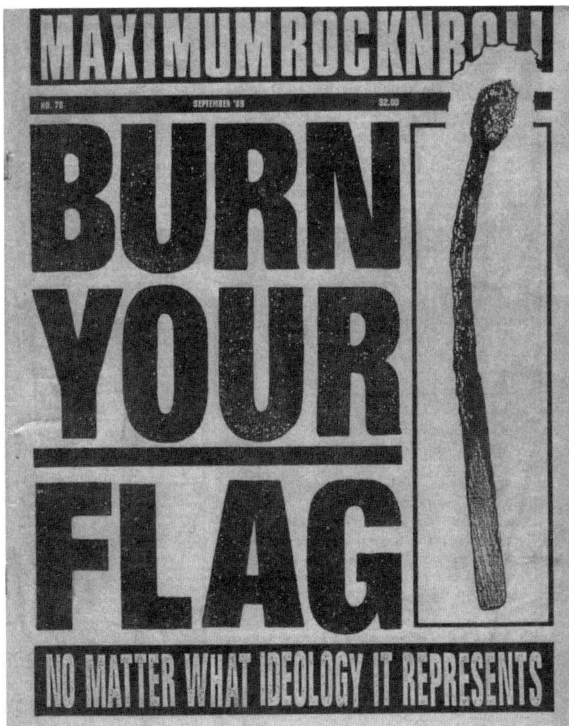

SHAWNA KENNEY: Our second show was supposed to be Gorilla Biscuits, Swiz, and In Your Face. Toby was living with some of the GB guys in NY by then and he put us in touch. Haile had booked local band Lucy Brown without telling us, for some reason, so they ended up playing and In Your Face canceled. According to my notes, 398 people paid to get into that show. After that, Haile was like, "Gorilla Biscuits—every weekend!" We had to explain to him that it didn't work like that.

Above: Maximum Rock-n-Roll, *1989.*

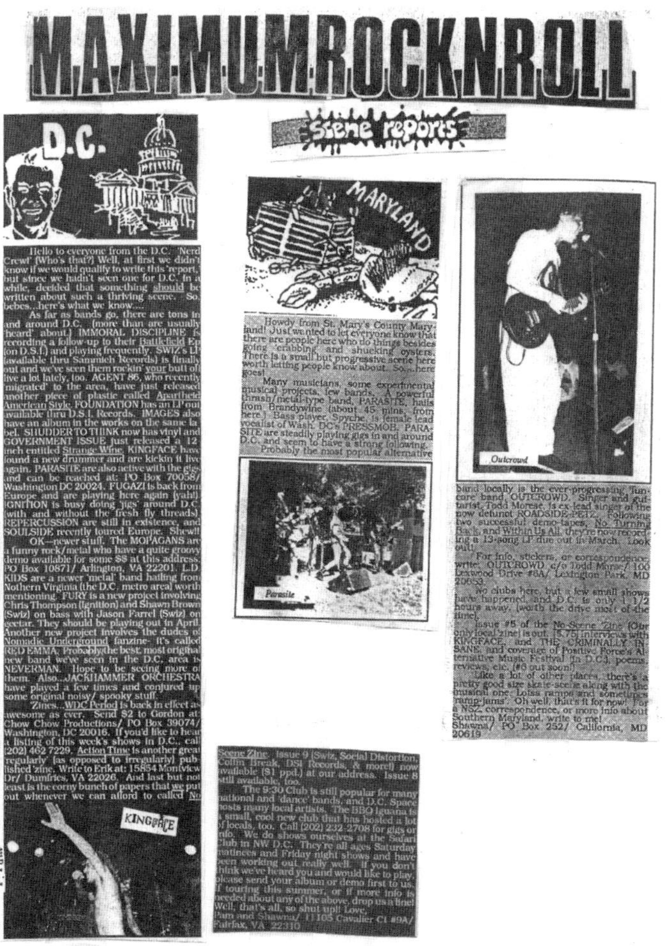

MAXIMUMROCKNROLL

scene reports

D.C.

Hello to everyone from the D.C. 'Nerd Crew!' (Who's that?) Well, at first we didn't know if we would qualify to write this 'report,' but since we hadn't seen one for D.C. in a while, decided that something should be written about such a thriving scene. So, bebes...here's what we know....

As far as bands go, there are tons in and around D.C. (more than are usually 'heard' about.) IMMORAL DISCIPLINE is recording a follow-up to their Battlefield Ep (on D.S.I.) and playing frequently. SWIZ's LP (available thru Sammich Records) is finally out and we've seen them rockin' your butt off live a lot lately, too. AGENT 86, who recently 'migrated' to the area, have just released another piece of plastic called Apartheid American Style. FOUNDATION has an LP out available thru D.S.I. Records. IMAGES also have an album in the works on the same label. SHUDDER TO THINK now has vinyl and GOVERNMENT ISSUE just released a 12 inch entitled Strange Wine. KINGFACE have found a new drummer and are kickin it live again. PARASITE are also active with the gigs and can be reached at: PO Box 70058/ Washington DC 20024. FUGAZI is back from Europe and are playing here again (yah!). IGNITION is busy doing 'jigs' around D.C. (with and without the fresh fly threads). REPERCUSSION are still in existence, and SOULSIDE recently toured Europe. Shew!!

OK—newer stuff. The MOPAGANS are a funny rock/metal who have a quite groovy demo available for some $$ at this address: PO Box 10871/ Arlington, VA 22201. L.D. KIDS are a newer 'metal' band hailing from Nothern Virginia (the D.C. metro area) worth mentioning. FURY is a new project involving Chris Thompson (Ignition) and Shawn Brown (Swiz) on bass with Jason Farrel (Swiz) on geetar. They should be playing out in April. Another new project involves the dudes of Nomadic Underground fanzine- it's called RED EMMA. Probably the best most original new band we've seen in the D.C. area is NEVERMAN. Hope to be seeing more of them. Also...JACKHAMMER ORCHESTRA have played a few times and conjured up some original noisy/ spooky stuff.

Zines...WDC Period is back in effect as awesome as ever. Send $2 to Gordon at: Chow Chow Productions/ PO Box 39074/ Washington, DC 20016. If you'd like to hear a listing of this week's shows in D.C., call (202) 462 7229. Action Time is another great 'regularly' (as opposed to irregularly) published 'zine. Write to Erik at: 15854 Montview Dr/ Dumfries, VA 22026. And last but not least is the corny bunch of papers that we put out whenever we can afford to called No Scene Zine. Issue 9 (Swiz, Social Distortion, Coffin Break, DSI Records, & more!) now available ($1 ppd.) at our address. Issue 8 still available, too.

The 9:30 Club is still popular for many national and 'dance' bands, and D.C. Space hosts many local artists. The BBQ Iguana is a small, cool new club that has hosted a lot of locals, too. Call (202) 232 2708 for gigs or info. We do shows ourselves at the Safari Club in NW D.C. They're all ages Saturday matinees and Friday night shows and have been working out really well. If you don't think we've heard you and would like to play, please send your album or demo first to us. If touring this summer, or if more info is needed about any of the above, drop us a line! Well, that's all, so shut up!! Love,
Pam and Shawna/ 11105 Cavalier Ct #9A/ Fairfax, VA 22310

KINGFACE

P: Pam

MARYLAND

Howdy from St. Mary's County Maryland! Just wanted to let everyone know that there are people here who do things besides going 'crabbing' and shucking oysters. There is a small but progressive scene here worth letting people know about. So...here goes!

Many musicians, some experimental musical projects, few bands. A powerful thrash/metal-type band, PARASITE, hails from Brandywine (about 45 mins. from here.) Bass player, Spyche, is female lead vocalist of Wash. DC's PRESSMOB. PARASITE are steadily playing gigs in and around D.C. and seem to have a strong following.

Probably the most popular alternative band locally is the ever-progressing 'funcore' band, OUTCROWD. Singer and guitarist, Todd Morese, is ex-lead singer of the now defunct ROADSIDE PETZ. Following two successful demo-tapes, No Turning Back, and Within Us All, they're now recording a 13-song LP due out in March. Look out!

For info, stickers, or correspondence, write: OUTCROWD c/o Todd Morse/ 100 Lexwood Drive #8A/ Lexington Park, MD 20653.

No clubs here, but a few small shows have happened, and D.C. is only 1 1/2 hours away. (worth the drive most of the time).

Issue #5 of the No Scene 'Zine (Our only local 'zine) is out. ($.75) interviews with KINGFACE, and THE CRIMINALLY INSANE, and coverage of Positive Force's Alternative Music Festival (in D.C.), poems, reviews, etc. (#6 out soon!)

Like a lot of other places, there's a pretty good size skate-scene along with the musical one. Lotsa ramps and sometimes 'ramp-jams'. Oh well, that's it for now! For a NSZ, correspondence, or more info about Southern Maryland, write to me!
Shawna/ PO Box 252/ California, MD 20619

Parasite

Outcrowd

Maximum Rock-n-Roll *scene reports, 1988.*

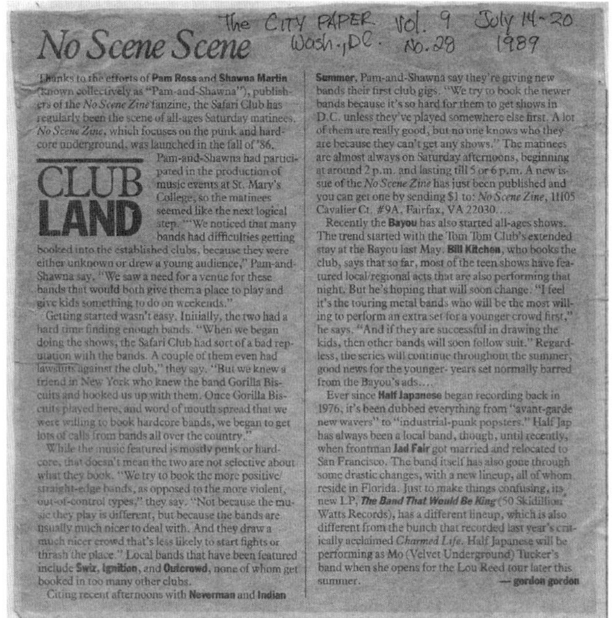

The CITY PAPER Vol. 9 July 14-20
Wash., DC. No. 28 1989

No Scene Scene

CLUB LAND

Thanks to the efforts of **Pam Ross** and **Shawna Martin** (known collectively as "Pam-and-Shawna"), publishers of the *No Scene Zine* fanzine, the Safari Club has regularly been the scene of all-ages Saturday matinees. *No Scene Zine*, which focuses on the punk and hardcore underground, was launched in the fall of '86.

Pam-and-Shawna had participated in the production of music events at St. Mary's College, so the matinees seemed like the next logical step. ""We noticed that many bands had difficulties getting booked into the established clubs, because they were either unknown or drew a young audience," Pam-and-Shawna say. "We saw a need for a venue for these bands that would both give them a place to play and give kids something to do on weekends."

Getting started wasn't easy. Initially, the two had a hard time finding enough bands. "When we began doing the shows, the Safari Club had sort of a bad reputation with the bands. A couple of them even had lawsuits against the club," they say. "But we knew a friend in New York who knew the band Gorilla Biscuits and hooked us up with them. Once Gorilla Biscuits played here, and word of mouth spread that we were willing to book hardcore bands, we began to get lots of calls from bands all over the country."

While the music featured is mostly punk or hardcore, that doesn't mean the two are not selective about what they book. "We try to book the more positive/straight-edge bands, as opposed to the more violent, out-of-control types," they say. "Not because the music they play is different, but because the bands are usually much nicer to deal with. And they draw a much nicer crowd that's less likely to start fights or thrash the place." Local bands that have been featured include **Swiz**, **Ignition**, and **Outcrowd**, none of whom get booked in too many other clubs.

Citing recent afternoons with **Neverman** and **Indian Summer**, Pam-and-Shawna say they're giving new bands their first club gigs. "We try to book the newer bands because it's so hard for them to get shows in D.C. unless they've played somewhere else first. A lot of them are really good, but no one knows who they are because they can't get any shows." The matinees are almost always on Saturday afternoons, beginning at around 2 p.m. and lasting till 5 or 6 p.m. A new issue of the *No Scene Zine* has just been published and you can get one by sending $1 to: *No Scene Zine*, 11105 Cavalier Ct. #9A, Fairfax, VA 22030....

Recently the **Bayou** has also started all-ages shows. The trend started with the Tom Tom Club's extended stay at the Bayou last May. **Bill Kitchen**, who books the club, says that so far, most of the teen shows have featured local/regional acts that are also performing that night. But he's hoping that will soon change. "I feel it's the touring metal bands who will be the most willing to perform an extra set for a younger crowd first," he says. "And if they are successful in drawing the kids, then other bands will soon follow suit." Regardless, the series will continue throughout the summer, good news for the younger- years set normally barred from the Bayou's ads....

Ever since **Half Japanese** began recording back in 1976, it's been dubbed everything from "avant-garde new wavers" to "industrial-punk popsters." Half Jap has always been a local band, though, until recently, when frontman **Jad Fair** got married and relocated to San Francisco. The band itself has also gone through some drastic changes, with a new lineup, all of whom reside in Florida. Just to make things confusing, its new LP, ***The Band That Would Be King*** (50 Skidillion Watts Records), has a different lineup, which is also different from the bunch that recorded last year's critically acclaimed *Charmed Life*. Half Japanese will be performing as Mo (Velvet Underground) Tucker's band when she opens for the Lou Reed tour later this summer.

— **gordon gordon**

Left: Washington City Paper, *July 14–20, 1989, mentions Safari Club shows. From the collection of Shawna Kenney.*

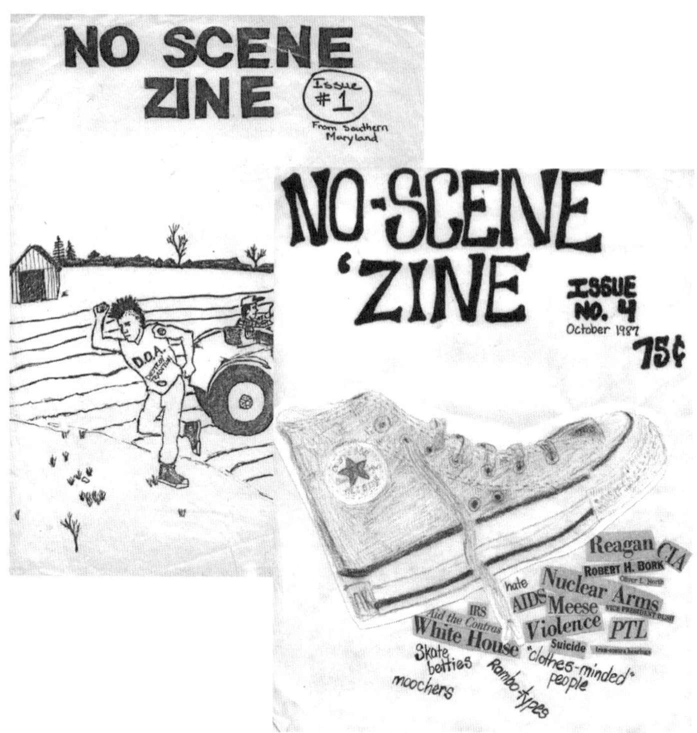

PAM GENDELL: Haile was a businessman, first and foremost. After that Gorilla Biscuits show, he saw an opportunity to cash in on our matinées. He started pushing us harder and harder on the money split and would argue that since he couldn't sell alcohol during our all ages shows we should pay a bigger percentage. It ended up being my job to battle with him every weekend to make sure the bands were paid fairly. Shawna and I were so into the scene at this point that all we wanted to do was book and promote our shows and go see other local shows. We even quit our jobs at a record store because our very first shift conflicted with a Soulside show in Bethesda.

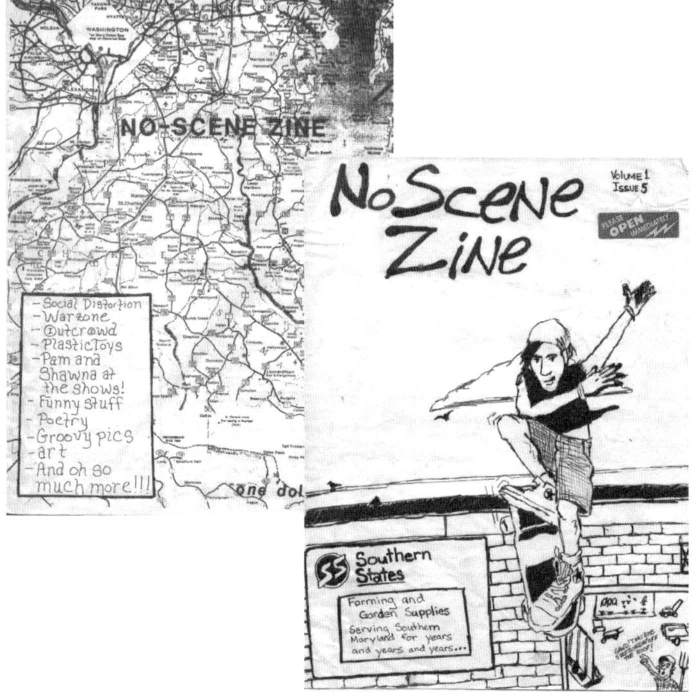

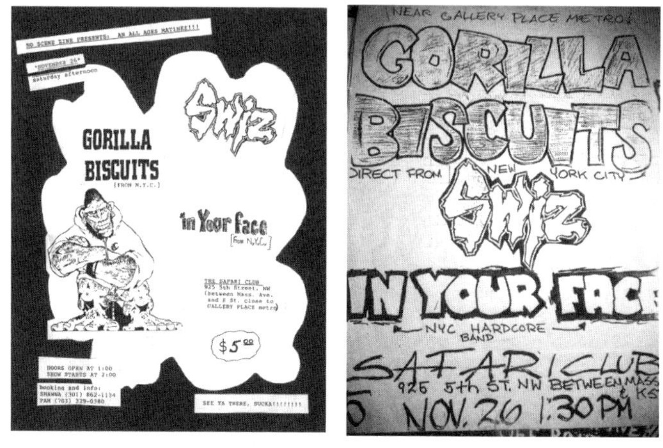

Left, above: No Scene Zines, *1986–1989. Archived in the* D.C. Punk and Indie Fanzine Collection, Special Collections, *University of Maryland Libraries.*

1989–1991

JOHN GALBRAITH: I graduated in '88 and was a college freshman. We went to almost every show Pam and Shawna did. I'd go to City Gardens, the Anthrax, CBGBs, ABC No Rio, too. Haile needed someone to help out at some of the go-go shows on Wednesdays, so I started with that. Sometimes he was difficult to deal with. He may have created some of the competition between us. I think it was around '89 when I started. There was some overlap there.

SHAWNA KENNEY: John thought we hated him and we thought he hated us, but we never really knew one another. We talked things out and made up years later.

JOHN GALBRAITH: I probably survived three years there then started doing occasional shows in other clubs around '92 or '93. I would do Fall Brawl at WUST and a few things at Kilimanjaro and Ibex, BBQ Iguana and the 15 Minute Club.

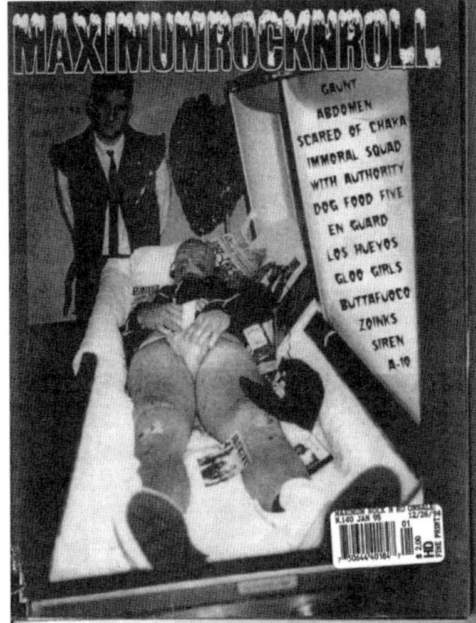

Left, below: zines of the era.
From the collection of John Galbraith.

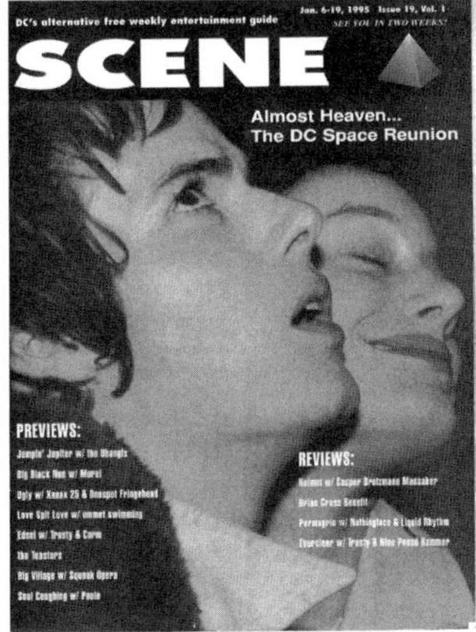

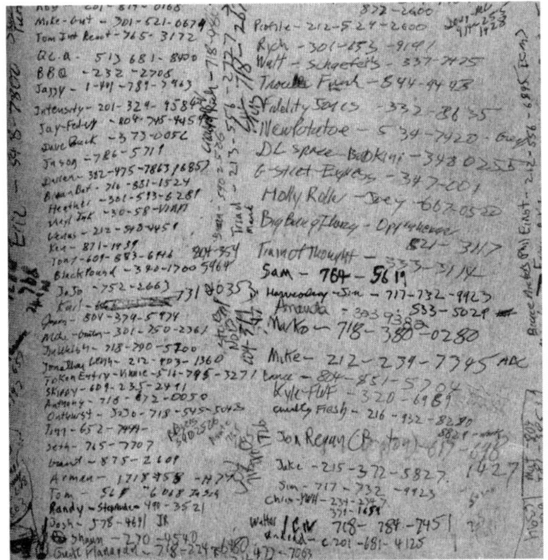

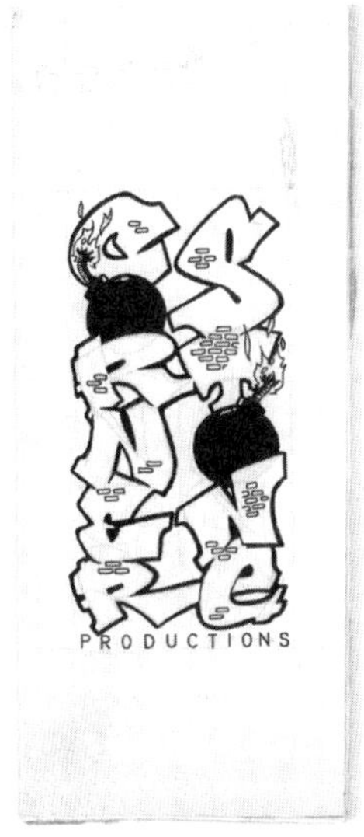

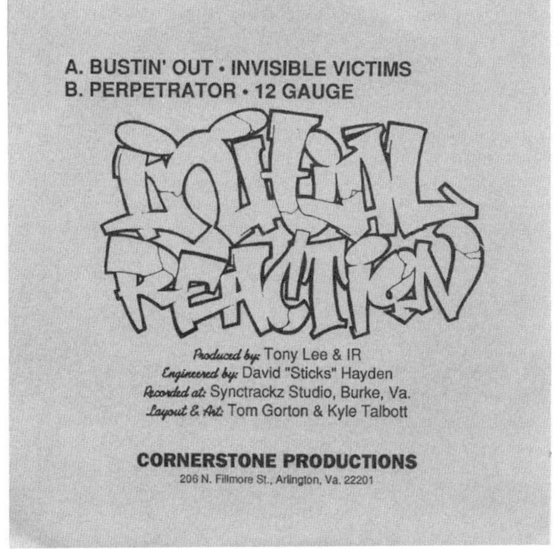

Left, center: John Cornerstone's phone list and business card, logo by Kyle Style.
From the collection of John Galbraith.

1992–1998

MARTIN CASTRO: When I started doing shows at St. Stephen's and different places, the idea was always to find a place. I remember talking to Jon Hennessee saying we've got to find a regular place to have shows. The DC scene at the time was dead. There wasn't any place of belonging.

JOHN GALBRAITH: I met Martin Castro there, who introduced me to Kyle Talbott. I did some shows with him and some with JR Glass. I introduced Martin to Haile. Martin and Jon Hennessee and Gabe Banner did shows together.

MARTIN CASTRO: The rebuilding was from Safari Club. When it started again, it was like "this is home." It wasn't just a booking relationship for me. I went to the club, I worked the door there, my roommate was a bouncer there, we'd just be hanging out. We were friends with the owners. Haile was out of the picture. I dealt with Palash and Dario. The bouncers were Pakistani dudes. We'd just chill there. I lived on Fifth and M at the time, five blocks up. It was like home to me. I did shows there from '92 or '93 to '97 or '98 when it burned down.

NO. 134
July 3 1990
RECEIVED FROM John Galbraith
One thousand five hundred fifty 00/100 DOLLARS
A Tribe Called Quest
Account Total $ 1,550.00
Amount Paid $ 1,550.00
Balance Due $ -0-
"THE EFFICIENCY LINE" AN AMPAD PRODUCT

Receipt for paying A Tribe Called Quest in 1990 (show was later moved from Safari Club).
From the collection of John Galbraith.

Facing page: newspaper ads for the Safari Club from the 1980s and 1990s.

Below: Martin Castro's business card.

The Safari Club & Restaurant
Nakfa Lounge

TH - 29 KAZZ NITE featuring KAZZ BAND, QUESADAS, THE END
FR - 30 THE ALMIGHTY SENATORS w/ MONKEY SPANK
SA - 1 Day Show UNDERDOG
WE - 5 LUCY BROWN, CADAVER, ZEN PARADE
TH - 6 SADDLETRAMP, PSYCHO GIRLS
SA - 8 CRUCIAL YOUTH, NEW JERSEY, SCREECHING WEASELS, TWO FACE JUDY

Free Parking available in Rear
925 5th St., NW
(between Massachusetts Ave. & K St., NW)
For Info Call 371-9275

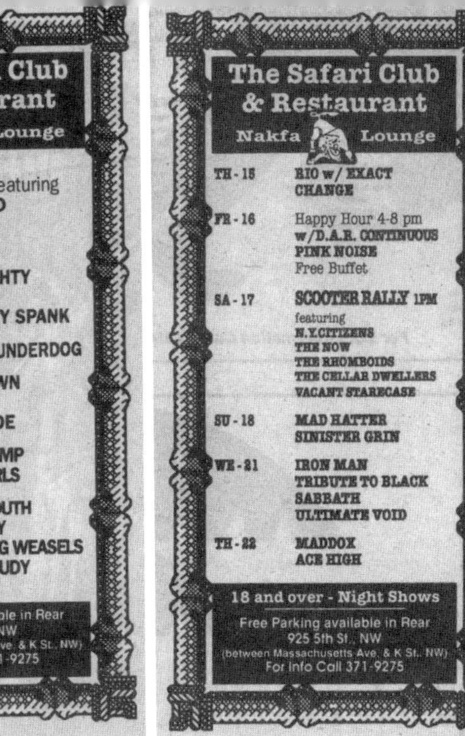

The Safari Club & Restaurant
Nakfa Lounge

TH - 15 RIO w/ EXACT CHANGE
FR - 16 Happy Hour 4-8 pm w/D.A.R. CONTINUOUS, PINK NOISE, Free Buffet
SA - 17 SCOOTER RALLY 1PM featuring N.Y.CITIZENS, THE NOW, THE RHOMBOIDS, THE CELLAR DWELLERS, VACANT STARECASE
SU - 18 MAD HATTER, SINISTER GRIN
WE - 21 IRON MAN TRIBUTE TO BLACK SABBATH, ULTIMATE VOID
TH - 22 MADDOX, ACE HIGH

18 and over - Night Shows
Free Parking available in Rear
925 5th St., NW
(between Massachusetts Ave. & K St., NW)
For Info Call 371-9275

The Safari Club & Restaurant
Nakfa Lounge

TH-6 Record Company Showcase w/ MITCH KERNUS, STILL LIFE
FR - 7 GOVERNMENT ISSUE, MOVING TARGETS, THE BAGS, ADMIRALS
SA - 8 Daytime All Ages Show 1 pm UNDERDOG, AMERICAN STANDARD, GUT INSTINCTS; Night Show - CIRCUS MIND, ALKALINE
SU - 9 Open Mike w/ NODES and Special Guests, THE SELVES
MO - 10 JOHNNY COHEN'S LOVE MACHINE, FATES, K.H.M.D.
TU - 11 Call Club for info
WE - 12 SKIRTS w/ Special Guests
TH - 13 BOOM SLANG, MAD ADMIRALS
FR - 14 LOUDMOUTH w/ SKELETON
SA - 15 JUNKYARD BAND, PURE ELEGANCE BAND, QUALITY BAND

18 and over - Night Shows
Free Parking available in Rear
925 5th St., NW
(between Massachusetts Ave. & K St., NW)
For Info Call 371-9275

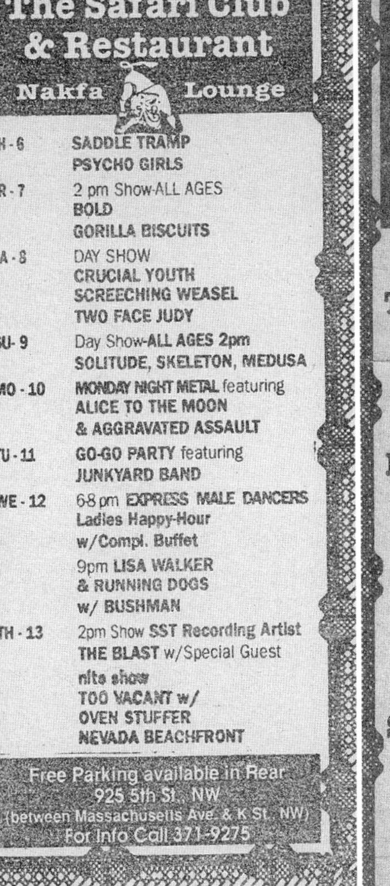

The Safari Club & Restaurant
Nakfa Lounge

TH - 6 SADDLE TRAMP, PSYCHO GIRLS
FR - 7 2 pm Show-ALL AGES BOLD, GORILLA BISCUITS
SA - 8 DAY SHOW CRUCIAL YOUTH, SCREECHING WEASEL, TWO FACE JUDY
SU - 9 Day Show-ALL AGES 2pm SOLITUDE, SKELETON, MEDUSA
MO - 10 MONDAY NIGHT METAL featuring ALICE TO THE MOON & AGGRAVATED ASSAULT
TU - 11 GO-GO PARTY featuring JUNKYARD BAND
WE - 12 6-8 pm EXPRESS MALE DANCERS, Ladies Happy-Hour w/Compl. Buffet; 9pm LISA WALKER & RUNNING DOGS w/ BUSHMAN
TH - 13 2pm Show SST Recording Artist THE BLAST w/Special Guest; nite show TOO VACANT w/ OVEN STUFFER, NEVADA BEACHFRONT

Free Parking available in Rear
925 5th St., NW
(between Massachusetts Ave. & K St., NW)
For Info Call 371-9275

The Safari Club & Restaurant
Nakfa Lounge

MARCH LISTINGS

TH - 23 SUB MENASAS, TONGUE & GROOVE, TRIAL & ERROR
FR - 24 All Ages Early Show 7-10pm N.Y. CITIZEN, THE NOW, I SPY; Night Show - after 10pm UNDERTOW w/Special Guest
SA - 25 Day Show INSTEAD, VISION, UPFRONT; Night Show TOO VACANT w/Special Guest
SU - 26 NODES Hosting Open Mike "Dead" Nite
MO - 27 LOUD MOUTH, JIMI SIN, TRASH IN DRAG
TU - 28 PUSH, TOO VACANT, LIQUID EYES
WE - 29 ON - XYZ w/SISTAH (from Detroit) - FOR FISHBONE LOVERS -
TH - 30 GREEN BONE, DANCE, FALL LINE, LIG; Early Show 5-9pm featuring Spoken Word

18 and over - Night Shows
Free Parking available in Rear
925 5th St., NW
(between Massachusetts Ave. & K St., NW)
For Info Call 371-9275

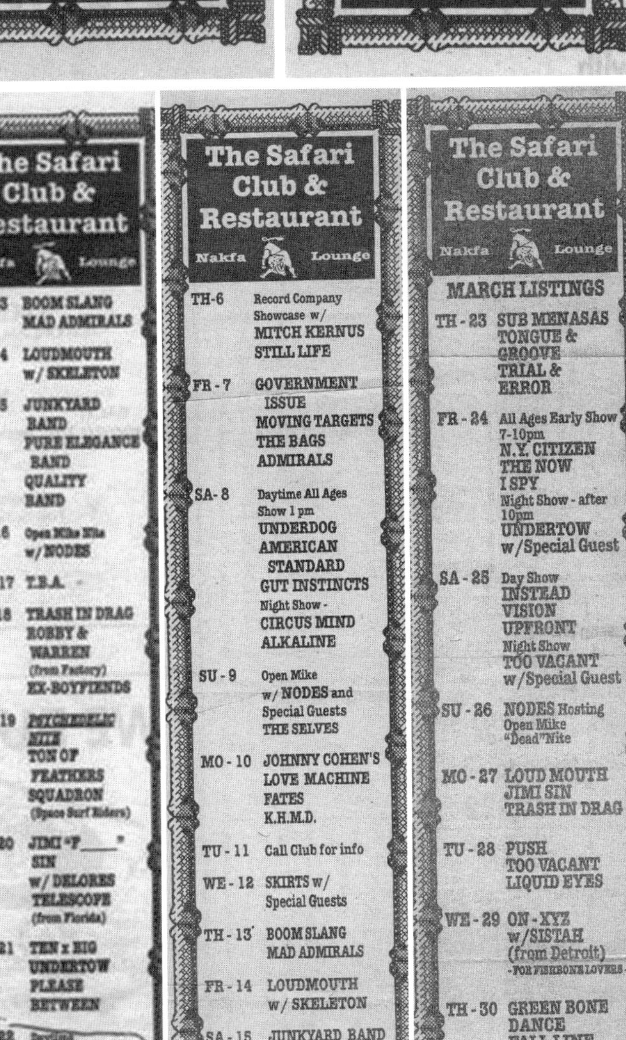

The Safari Club & Restaurant
Nakfa Lounge

TH - 13 BOOM SLANG, MAD ADMIRALS
FR - 14 LOUDMOUTH w/ SKELETON
SA - 15 JUNKYARD BAND, PURE ELEGANCE BAND, QUALITY BAND
SU - 16 Open Mike Nite w/NODES
MO - 17 T.B.A.
TU - 18 TRASH IN DRAG, ROBBY & WARREN (from Factory), EX-BOYFIENDS
WE - 19 PSYCHEDELIC NITE TON OF FEATHERS, SQUADRON (Space Surf Riders)
TH - 20 JIMI "F____" SIN w/ DELORES TELESCOPE (from Florida)
FR - 21 TEN x BIG, UNDERTOW, PLEASE, BETWEEN
SA - 22 Daytime STICKS - STONES, KINGFACE, FOUNDATION

18 and over - Night Shows
Free Parking available in Rear
925 5th St., NW
(between Massachusetts Ave. & K St., NW)
For Info Call 371-9275

The Safari Club & Restaurant
Nakfa Lounge
TH-6 Record Company Showcase w/ MITCH KERNUS, STILL LIFE
FR - 7 GOVERNMENT ISSUE, MOVING TARGETS, THE BAGS, ADMIRALS
SA - 8 Daytime All Ages Show 1 pm UNDERDOG, AMERICAN STANDARD, GUT INSTINCTS; Night Show - CIRCUS MIND, ALKALINE
SU - 9 Open Mike w/ NODES and Special Guests, THE SELVES
MO - 10 JOHNNY COHEN'S LOVE MACHINE, FATES, K.H.M.D.
TU - 11 Call Club for info
WE - 12 SKIRTS w/ Special Guests
TH - 13 BOOM SLANG, MAD ADMIRALS
FR - 14 LOUDMOUTH w/ SKELETON
SA - 15 JUNKYARD BAND, PURE ELEGANCE BAND, QUALITY BAND
18 and over - Night Shows
Free Parking available in Rear
925 5th St., NW
(between Massachusetts Ave. & K St., NW)
For Info Call 371-9275

The Safari Club & Restaurant
Nakfa Lounge
MARCH LISTINGS
TH - 23 SUB MENASAS, TONGUE & GROOVE, TRIAL & ERROR
FR - 24 All Ages Early Show 7-10pm N.Y. CITIZEN, THE NOW, I SPY; Night Show - after 10pm UNDERTOW w/Special Guest
SA - 25 Day Show INSTEAD, VISION, UPFRONT; Night Show TOO VACANT w/Special Guest
SU - 26 NODES Hosting Open Mike "Dead" Nite
MO - 27 LOUD MOUTH, JIMI SIN, TRASH IN DRAG
TU - 28 PUSH, TOO VACANT, LIQUID EYES
WE - 29 ON - XYZ w/SISTAH (from Detroit) - FOR FISHBONE LOVERS -
TH - 30 GREEN BONE, DANCE, FALL LINE, LIG; Early Show 5-9pm featuring Spoken Word
18 and over - Night Shows
Free Parking available in Rear
925 5th St., NW
(between Massachusetts Ave. & K St., NW)
For Info Call 371-9275

The Safari Club & Restaurant
Nakfa Lounge
TH - 6 SADDLE TRAMP, PSYCHO GIRLS
FR - 7 2 pm Show-ALL AGES BOLD, GORILLA BISCUITS
SA - 8 DAY SHOW CRUCIAL YOUTH, SCREECHING WEASEL, TWO FACE JUDY
SU - 9 Day Show-ALL AGES 2pm SOLITUDE, SKELETON, MEDUSA
MO - 10 MONDAY NIGHT METAL featuring ALICE TO THE MOON & AGGRAVATED ASSAULT
TU - 11 GO-GO PARTY featuring JUNKYARD BAND
WE - 12 6-8 pm EXPRESS MALE DANCERS, Ladies Happy-Hour w/Compl. Buffet; 9pm LISA WALKER & RUNNING DOGS w/ BUSHMAN
TH - 13 2pm Show SST Recording Artist THE BLAST w/Special Guest; nite show TOO VACANT w/ OVEN STUFFER, NEVADA BEACHFRONT
Free Parking available in Rear
925 5th St., NW
(between Massachusetts Ave. & K St., NW)
For Info Call 371-9275

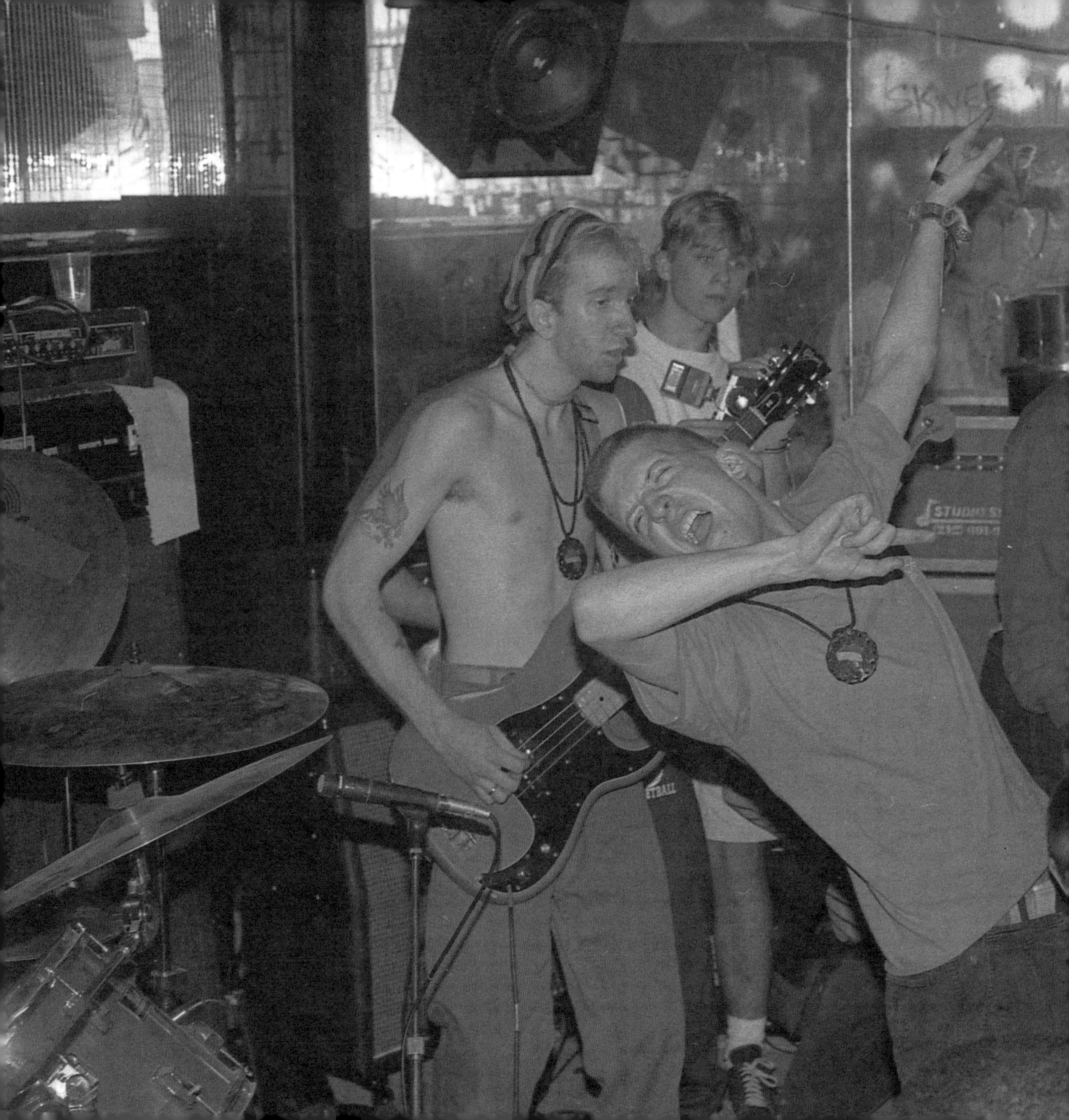

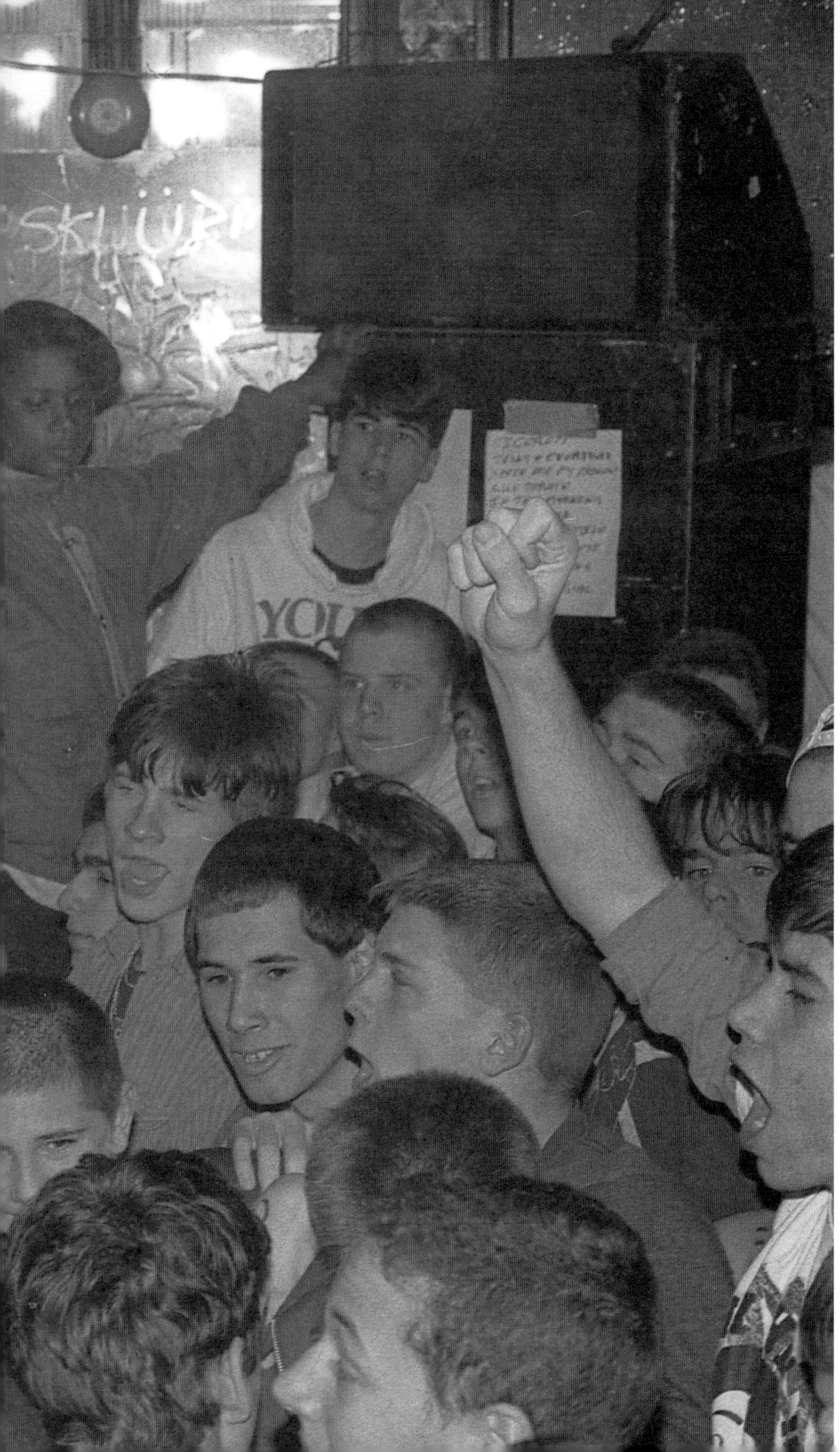

On the end of that **Gorilla Biscuits: Live at the Safari Club** *7-inch, you can hear "stick around, Four Walls Falling is up next!" as everyone faded out of the club.*
—Taylor Steele

Four Walls Falling.
Photo by Joe Wongananda.

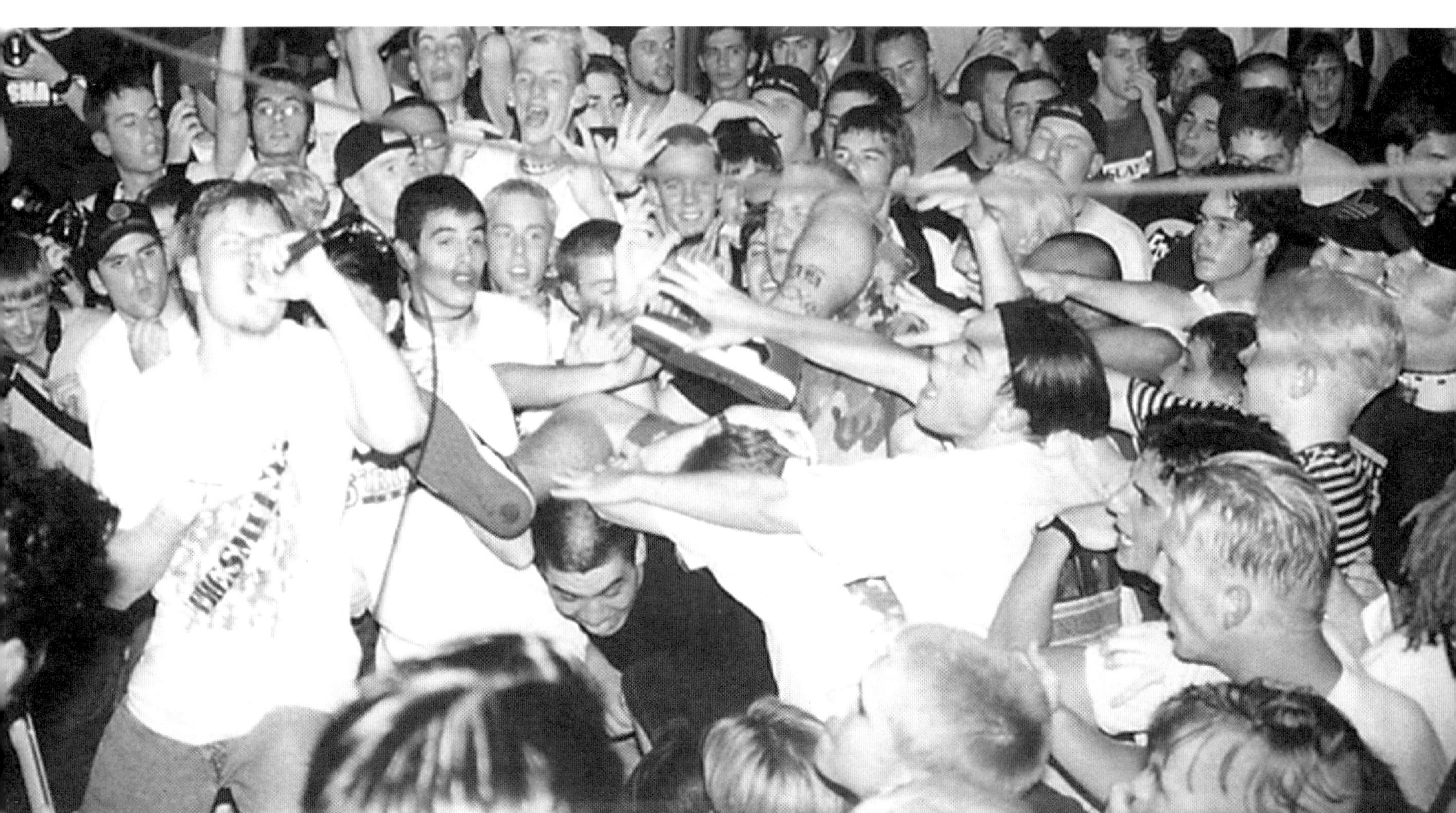

Unbroken. Photo by Jim Wilson.

CHAPTER 2: JUST LOOK AROUND

TOMMY ANTHONY: At a time when all the corporate venues in DC seemed to only have shows on weeknights with age limits, to have a new venue that did all ages matinée shows on weekends was amazing for us youngins/smallies! Finally accessible, as punk and hardcore should be.

CHUCK COPELAND: I first heard about the club from John Galbraith. Our DC crew and Baltimore's CCS crew were all friends, and when the Oi skinhead stuff was fading out, we noticed bands incorporating more breaks in the music, Doc Martens were replaced with Adidas, and jeans and Fred Perrys turned into Champion hoodies and sweats. So we started going with John and Kyle Style to Safari, and that's when I met Shawna and Pam.

JASON FARRELL: It's hard to think back to when it became something. We played the 9:30 Club but didn't really fit in there and everything else was pretty much Positive Force and they had sort of a monopoly on the majority of shows that would happen. They had a certain vibe about them where maybe you didn't want every one of your shows to be like that. Swiz was not of any one scene at the time. As much as we wanted to be part of and on Dischord, we were easily six to eight years younger than those guys and doing something they had abandoned and not really sounding like Fidelity Jones or whatever else they were putting out at the time. I don't think we had much of a response at the 9:30 Club. The Safari Club ended up being its own scene—something that was an alternative to some of these things that were sort of set.

KEN OLDEN: Safari was almost the first steady matinée situation, which was perfect for that crowd. You could tell that kids had almost been waiting for that—kids like us, who were out in the suburbs knowing each other and hanging with each other but the only other thing you had was the 9:30 Club so sometimes you would get a couple shows catering to the hardcore crowd like Cro-Mags or Sick of it All coming through. That was the height of the "murder capital" era. Here we are a bunch of suburban kids, going into the most dangerous city in the country—almost the most dangerous city in the free world.

"That is the place where underage kids like myself could go see all kinds of heavy metal bands from hardcore to thrash to death metal."
—Sparky Voyles, *Extremity Retained: Notes From the Death Metal Underground*

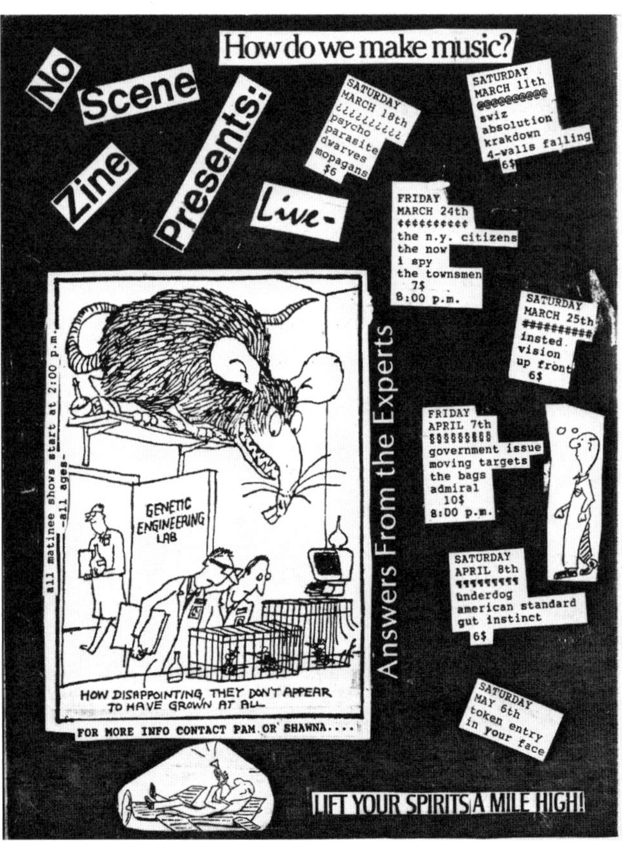

DAVE CHELSEA-SIEFERT: In the late eighties the DC scene was basically two clubs—9:30 and DC Space. There were some venues that had shows infrequently or for a span of several months, but either they weren't regular enough to be a reliable source of good punk shows or they stopped having shows as soon as they got a good booking schedule going. Both Space and 9:30 were great and booked awesome bands, but they each had a pretty diverse sampling of acts and genres, so hardcore shows didn't occur there as often as a lot of us kids wanted. The Safari Club was great because they had hardcore and harder-edged punk shows every week all year long!

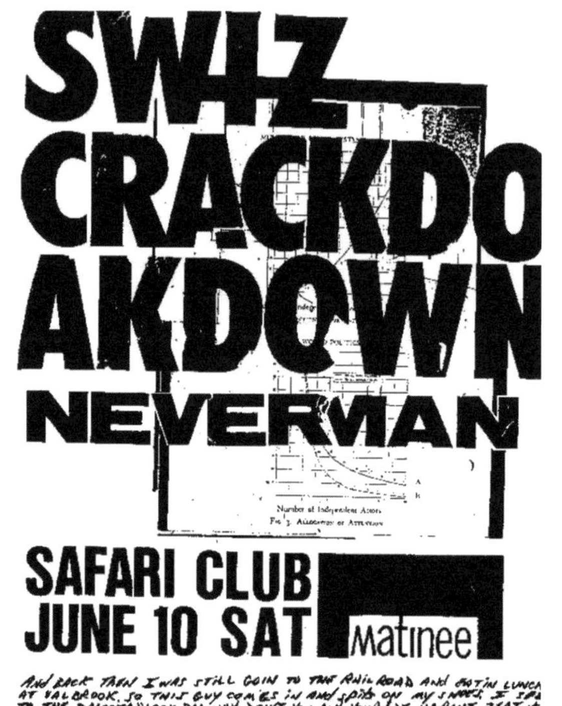

CF BEST: I loved the fact that I could go see shows there in the afternoon. If I was grounded, my parents didn't care that I went out in the afternoon.

BEN CHUSED: At the time I was living in Southeast DC, Capitol Hill. Since a lot of the hardcore shows at Safari Club were matinées, I could just walk from home a couple miles to downtown DC and I didn't need to argue with my parents to stay out late. Half the time, I don't even think I told them where I was going.

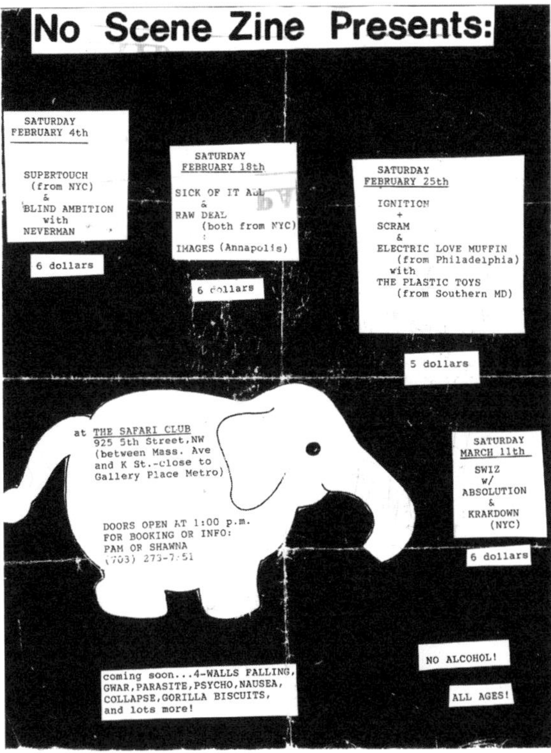

SEAN DORSEY: Flyers at Smash in Georgetown or word of mouth were really the only way I found out about Safari shows until I became friends with people in the scene actually doing the shows like Jon and Martin, who would then give you a heads up. The Hardcore Calendar that Martin put out one summer was epic for sure.

TIM OWEN: Safari was the perfect layout, perfect size, and perfect stage height. All the barriers were broken down. You could meet the bands. You could be on stage. You could take photos. I remember being outside on the sidewalk and a band would roll up and you'd get so excited.

MARK ADAMS: I just remember the club being really dark, even during the matinée shows. You'd walk outside and be completely blinded as your eyes would adjust. That, and the giant gorilla on the side of the stage! The neighborhood was really freaky as it had a strip club next door, a liquor store on the other side of the street, and a crackhouse next door. It was one of those neighborhoods where any minute you'd be expecting The Warriors to be rounding the corner, walking down the sidewalk.

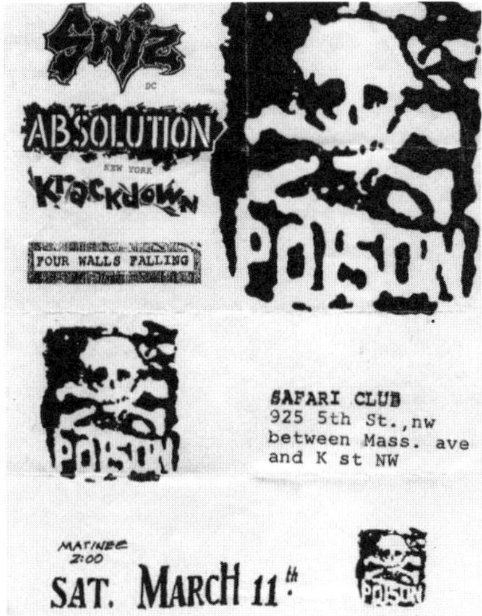

CHRIS LYMAN: The space was like a thousand places I have seen since then. It had mirrored walls, a dirty floor, a nice medium-high stage. The neighborhood, however, was fascinating: part drug market, part war zone, all wonderful to a wide-eyed suburban kid like myself.

MOE SHORTER: It was on the underground circuit of venues/not in the mainstream. It was dark, had no glitz or glam, very raw—lacking furniture, fixtures, and adornment, but cozy. It was definitely a spot where "you could get your freak on."

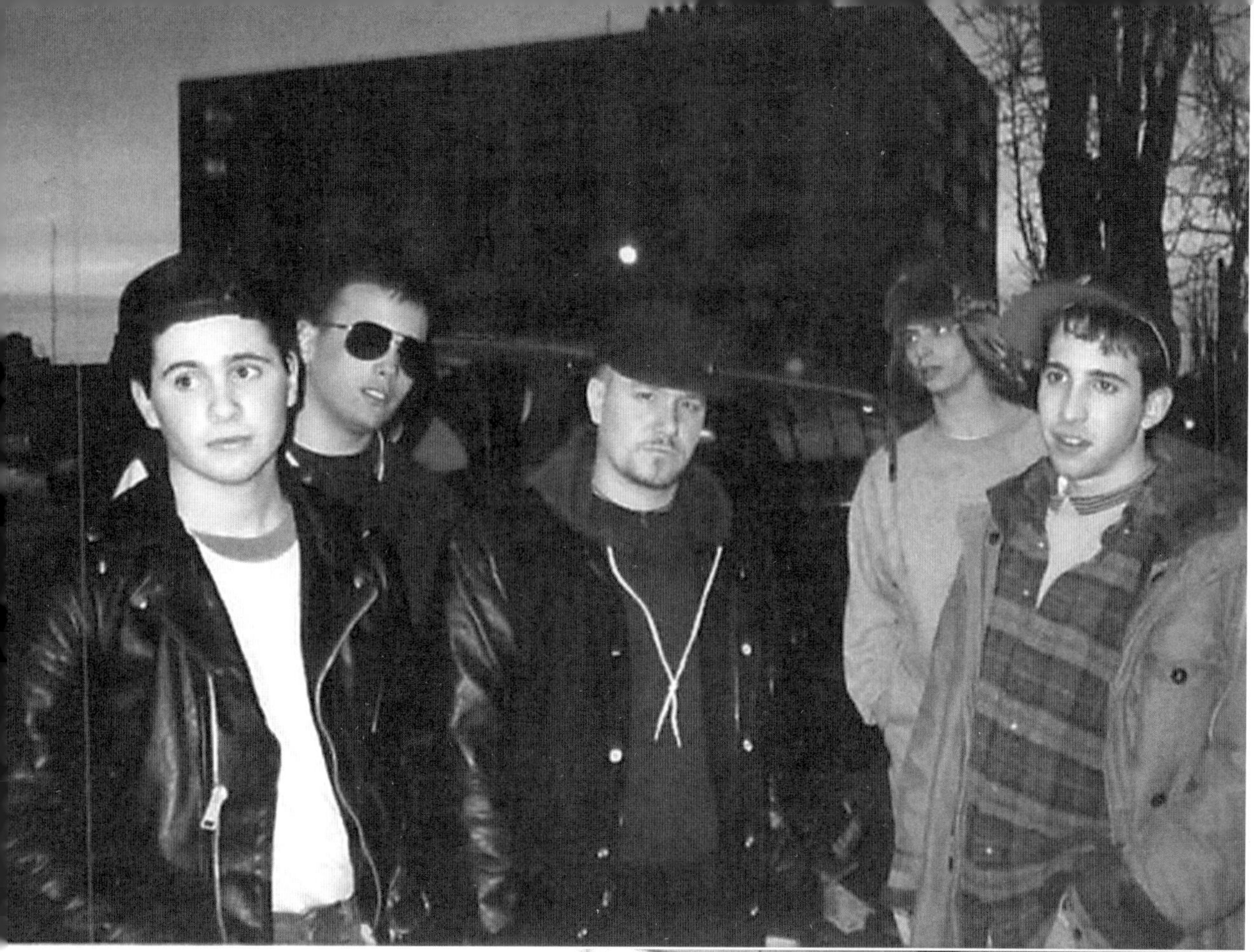

It was a cool space with those animals inside. Kind of campy. The neighborhood was like every hardcore club's hood. Crap. That's how you knew you were in the right place.
—Anthony Communale

Above: Anthony Drago, Bill Wilson, Pete Koller, Derek, and Carl Porcaro hanging out, 1988. Photo courtesy of Bill Wilson.

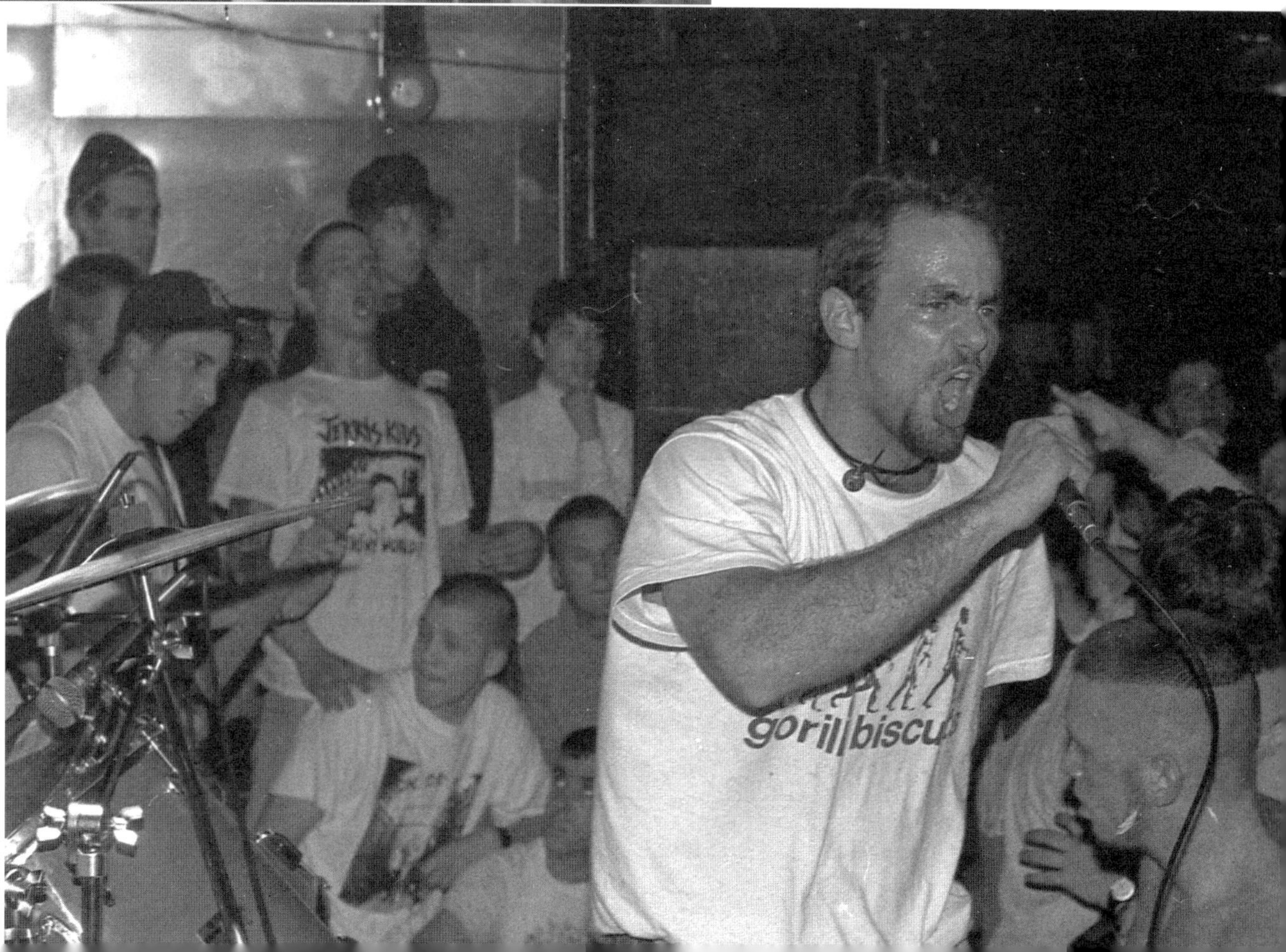

Raw Deal, 1988.
Photo by Joe Wongananda.

PHIL BAXLEY: The neighborhood was awful but I didn't care. I felt like "I'm a hardcore kid. I'm going to see a show," like a ridiculous badge of honor and nothing would happen to me. I never got the sense of danger. You'd get off the metro and you'd always see groups of hardcore kids. I met Jason Hamacher that way—just walking to a show.

RICH DOLINGER: I lived in Alexandria and we used to catch the metro at Huntington Station. There we met up with all the Woodbridge kids wearing Bold and GB shirts. We were like a pack of suburban youth rolling into Chinatown.

MEREDITH WRIGHT-DOWELL: I remember waiting outside the Safari Club waiting for the doors to open and hearing talk about people from the show *America's Most Wanted* having been there looking for a runaway or missing kid. I never saw anything about it on the show but, admittedly, I didn't watch it that often.

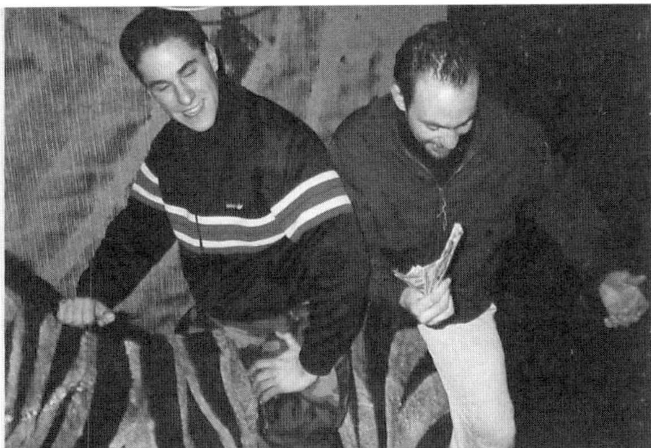

ANTHONY COMMUNALE: It was a cool space with those animals inside. Kind of campy. The neighborhood was like every hardcore club's hood. Crap. That's how you knew you were in the right place. We never played in a decent area back then.

ARTHUR SMILIOS: I always thought that club was a gas. Then there was just the idea of playing DC to all of us from New York—no Minor Threat, no Gorilla Biscuits—not that we're in their league, ever, but just playing that city was special.

WALTER SCHREIFELS: It might have been our first show in DC. I thought it was cool that "there were these two girls" doing the shows—that was unusual.

MARK ANDERSEN: Given this high level of testosterone, it was quite a surprise to discover that the main show organizers were two hard-working and upbeat young women, the ubiquitous Pam-n-Shawna. A reminder not to judge too quickly or easily, no doubt.

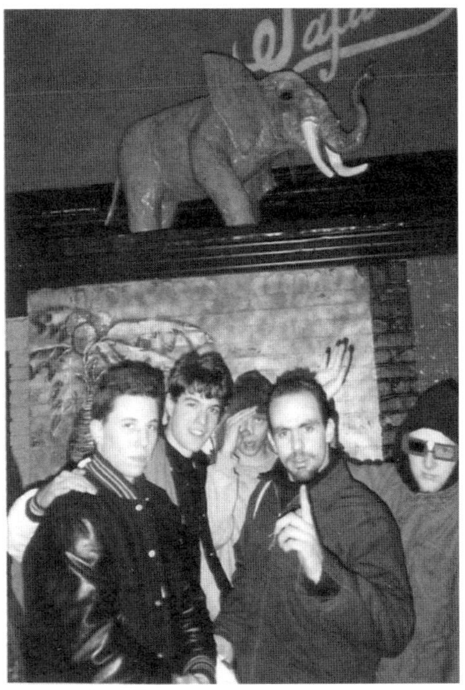

CHUCK TREECE: DC was a place I always associated with HR. This place was more like a place where the kids were more involved versus a club owner. It was easy for Richie to get off the phone and say, "Oh, we're going to play Safari Club." The scene was already there, the crowd was already there,

Above: Armand Majidi and Anthony Communale horse around on the stuffed zebra inside the club. 1988. Photo by Bill Wilson.

Above: Craig Setari, Arthur Smilios, Derek, Anthony Communale, and Chance inside of Safari Club, 1988. Photo by Bill Wilson.

and Pam and Shawna were involved with it, so it was like a home versus a weird VFW hall.

KATYA ODDIO: The most amazing thing about the Safari matinées was that here you had two girls who were about the same age as my friends and I, who were making their dreams come true. They were uniting hardcore scenes from New York, New Jersey, and all over the country. They were bringing them all together. That was super cool. They were really fucking doing it. You know? That was incredible, especially when it was such a testosterone heavy scene, to have teenage girls making it happen. In cooperation with *No Scene Zine, Clockwork Fanzine*, and *Take a Stand*, they organized shows with legendary bands!

CHRIS HARTNETT: Many bands from NY ran through the Safari Club. Two major reasons for success of hardcore in the DC area were Vinyl Ink and Safari Club Saturday afternoon gigs, no bullshit.

SHAWNA KENNEY: I remember Pam and I looking at *The Way It Is* and saying "let's book every band on this album." We didn't get them all, but we at least called someone from every band on there.

JASON FARRELL: The straight edge bands—most of our dislike of them was purely rooted in envy. They were doing very well and we were frustrated about that. At the same time, that's not excluding all NY bands. Absolution, American Standard, Krakdown—these are bands that didn't go with what we thought was the easy route of straight edge mosh breakdown parts or what we perceived as a formula. Krakdown seemed legitimately dangerous. They looked real. They didn't wear big puffy shoes. They were more Void than Youth of Today. To me, that was way more interesting.

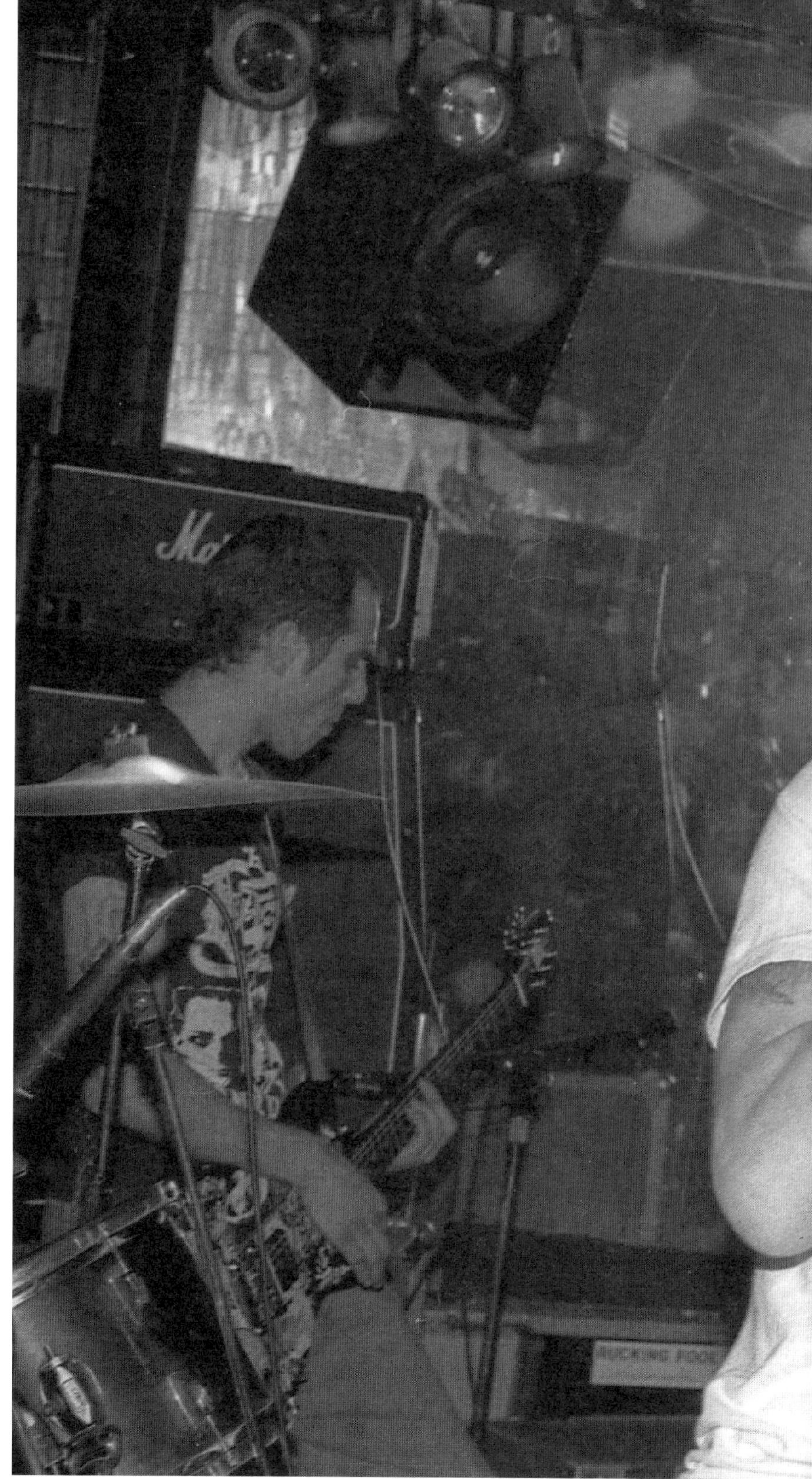

Krakdown, March 1989.
Photo by Joe Wongananda.

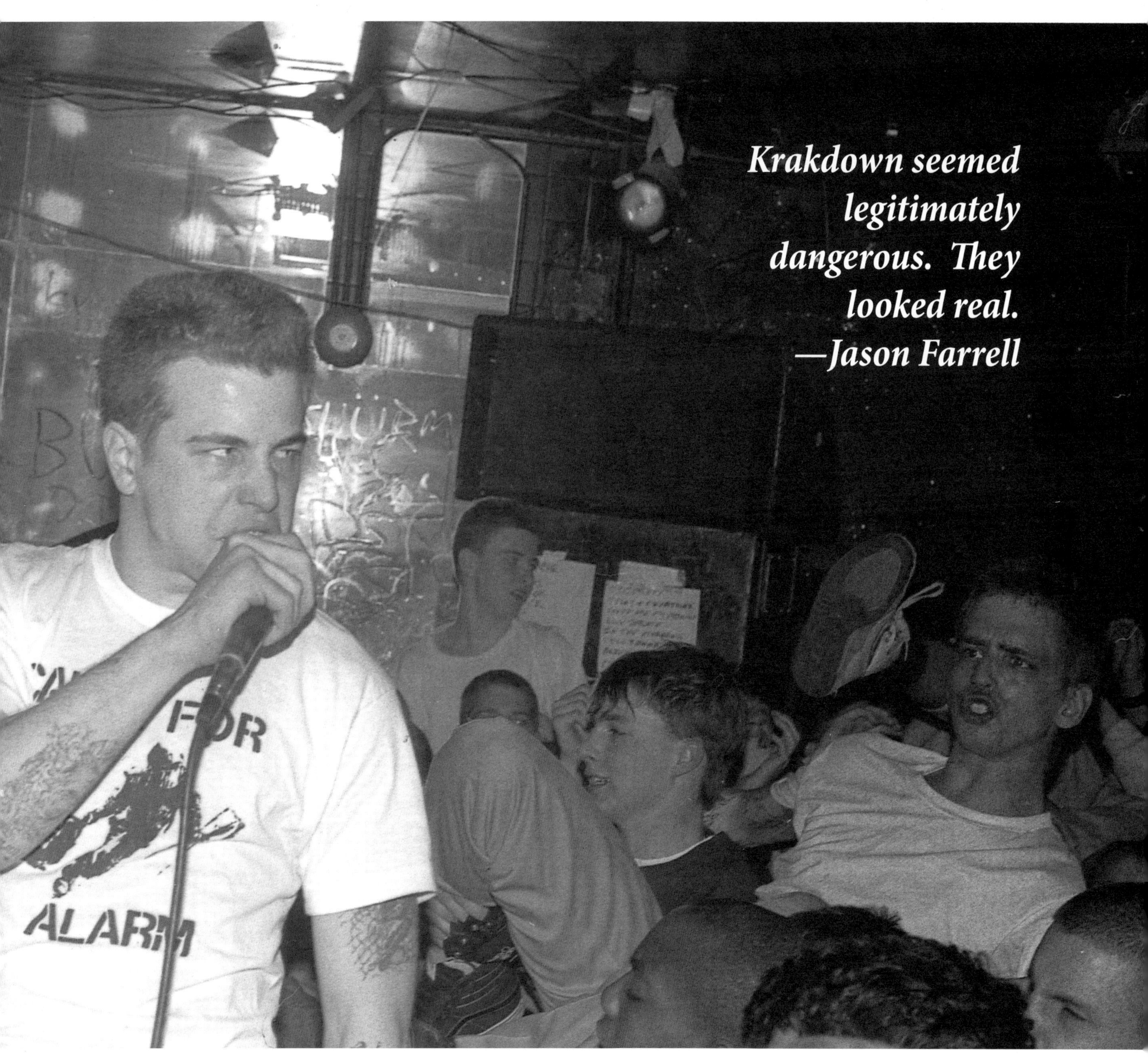

Krakdown seemed legitimately dangerous. They looked real.
—Jason Farrell

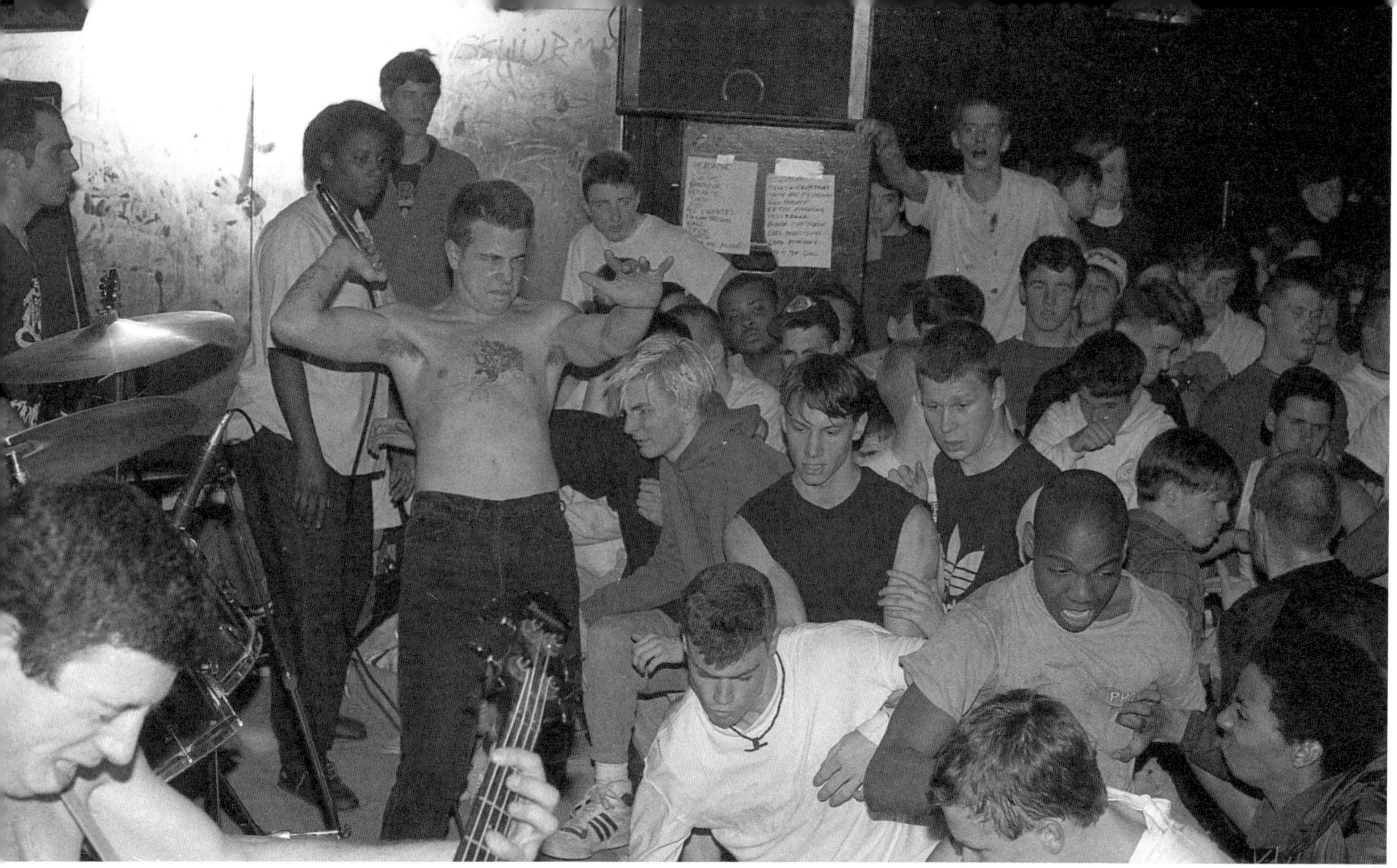

Krakdown, March 1989.
Photo by Joe Wongananda.

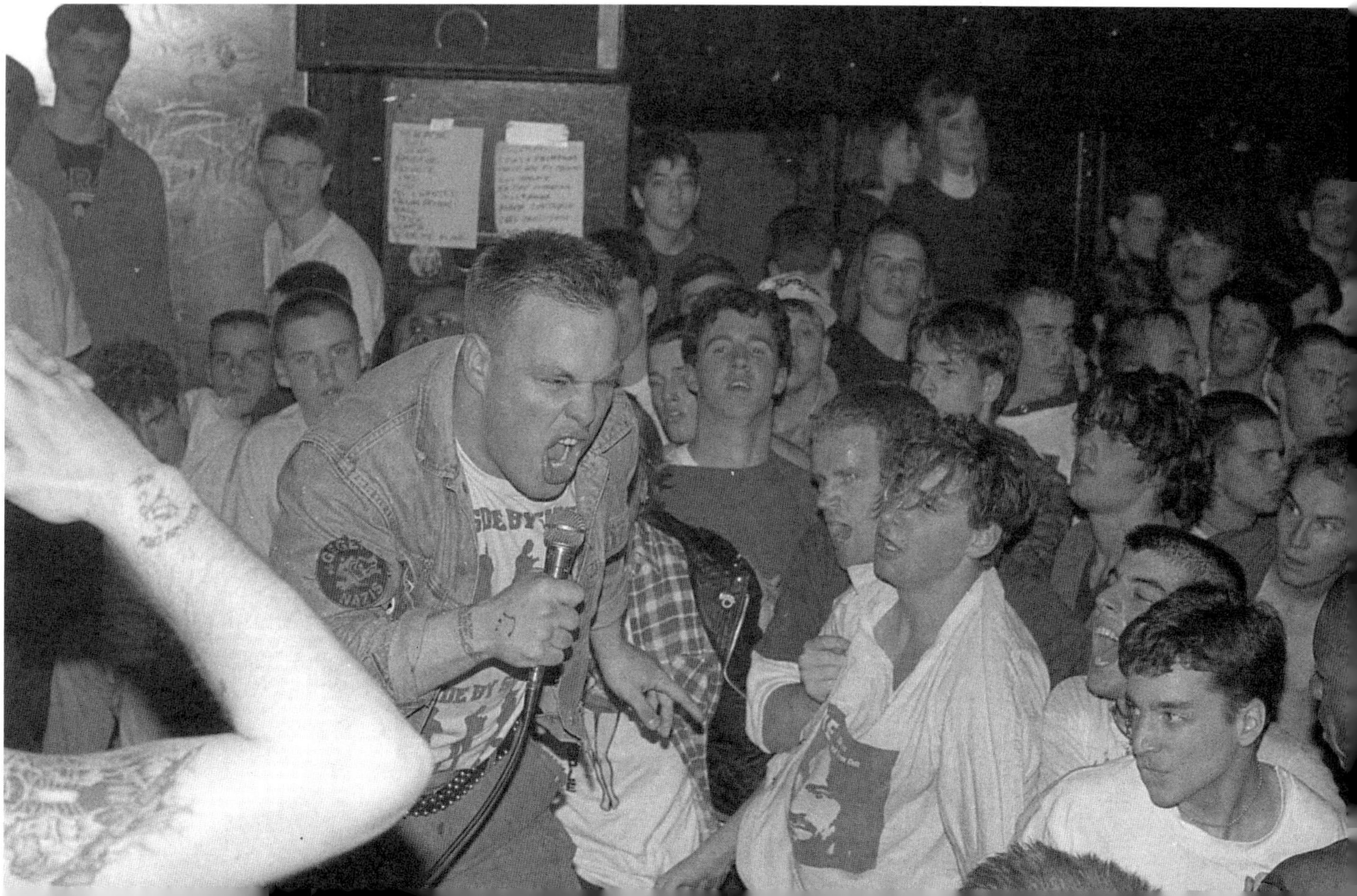

Gavin Van Vlack (of Absolution) takes mic during Krakdown set, March 1989.
Photo by Joe Wongananda.

RICHI KRAKDOWN: My favorite band is Void. To me, that's hardcore. That's the level you have to play at. You have to take that guitar and you have to bash it, feedback out of control. If you look at the Faith/Void split album, you can see the bass player. He's wearing a black ski cap. And he looks so fucking hardcore. You're like "who wears shit like that?" We always thought that was totally fucking cool. And guess what… We get into DC and it's freezing cold out. We head into a liquor store. I see this cardboard box sitting right in front of the counter. I look inside of the box and inside there's a black ski cap for $1.99. I was like, "Squirm, check this shit out. VOID CAPS!!!" They were like, "NO WAY!" I put that shit on, and I was like, "Yo, we're in DC now! Holy shit, this is hardcore." I have a picture of me the next day at CB's and I'm wearing that hat while playing guitar. I never took it off that whole weekend. I slept in it.

DAN CAV: I went with a bunch of bands from New Jersey—Turning Point, Release, and all the New York bands—GBs and others. We'd always go down in mass groups. Every time time we went there it seems like we'd get lost. For some reason we couldn't navigate letters, numbers. The grid system with circles is tough.

JOE SONGCO: Oh man, it was like you had this idea of "Washington, DC" in your head—the monuments, the government buildings, etc.—and you thought it was going to be this different world. Then you saw New York Ave and the area where the club was and it was like "hey, this isn't so

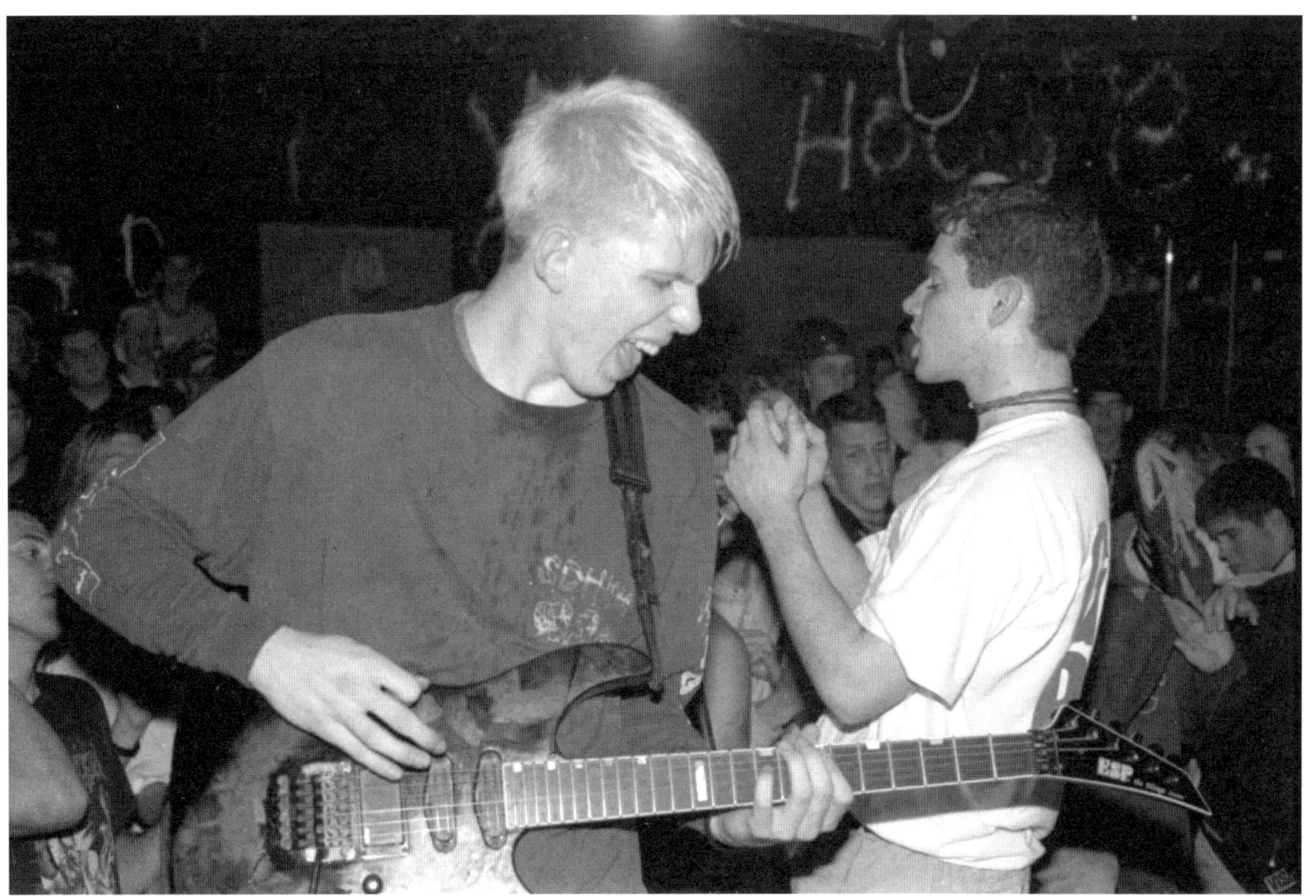

Turning Point. Photo by Chris Yormick.

different from home." I'm born and raised in New York City, but the biggest street rat I've ever seen in my life, I saw on the streets of DC.

DAVE CHELSEA-SEIFERT: The club itself was notable mostly for all of the shabby stuffed wild animals all over the place. I seem to remember that some of them were missing patches of fake fur, kind of like they had mange. It was fairly large by the standards of DC clubs at the time, and the stage wasn't that high, so it was easy to stage dive. It smelled better than 9:30, you didn't feel like there was a danger of hitting your head on the ceiling like you did at DC Space, and it wasn't freezing like the BBQ Iguana.

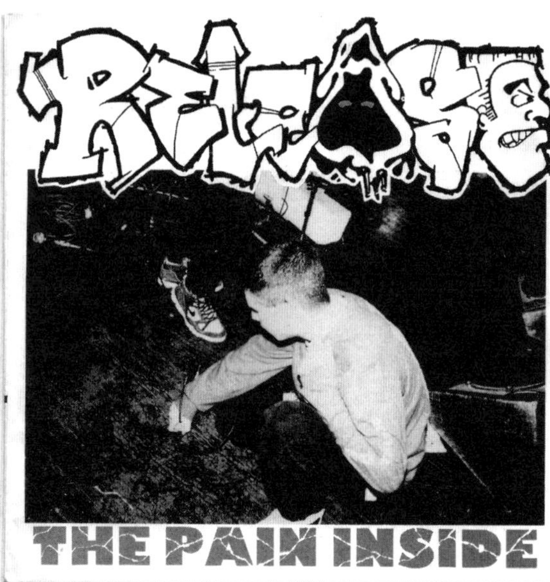

ALEX DANIELS: They had stuffed animals that must have been there from 1964 or something. All discolored with grease on them. Cigarette smoke had discolored them over the decades. I just remember thinking these were fire hazards. Something's going to fall on them, someone's going to light one of them and they're gonna blow the whole place up.

KURT UBERSAX: I remember that damn gorilla! First time I walked in, I remember the thing just standing there, like some stuffed bouncer. It was surreal. Is this the place I've been hearing about?

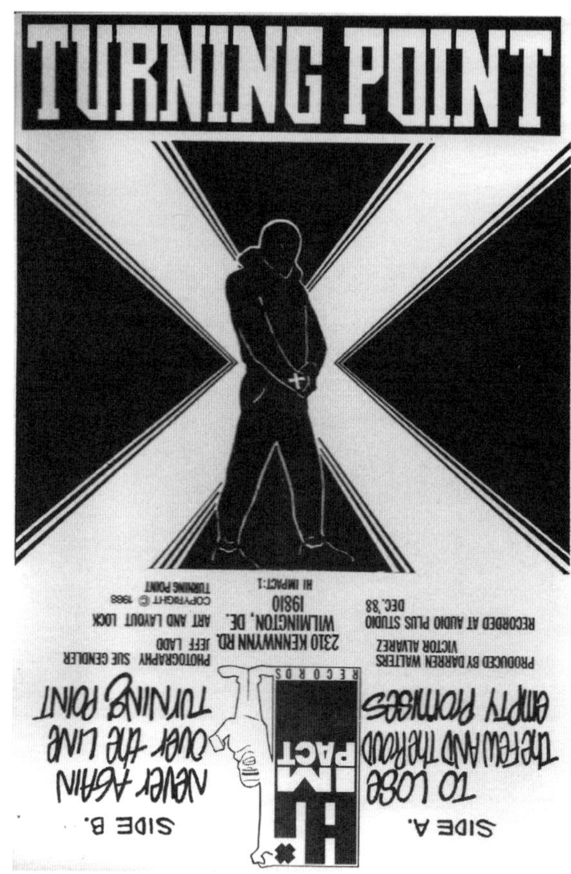

DAVID BYRD: I had heard about Safari Club while living in Florida and seen pictures in zines and stuff so you think it's this grandiose place and then you show up and it's like a typical shithole. But it was also a place where you thought, *Wow, this is a place where all these bands played and in Florida we don't get to see those bands.* It was kinda like going to CBGBs for the first time, where you show up and it's just a long closet with stickers all over it. It was perfect for hardcore shows.

DARREN WALTERS: Karl [Hedgepath] and I were best friends growing up—he went to Salisbury State. I think him and his roommate John Galbraith found out about the shows in DC, met Tim [Owens] who I do Jade Tree with. I got introduced to Tim from going to Safari Club. They told me about the shows and I started to come down and meet those guys.

JASON ORR: My dad would drop me and my friends—a bunch of thirteen-year-olds—off in his cab. I was coming from Woodbridge. He knew the area. He knew when next door was the Brass Rail, a notorious drug and gay club. He had faith in me.

JAY MARTIN: Just the idea of parking in the neighborhood of the club was pretty disconcerting. Fortunately, I never had my car broken into, but Earl Hudson wasn't so lucky. He came down to see a show that, as I recall, Ignition was to play, and he had the back window of his car broken in to. I think it was then that we realized the Bad Brains probably wouldn't ever be playing a Safari Club matinée during our time.

KENNY INNOUYE: I used to go there semiregularly to check out bands when I was booking 9:30 Club. The neighborhood was pretty sketchy, even by DC sketchy neighborhood standards. I remember I only used to go there when it wasn't raining because I would only go there on bicycle. I wouldn't drive there because I didn't want to bother with the hassle of my car getting broken into. Going to shows in DC, I used to get my car broken into at least five or six times a year, and going to Safari was just a huge invitation for getting your car fucked with. It got to the point that I used to always have a bunch of towels in the trunk of the car, so that when someone smashed the car window all I'd have to do is throw the towels over the broken glass and drive off. I did this because a lot of times folks will wait around and hide after they break in your car for you to come back and then mug you while you're busy cleaning out the glass in your car. I never gave them that chance.

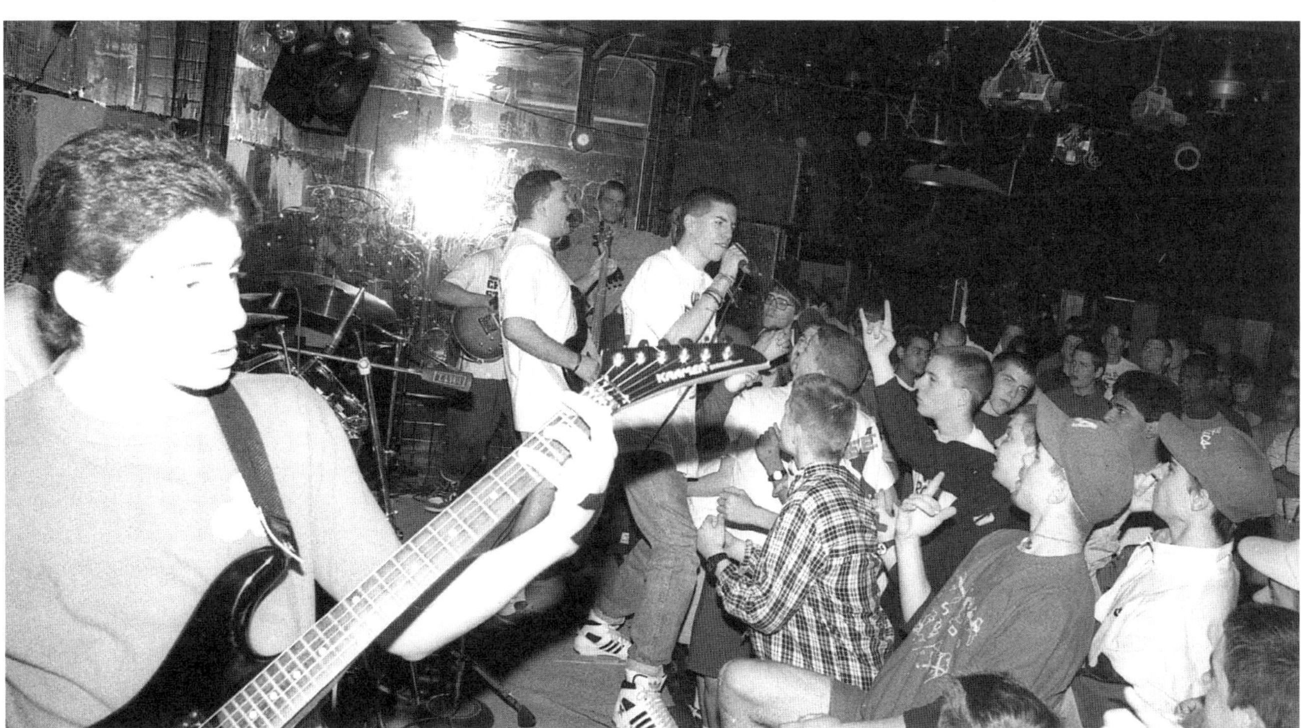

Release. Photo by Joe Wongananda.

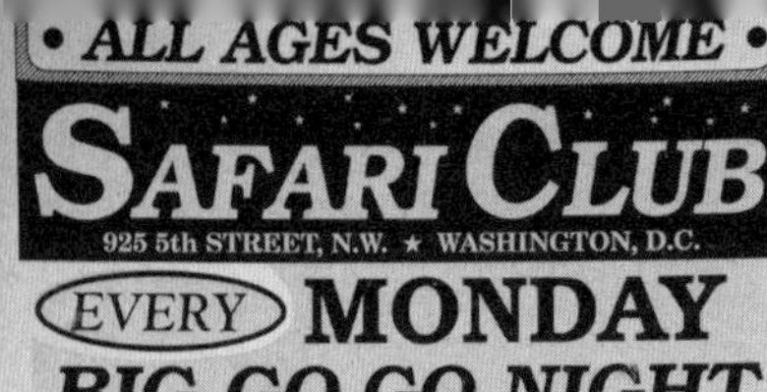

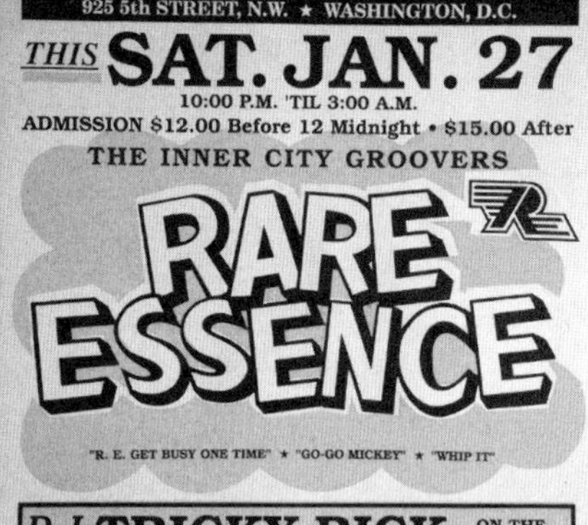

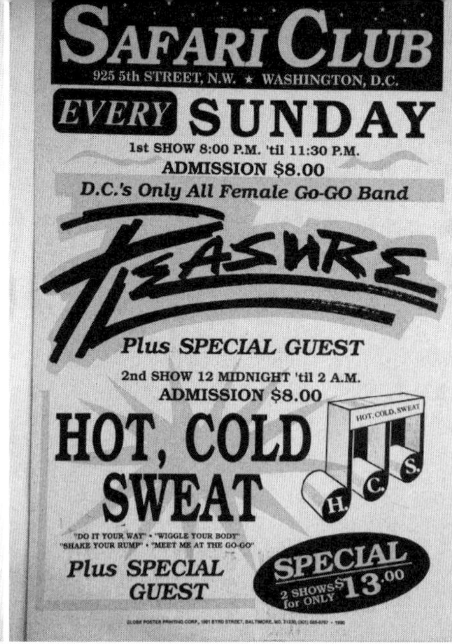

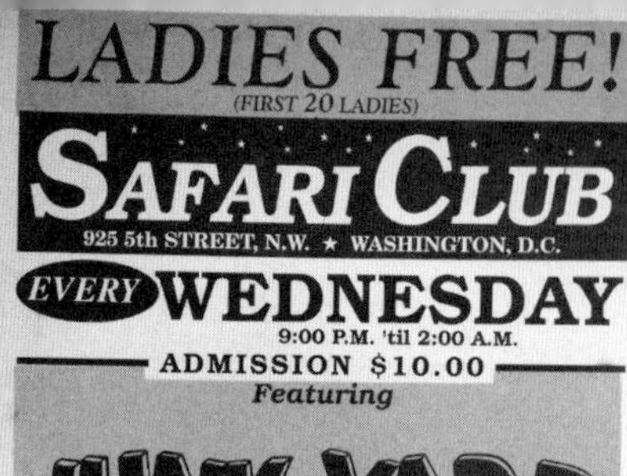

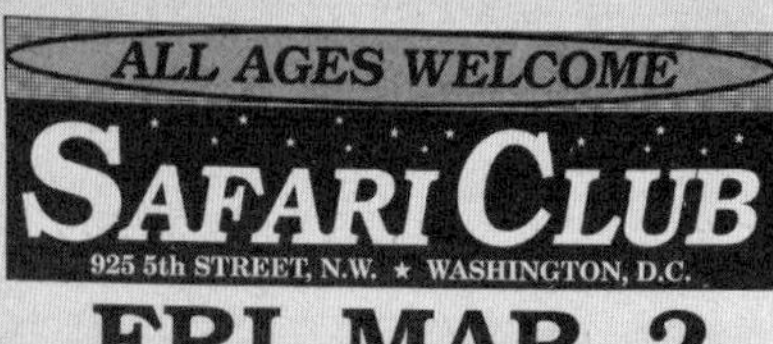

SAFARI CLUB
925 5th STREET, N.W. ★ WASHINGTON, D.C.
SAT. APRIL 7
10:00 P.M. 'til 3:00 A.M.
ADMISSION $10.00 Before 12 Midnight — $12.00 After —
Featuring
The BEST GO-GO BAND IN TOWN!
JUNK YARD BAND
"BRAND NEW FUNK" "WORK YOUNGIN'"
"FREAK-A-DEKE ZONE" "MOVIN' & GROOVIN'" "PUSH IT"
"TAKE ME OUT TO SEE JUNK YARD"
Security by METROPOLITAN POLICE
24 HOUR HOT LINE 371-9275
NO IN's & OUT's • NO REFUNDS • NO RECORDING SOUND SYSTEMS
The SAFARI is FREE of DRUGS & VIOLENCE

The BEST GO-GO BAND IN TOWN!
SAFARI CLUB
925 5th STREET, N.W. ★ WASHINGTON, D.C.
SAT. MAR. 24
10:00 P.M. 'til 3:00 A.M.
ADMISSION $10.00 Before 12 Midnight — $12.00 After —
Featuring

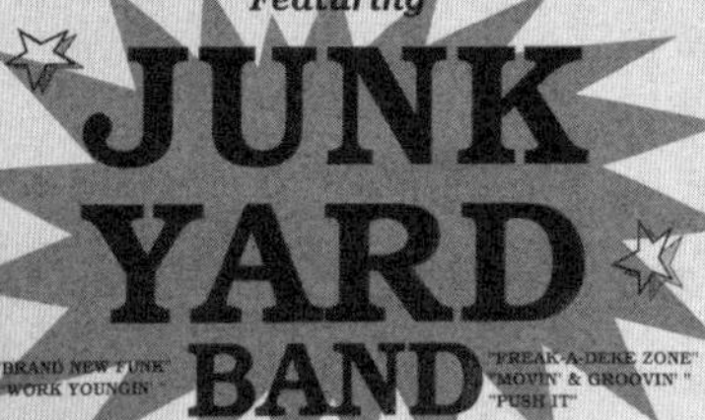

Security by METROPOLITAN POLICE
24 HOUR HOT LINE 371-9275
NO IN's & OUT's • NO REFUNDS • NO RECORDING SOUND SYSTEMS
The SAFARI is FREE of DRUGS & VIOLENCE

The BEST GO-GO BAND IN TOWN!
SAFARI CLUB
925 5th STREET, N.W. ★ WASHINGTON, D.C.
SAT. MAR. 3
10:00 P.M. 'til 3:00 A.M.
ADMISSION $10.00
LADIES Before 11 P.M. $8.00
Featuring
JUNK YARD BAND
"BRAND NEW FUNK" "WORK YOUNGIN'"
"FREAK-A-DEKE ZONE" "MOVIN' & GROOVIN'" "PUSH IT"
"TAKE ME OUT TO SEE JUNK YARD"
Security by METROPOLITAN POLICE
24 HOUR HOT LINE 371-9275
NO IN's & OUT's • NO REFUNDS • NO RECORDING SOUND SYSTEMS
The SAFARI is FREE of DRUGS & VIOLENCE

ALL AGES WELCOME
SAFARI CLUB
925 5th STREET, N.W. ★ WASHINGTON, D.C.
SAT. FEB. 17
10:00 P.M. UNTIL
ADMISSION $8.00 Before 12 Midnight ★ $10.00 After
D.C.'s Sharpest New Go-Go Band
3rd DIMENSION BAND
Special Guest
BACK YARD BAND
FOR MORE INFORMATION CALL: 371-9275
Security by METROPOLITAN POLICE

SAFARI CLUB
925 5th STREET, N.W. ★ WASHINGTON, D.C.
SAT. JULY 28
10:00 P.M. 'til 3:00 A.M.
ADMISSION $10.00 Before 12 Midnight • $12.00 After
STARRING
JUNK YARD BAND
"SARDINES" "WORD"
"TAKE ME OUT TO SEE JUNK YARD"
ALL GIRL GO-GO BAND
PRE'CIS
"YOU JINGLING BABY"
• Formerly Members of PLEASURE •
Featuring SWEET SHELL
BODY SWEAT BAND
FOR INFORMATION CALL: 371-9275

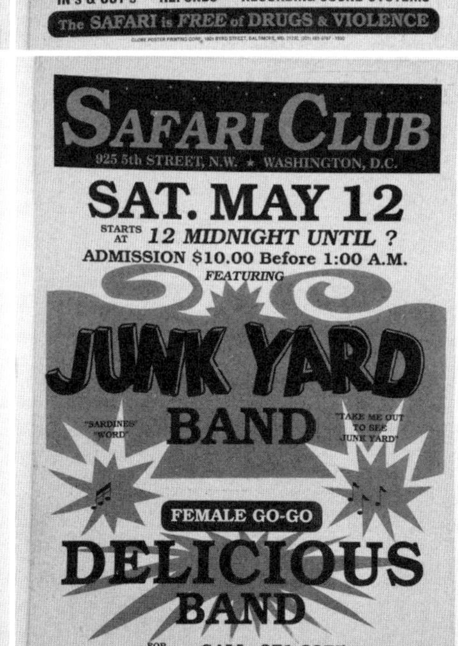

MY MAIN MAN . . . HALLE'S BIRTHDAY
SAFARI CLUB
925 5th STREET, N.W. ★ WASHINGTON, D.C.
SAT. MAY 5
9:00 P.M. 'til 3:00 A.M.
ADMISSION $10.00 Before 12 Midnight
Featuring
JUNK YARD BAND
"SARDINES" "WORD"
"TAKE ME OUT TO SEE JUNK YARD"
The GOOD JUNK

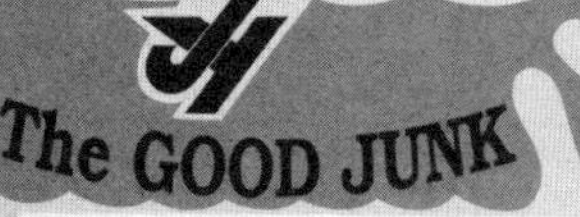

FOR INFORMATION CALL: 371-9275

RODNEY BUTINELLI: There was always that trifecta of people going from Safari to DC Space to 9:30. You would walk that four or five block radius knowing there's gotta be something going on. People would walk back and forth.

SEAN DORSEY: The DC Chinatown neighborhood was very raw and had a lot of soul. The better shows were always in the humid DC summers, and the Safari Club was always twenty degrees hotter than outside, which seemed to make the shows that much more intense. The black walls and black exterior added to the underground aesthetic of the space. DC has always been a city where one block is baller and the next block over will be sketchy. The area where Safari Club was at the time was very much the latter. One time, everyone left a show and headed out to the parking lot to find out that every single car had their windows smashed out and had been broken into.

JASON ORR: Once, I think if I'd been dropped off ten minutes later I wouldn't be the same person because right after [my dad] pulled away, a guy fell off the front stoop of the methadone clinic and his feet were on the sidewalk and his head was in the building and I think if my mom had seen that I probably never would have been allowed out again.

STEVE SQUINT: It had a methadone clinic across the street. [The owner] was pimping out transvestites.

NATHAN LARSON: Was the club owned by Ethiopian gangsters? It seemed like Pam and Shawna were always dealing with some shadiness behind-the-scenes.

PAM GENDELL: Haile, the owner, told us he was Eritrean—not Ethiopian. And he had an older friend who would hang out sometimes who had a fake wooden hand—he said his hand had been blown off in the war.

SHAWNA KENNEY: Medupe was the manager—he was a young guy from Kenya, maybe? His sister bartended there, too. She was really nice and played in an all-woman go-go band called Pleasure.

MOE SHORTER: One of my most vivid memories of Safari was Haile Daniels. Quite often when Haile would see me he would say, "Moe—my man… Monnnnney, I like money" (while rubbing his fingers together). He made good money on the nights Junkyard would play.

JOHN GALBRAITH: When Junkyard stopped doing Wednesday shows there that hurt his money flow. I figured out he was making about $20,000 a week between all the shows. Sometimes I felt bad for him because the club would get destroyed. People would purposely try to kick the disco ball, and who knows what happened to those stuffed animals. I'd say a quarter of all clubs in DC were owned by someone of Ethiopian or Eritrean descent.

ED LINTON: We had to replace so many microphones after the punk shows. Sometimes they'd get flattened at the go-go shows, too.

MICHAEL STRAIGHT: I told my parents I was booking shows in College Park. If I told my dad where it really was, they wouldn't have let me go.

JOHN ENGLE: I met a few straight edge kids at my new school in Montgomery County. They brought me to my first Safari show—actually my dad dropped me off. They lied to their parents about going to the mall. Bold was headlining.

SHAWNA KENNEY: We got calls from parents sometimes. Haile would tell us to pick up the phone in the office because "somebody's dad wants to speak to Pam or Shawna." Parents wanted to know if there was "supervision." We were like "yeah—us!" Probably not very comforting considering I was eighteen and Pam was nineteen.

Facing page: classic go-go band posters. From the collection of Roger Gastman.

JAY MARTIN: I was not quite old enough to be grandfathered in when the drinking laws in DC changed from eighteen to twenty-one, so I used to buy beer at that liquor store across the street because they never carded anyone.

CHUCK COPELAND: I remember the first time we went inside Safari Club, I was like, OK now I see why this place has its name. The big stuffed gorilla and other animals around the place. Fifth and K St. was not the place back in the day for the faint at heart. Hookers, pimps, drug dealers, homeless people, etc. Shit was live back then! Oh, and when the bums use to throw bottles at us from the rooftop across the street!

ANTHONY ONLEY: Chuck (the bouncer) was bigger than I am. He was a big dude that we all respected. I was scared of him. I was a little kid, though! We were like sixteen, seventeen. Chuck was a big deal. Chuck was awesome because he would always get the kids off the monitors. Kids used to walk on kids' faces and shit from the monitors. If you got on the monitors, Chuck would always stop the show. I call it "pulling a Fugazi." He'd stop the show and do a little speech. "If these monitors fall off the ceiling and bust your head and kill one of y'all, that's YOUR ASS!" It got to the point where you knew what he was gonna say, so at the end of his speech—it'd be different all the way until the end—but then we'd all yell, "That's your ASS!" and he'd walk off and the show would start. Nobody would fuck with the monitors until the next show.

Everything was word of mouth. If a band played at a venue and had a great experience with it, they'd go tell everyone, "Yo, this is the spot."
—Toby Morse

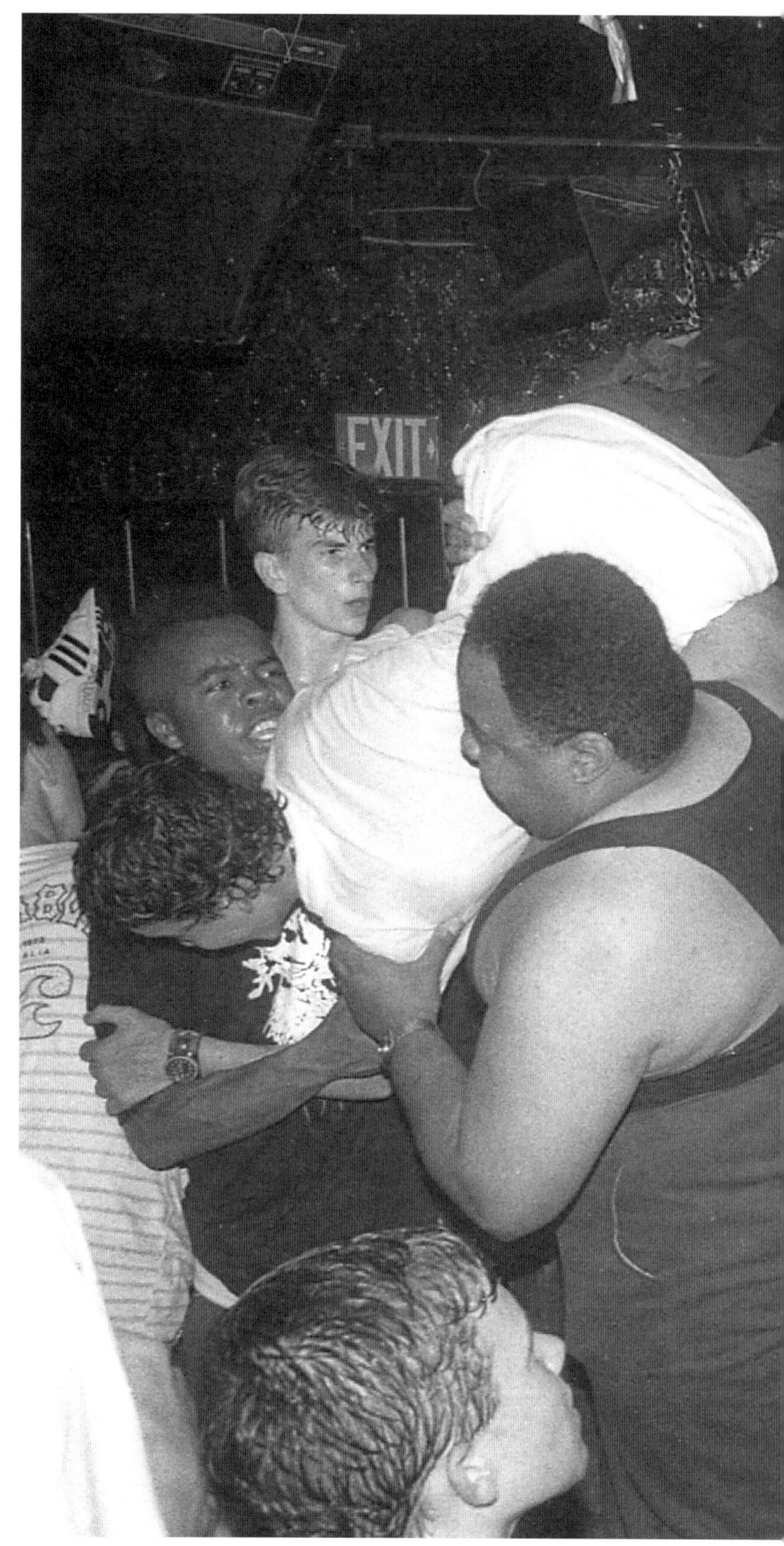

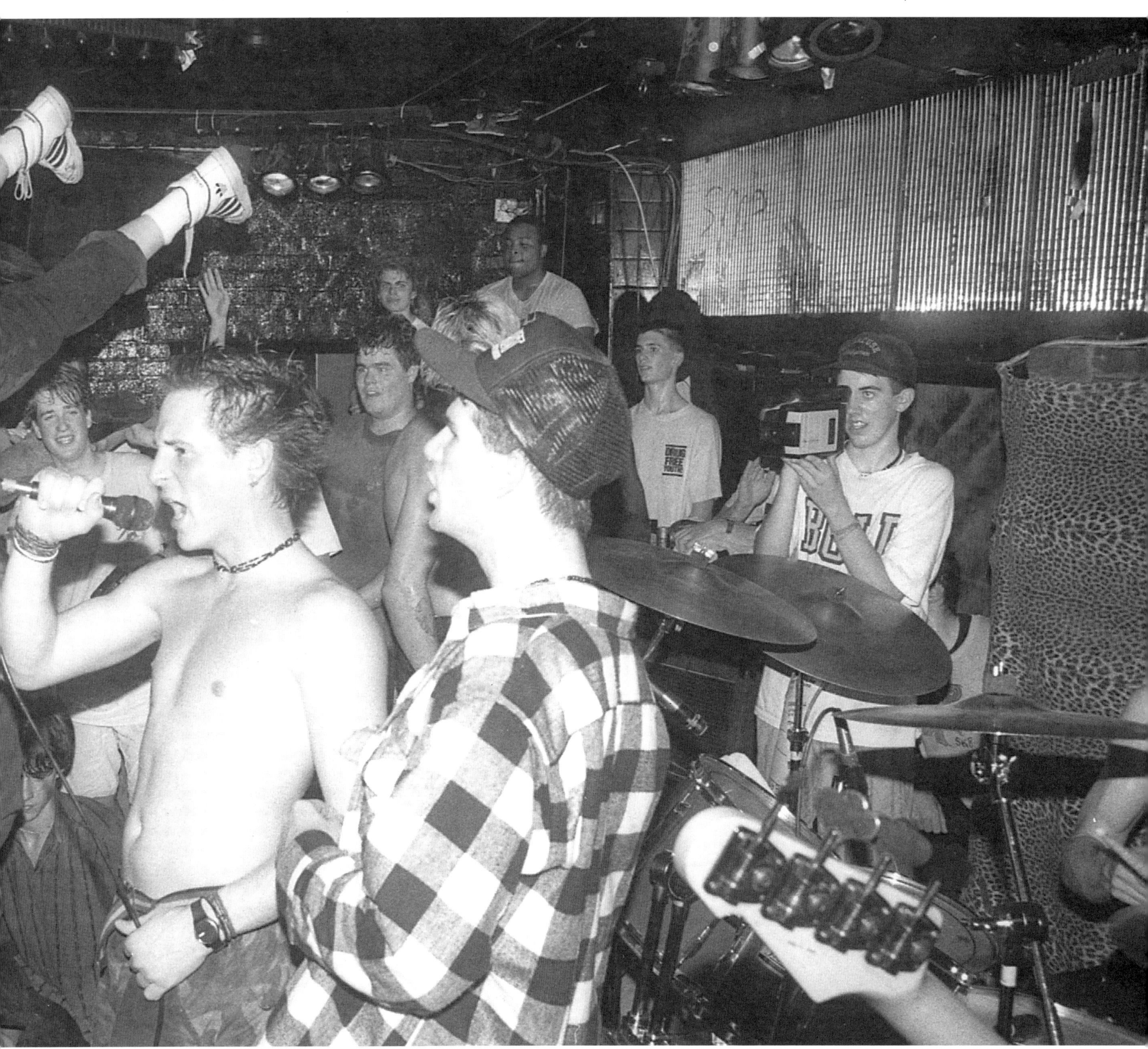

Toby Morse on mic during Token Entry set. Big Chuck the bouncer, in foreground. Photo by Joe Wongananda.

PAM GENDELL: The club owner wanted us to pay for his whole security team at first. These were guys he hired for go-go shows. We refused and said we could police our own scene. Chuck was the only one of the original guys we kept on. He worked security at the Cap Center, too.

GLENN BURNS: I missed the first show so I don't know what it was like, but THIS one, Big Chuck got up on stage, overwhelmed by the pit and the stage diving, and stopped the band from playing, Shawn Brown of Swiz at this point got up and explained exactly what was going on, something to the effect of "this is what we do." Chuck stepped back, and the show resumed as usual, into the chaos

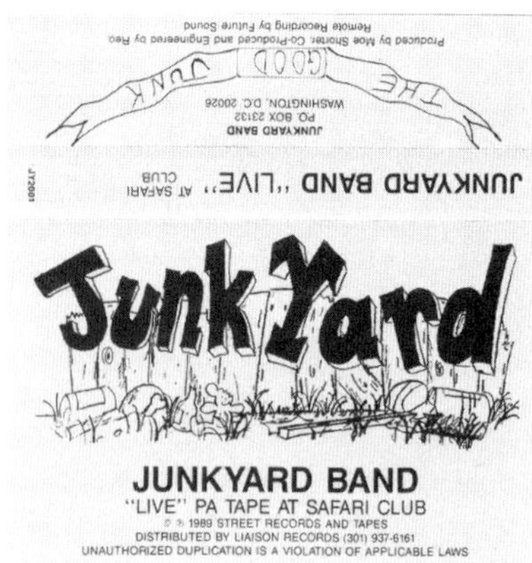

CHRIS LYMAN: One of my absolute favorite parts about the Safari Club was "Big Chuck," the brother that ran the place. He took care of us and ran the club while simultaneously conducting business on the street with some of the go-go bands that he knew. There were a lot of wild rumors about "Big Chuck," but all I do know is that we all felt safer when he was around. He even let me hang out a few times when the club was getting ready for the night (all of the hardcore shows were matinées) and watch go-go bands doing sound checks. I will always be grateful for that.

CHRIS BATTISTA: When the bouncer got too concerned about too many people hanging out next to the equipment to get a view at one show, he stopped the show and said something like, "All of you hanging out up here have got to take two steps back. Back up! Don't look at me like I'm stupid. You gotta do it today, not tomorrow. You go to church tomorrow."

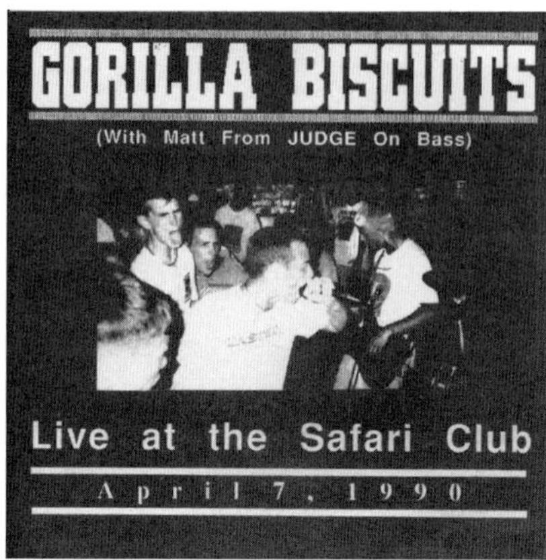

STEVE ZEITZOFF: I remember the big dude bouncer because I would go see hip-hop superfests at the Capital Center and see him. Then there was that woman just yelling at everyone, saying "we're gonna shut it down!"

MARTIN CASTRO: The go-go shows were on Sunday. It was ill. People got shot. Spanish gangs shot each other. There was an AA meeting across the street. It wasn't a nice building. On the corner you had hookers and a transvestite hooker bar. Crackheads. Everything. That was DC in the early nineties.

SAMMY SIEGLER: My main memory of it is that it turned into a go-go club. We'd clear out and the go-go crowd would come in. I grew up in New York City and I wasn't familiar with the go-go scene, so I was fascinated by it.

MOE SHORTER: I can proudly say that Safari Club was our (Junkyard Band's) "spot." Most premier go-go bands can lay claim to some venue where they had a sense of exclusivity among go-go bands. We played there every Tuesday for almost two years from 1989–1991. Some times we would play Friday, Saturday, or Sunday in addition to Tuesday because it was a win-win for the club and the band.

Left: Junkyard Band's cassette, Live at the Safari Club, *1989.*
Above: Gorilla Biscuits unofficial release 7-inch, Live at the Safari Club, *1990.*

KATYA ODDIO: The stage was tall enough that you could hang back at the bar and still see the band. The whole place was painted dark, and by the end of the shows the walls wept with perspiration. Even as kids we could see the similarities between the punk teens in the afternoon and the go-go twenty-somethings in the evenings. These were two groups of young people into peripheral music genres who were making and supporting the music themselves.

MARK ANDERSEN: I remember the sometimes chaotic scene outside the club, with neighborhood kids mixing with the punks, sometimes scary stories about the violence and drugs in the low-income housing complexes up the street—Sursum Corda, Temple Courts, and the Golden Rule Center.

"It was a particularly murderous time in DC, with crack wars still in effect and over five hundred murders a year." —King Fowley, *Extremity Retained: Notes From the Death Metal Underground*

ETHAN MINSKER: Its disco ball and lights from an era definitely gone by. The neighborhood was shit, but you could always find someone on the block who wouldn't mind buying you some beers as long as you got them some, too. Sometimes a girl from the suburbs might have her window broken and the radio stolen, but for the most part nothing too bad really happened. It was a time when punkers were looked at as crazy, not in a crazy wild way, but in an institutional way, especially within Washington's black community, so most of the neighbors kept their distance.

MICHELLE MENNONA: Safari Club was the club that you prepared to go to. What I mean by that is you went to the bathroom about six times before you left your house and you prepared yourself for the smell. I'm not saying it was a bad smell. Well, then again, on a hot summer's day it was pretty particular.

SEAN DORSEY: I remember when someone accidentally broke the ceiling's lights with their fist during Shelter and Endpoint and people were dancing in complete darkness as the band didn't know what to do.

RODNEY BUTINELLI: People who didn't know DC were freaked out about it. People who knew it, it was just another place to go. Some people would call it sketchy back then, sketchier than where DC Space was located. It wasn't as well-lit because back then the government was doing their rolling brown-outs with power. It looked like this nondescript building, like it was condemned. You would see people hanging out on all the corners. You didn't know who was who until you looked and saw studs or leather or skinheads or people that you knew you, and you go "oh this must be the right place." You go in and it was a restaurant by day.

BEN CHUSED: The Safari Club makes me think of all of the latest style of Vans and Doc Martens, Hare Krishnas selling little books on reincarnation and "Razor's Edge" fanzines, literature on vegetarianism and PETA, Big Adam on stage during every band just tossing kids around, that disco ball right above the pit, and Gut Instinct opening almost every set with "Disturbing the Peace."

CHRIS HARTNETT: In those days, I wore a lot of gold jewelry and a clock around my fuckin' neck, probably the only person in the club who looked like that. Used to go to hardcore shows on Saturday afternoons and go-go shows on

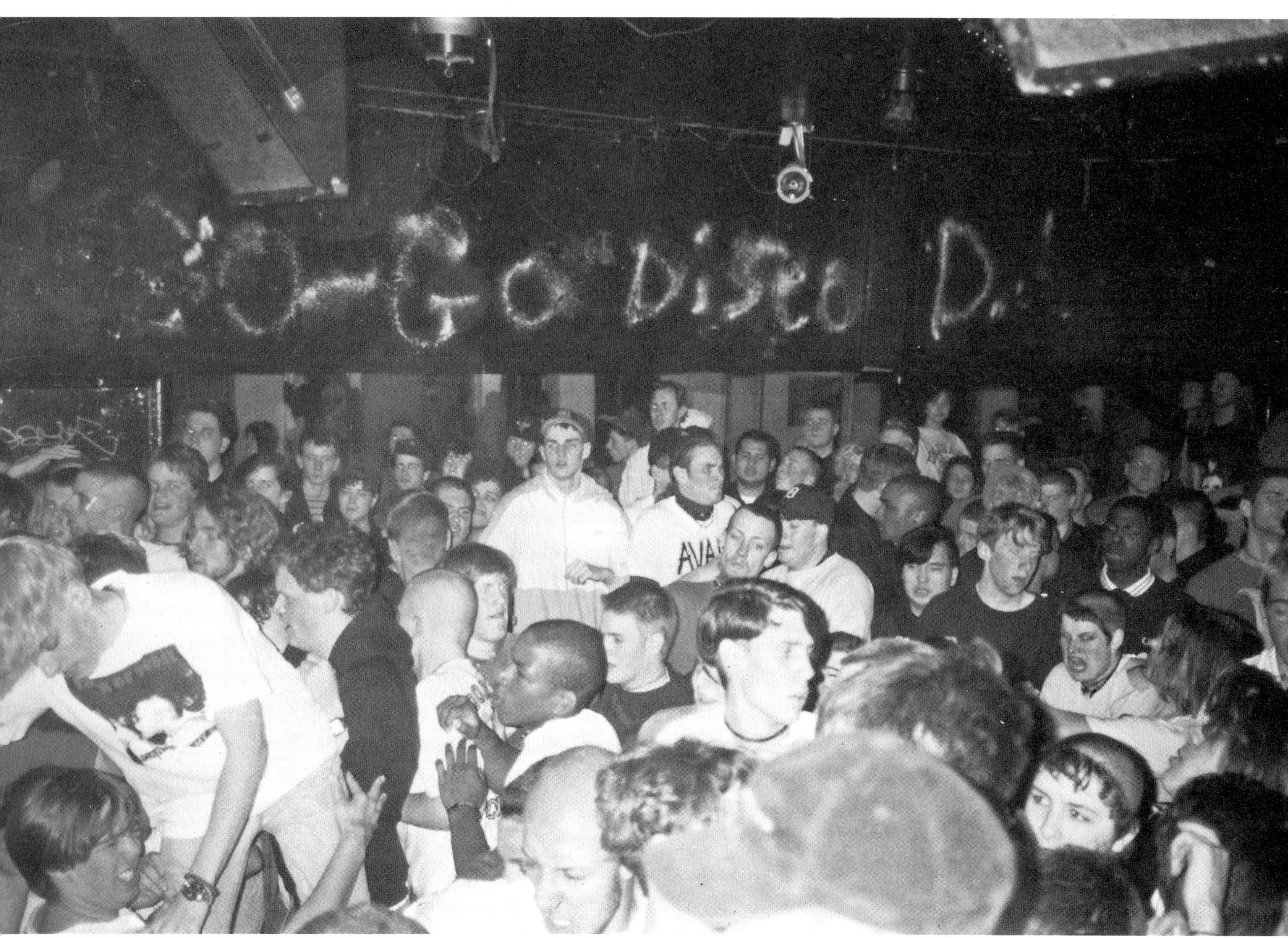

Crowd at a Gorilla Biscuits show.
Photo by Eric Hochberg.

Sunday nights. I had nothing to do with the punk scene other than going to shows. Didn't go to parties, didn't date punk girls, didn't know anybody there, just dug the music. Most people who went to gigs with me there were in the same boat. I audiotaped many shows. My biggest nonaccomplishment was trying to sleep with the hot Ethiopian female bartender. Unfortunately, that never happened.

JAY MARTIN: There was the night show we did with The Accused from Seattle, Washington. It was strange because one, it was a metal band and two, because it was a night show. Not many of either of those really happened during the Shawna/Pam era. I was working the door and acting as "security" (like usual), which is funny in retrospect because I think I only weighed about one hundred pounds. at the time. There was nothing "secure" looking about me. At some point in the evening, we were approached at the door by a guy (homeless, or just thuggish) demanding all of the money from the till box. The counter was just in from the door on the right-hand side when you entered. Across from that was just the interior wall of the hallway, brick as I recall, that led in to the main entrance/room. The guy was all loud and aggressive, saying "we better give him all the money or someone's gonna get hurt." I tried to reason with the guy but he wouldn't let up. It went on like this for a bit. I remembered that we had a small fire extinguisher under the counter, and I told him I'd use it on him if he didn't just turn around and leave. That didn't work and he kept yelling. So I proceeded to pull it out from under the counter and I pointed it at him. He was still being aggressive and yelling and it seemed that he was going to really become violent, and I was getting pretty freaked out myself. I gave him one last chance, and he told me "he knew I wouldn't use it," so I did. I just hit the pump with one quick blast and it shot all over him. He screamed and cussed and ran out of the front door and down the street continuing to yell and scream, covered in white fire extinguisher powder. I just sat there shaking, but cracking up because on the opposite side of the wall from me/the counter, you could see his silhouette in the wall, with the white powder forming the outline. If the cops had come, we could have used that as his profile to gauge how tall he was.

GINI CROWDER: Once I was working the door with Jay and he had some mace that he wanted to "test out," so he sprayed a little bit with the nozzle turned toward the door and the wind wafted it back in our faces. I was blind for a few minutes and Chuck Treece walked me to the bathroom to rinse my eyes out.

KEN OLDEN: One time, we were walking and this guy was like "hey, you got a dollar?" and we didn't have a dollar because we were a bunch of broke kids who barely have enough to get to the show and back. And the dude was like "you know, if it was night time, I would just take it from you." I'm thinking "that guy is fucking serious! If this show ends a little late, we might have a problem getting back to that metro."

MIKE MCTERNAN: When you're leaving, it's dark out but you're so amped and have so much adrenaline. You're leaving with everyone from the show and you definitely feel safer.

JASON FARRELL: By the time we got known for playing Safari Club, our friends like, Kevin Haley and the guys in

Kingface, would make fun of us by saying "yeah, I meant to come to your show but I don't get up that early." I'd be like "fuck you, man." It was so relatively early in the day that anyone who would have been dangerous was still sleeping—but if it went too late, like GB's first show, people sat there waiting four or five hours. When they were supposed to go on stage they got in their car to drive from NY. When it got late, people accelerated their departures because it was a different world and not one that was very comfortable. Being there in the middle of the day was like "sneaking in."

> ***The scene was a generally welcome "nudge" to us "old-timers," underlining the fact that younger folks were making their own sounds and community.***
> ***—Mark Andersen***

MARK ANDERSEN: The scene was a generally welcome "nudge" to us "old-timers," underlining the fact that younger folks were making their own sounds and community.

Sometimes it could be a bit jarring, like the time Ian MacKaye and I happened to pick up a flyer for a "DC straight edge" show—something that in principle you'd think we would tend to know quite a bit about—only to discover we didn't recognize a single one of the bands playing! Again, an invitation to some humility…

CARA BRUCE: I remember being so intimidated going to shows when I was younger. There were not a lot of girls at the shows back then (and some of them were a little scary). But when my friends in LDK played, almost everyone from Reston went to support them. It was exciting, seeing a band who had played in my parents' garage playing at a real punk club in DC. The funny thing is that I realized all of the clubs were in really bad neighborhoods but that never scared me… just some of the girls.

CF BEST: I loved the ambiance. It was about the people who were there. That's what gives any space its flavor anyways. It doesn't matter how horrible the place is. The fact is, people showed up and the energy was amazing.

ADAM HELFER: We were in a bit of a lull in the scene. I don't recall much going on at other clubs, or in general. And given DC's prolific past, it seemed the best years were perhaps all behind us. But stepping into the Safari Club was like stepping into a parallel universe. Seemingly out of nowhere, a happening scene, fresh faces, and good music.

TOBY MORSE: Everything was word of mouth. If a band played at a venue and had a great experience with it, they'd go tell everyone, 'yo, this is the spot. This is the place to play.' That's what hardcore's about—word of mouth and fanzines. That's what contributed to how many bands did come through the Safari Club. It was definitely the club that bands wanted to play in DC. They didn't want to play a venue with a barricade and crazy ticket prices. They wanted to play a show where they'd be taken care of and feel like a family vibe there.

PHIL BAXLEY: I remember seeing Lars Frederiksen there at an H2O show and I was unexpectedly starstruck. I think he was wearing moccasins.

Finally we found the place—in the worst neighborhood of all time—and I think all they had was orange juice, straight edge cocktails? —Lars Frederiksen

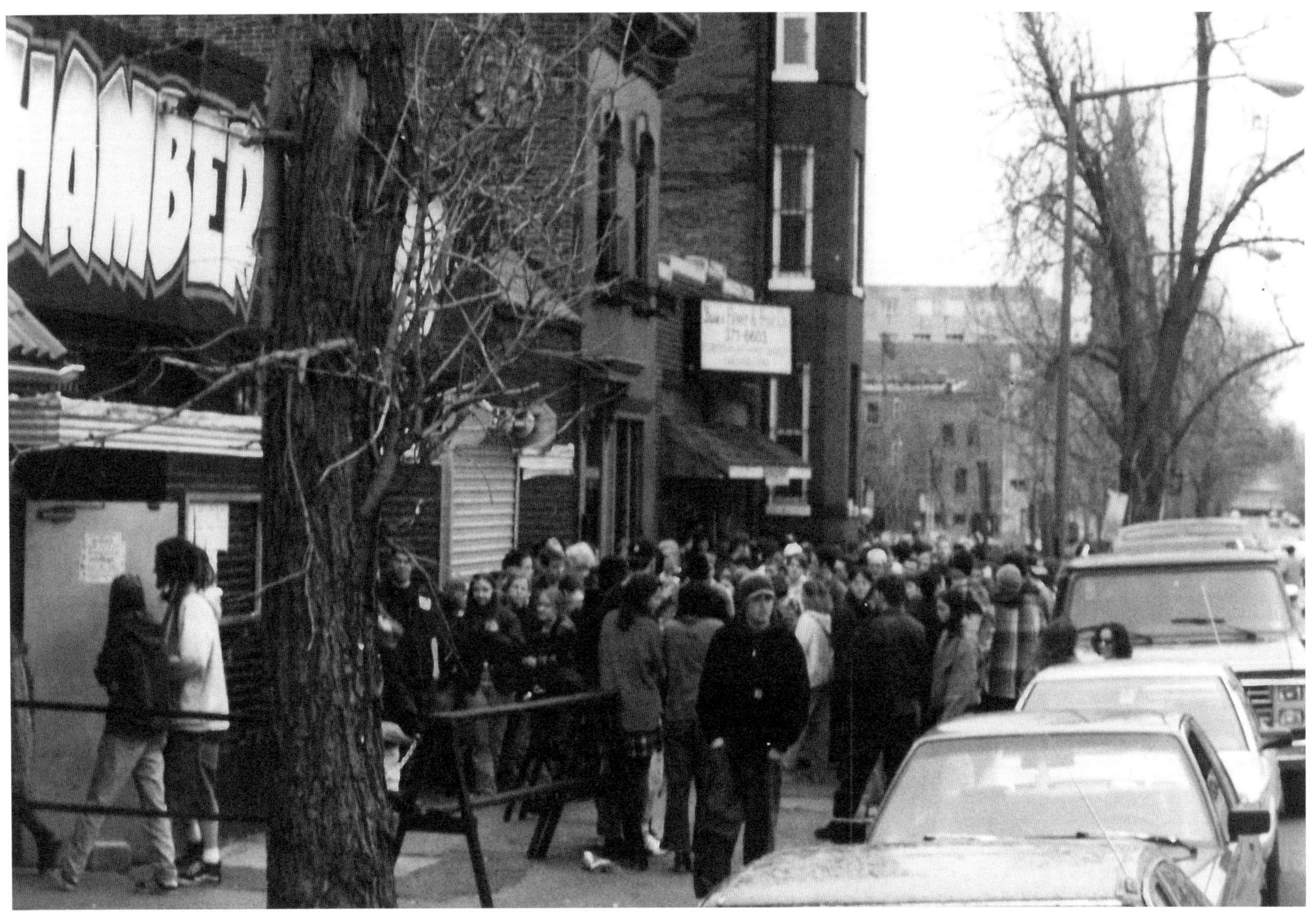

Front of Safari Club after name change to Chamber of Sound.
Photo by Dave Brown.

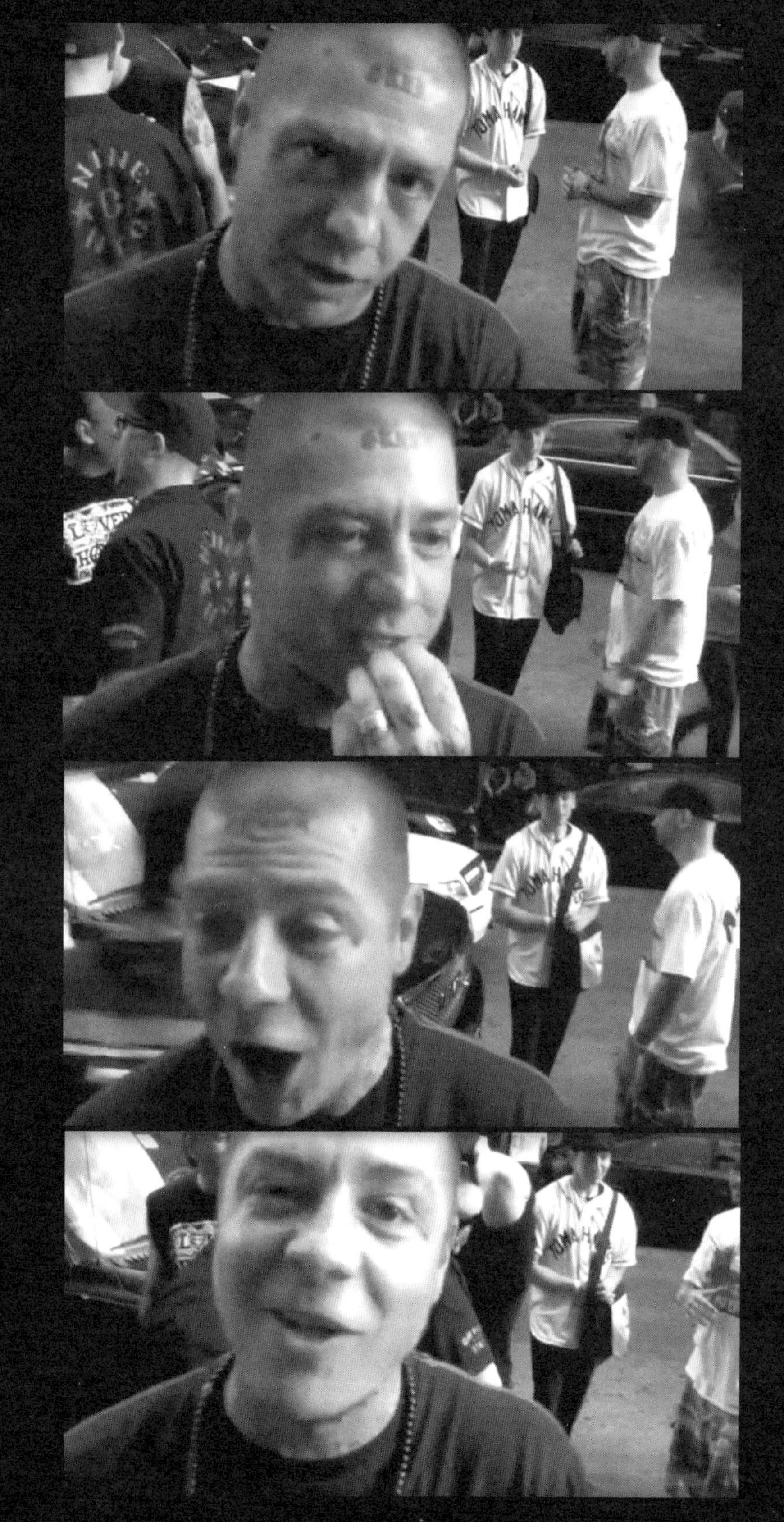

LARS FREDERIKSEN: We were going to Crown of Thornz, H2O, whatever…me and Tim Shaw from Ensign and Jere, we'd get in Jere's little Honda Civic and we take the drive from New York City all the way to DC. We wake up hellish early in the morning just so we can go see Crown of Thornz and Lord Ezac. So we're at a stop sign, and Jere's kinda clueless. All the homies come out, with the pacifiers and the wheelchairs, and they're about to roll us, and Tim Shaw's like "we gotta go! We gotta gooooo!" So we floor it through. Finally we found the place—in the worst neighborhood of all time—and I think all they had was orange juice, straight edge cocktails? And then we played "My Love is Real."

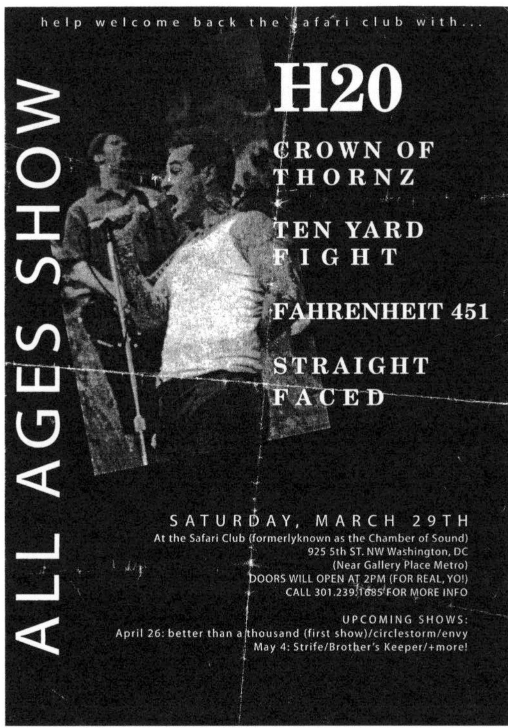

TOBY MORSE: We were opening up for the Bosstones at the 9:30 Club, where the tickets were really expensive, so we wanted to do a show for H2O kids, so we did a show at three o'clock on the day of that show at Safari Club. For some reason Lars was with me and Ezac and Tim from Ensign, and I remember Lars from Rancid played guitar with us. It was one of our first shows and I was completely bald. I think Lars played "Five-Year-Plan" with us, and Ezac and Tim Shaw took turns playing "My Love is Real."

BRADFORD REID GOODWIN: For a while, Safari was where EVERYTHING happened. I thought the name said everything. Going there to see bands play was like trekking into the jungle to glimpse panthers gliding through the vegetation on their nocturnal hunting forays. Which pretty much describes the stagediving that went on there, too… I had never seen anything on that large a scale. It hooked me completely, and everything else—including my forming friendships with the people who later became my bandmates—can be traced back to those initial experiences.

GABE ONRUBIA: It was a hidden playground. I was like fifteen when I started going. I remember not even knowing what Gorilla Biscuits or anyone sounded like. It's opposite of now, when people do their research, know a band's whole history and all their songs before going to a show.

MATT BURGER: It was absolute chaos and run by hardcore kids, which made it different than any other club that I'd ever been to. It was like there was no authority at all.

STEVE ZEITZOFF: If you saw somebody at a skate shop or mall with a hardcore shirt on that you knew went to Safari Club shows, you took note, because at the time it seemed like a secret world.

CHRIS LYMAN: I can't say when I first heard about it, but before the Safari Club the bands that we loved (typically from New York) would play at whatever hall could host them. There was never any chance to develop that relationship

Facing page: screen captures of Lars Frederiksen interviewed at Black N' Blue Bowl 2011, New York City. Shot by Rich Dolinger.

which forms between the venue and it's patrons. A new place would open and close in a weekend. The Safari Club changed all of that. It stayed open long enough and provided a safe enough environment that bands from all across the country could depend on to both host them and provide a packed show. There was a great support network built up to take care of out-of-state acts and local bands were always selected to open when possible, which gave many of these bands (including my own) a chance to play with their heroes. Personally, I absolutely loved the fact that it was a go-go club by night because I have always had a deep love and respect for that style of music.

MOE SHORTER: I did briefly pop in one day during a performance. It was amazing and so reminiscent of go-go in the sense that the crowd gets lost in the music and just wants to have fun. I loved it.

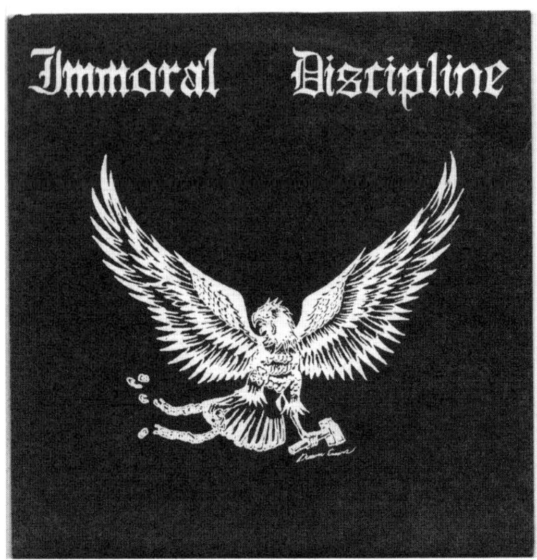

The most amazing thing about the Safari matinées was that here you had two girls who were about the same age as my friends and I who were making their dreams come true. They were uniting hardcore scenes from New York, New Jersey, and all over the country.
—Katya Oddio

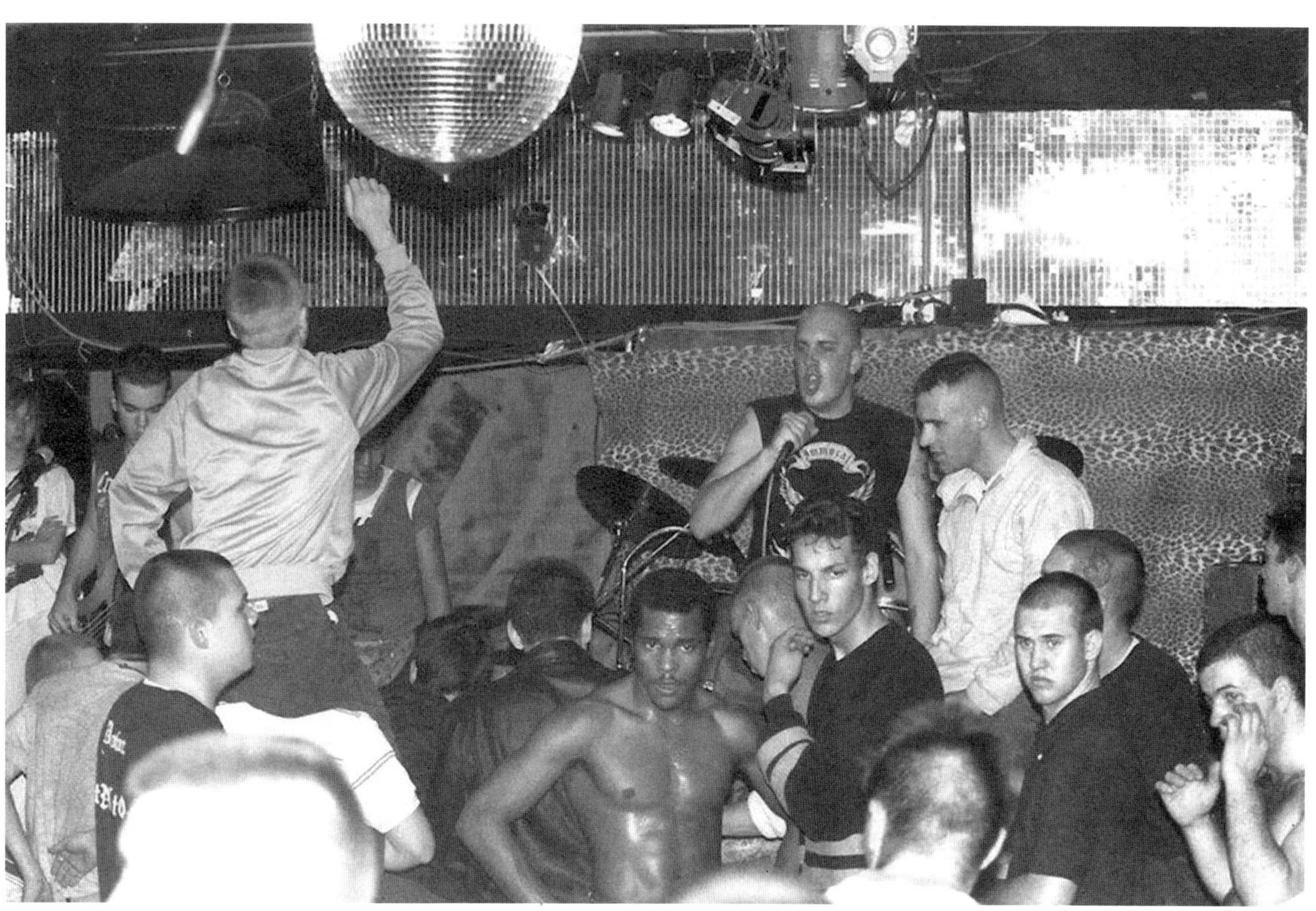

Immoral Discipline show. Photo by Ethan Minsker.

Token Entry was my favorite show. I see this guy running around in his boxers. It was Toby. He wasn't trying to be tough. He was just having fun. That's what it was all about. —Bill Anderson

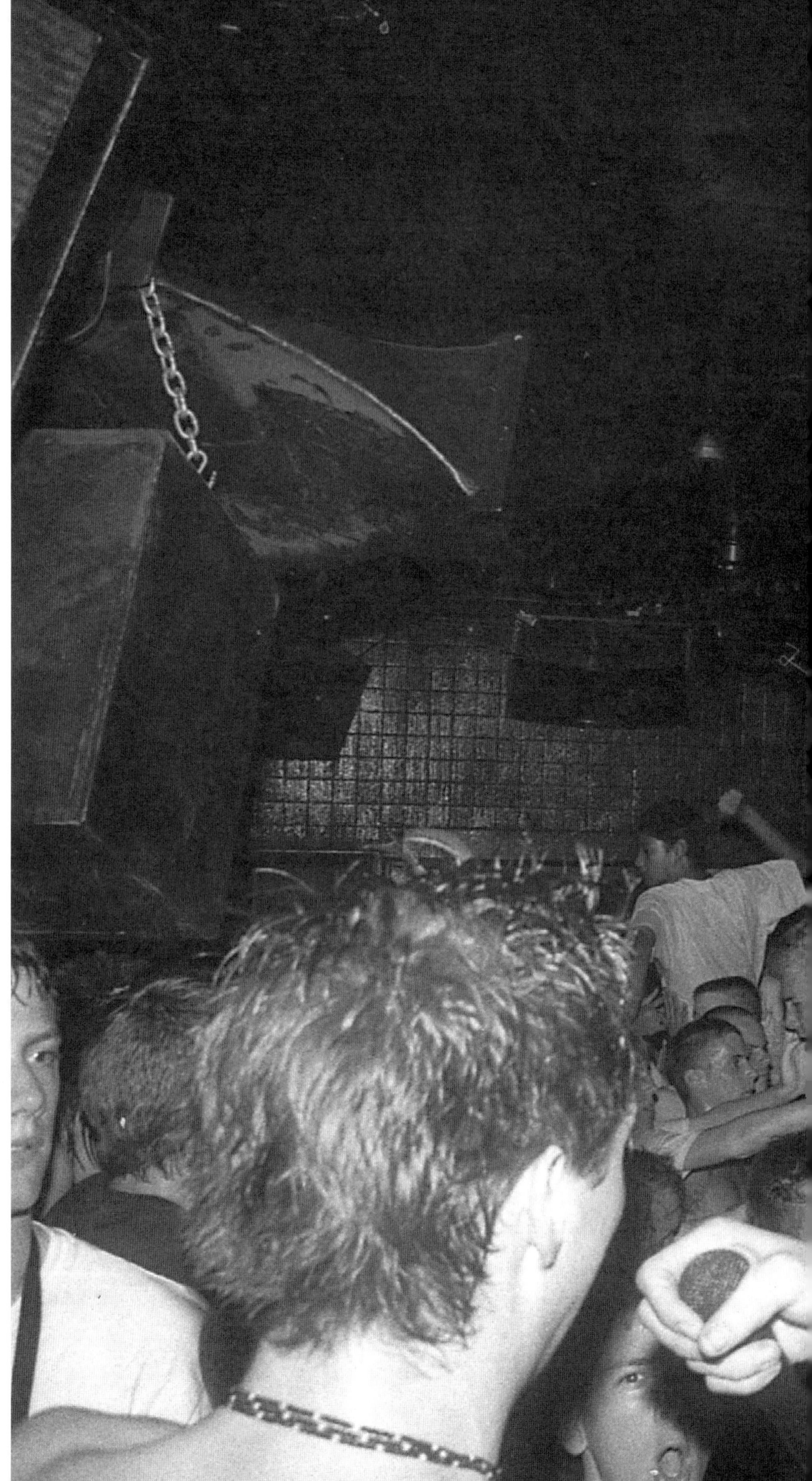

Timmy Chunks of Token Entry offers mic to Toby Morse, 1988. Photo by Joe Wongananda.

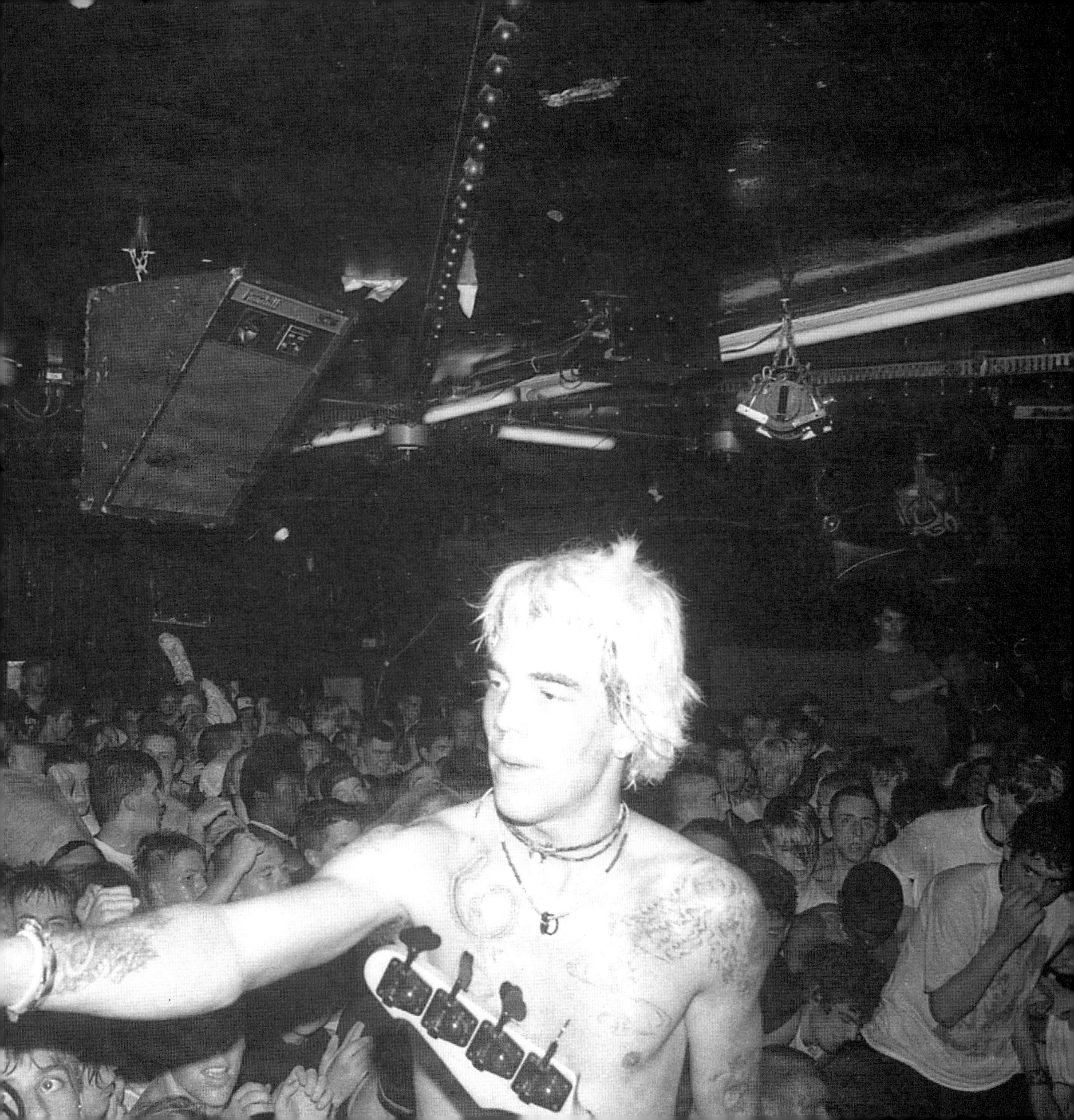

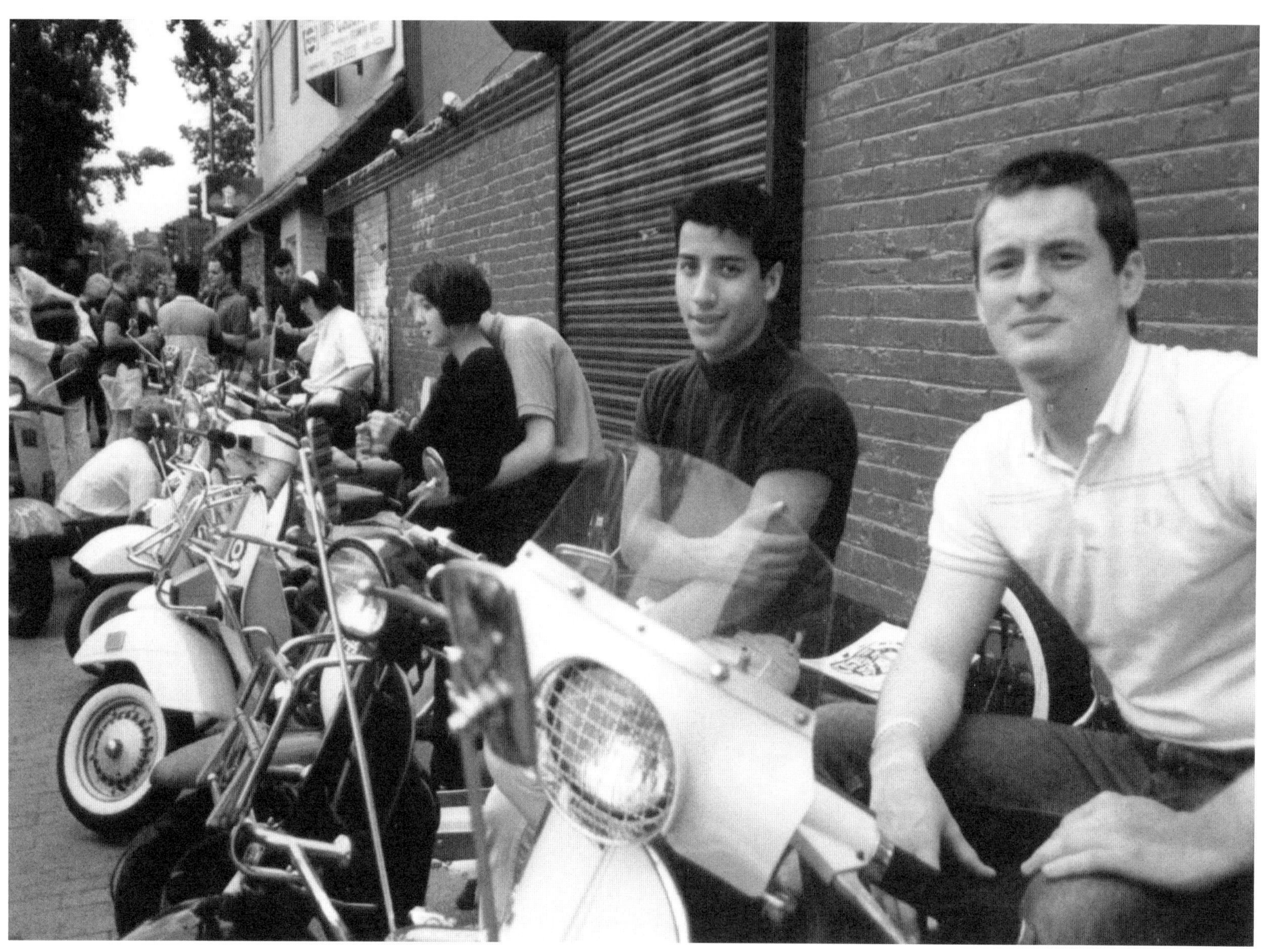

Scooters in front of Safari Club at The Now and Rhomboids show, June 17, 1989.
Photo by Karen Crespy.

CHAPTER 3: BONDS OF FRIENDSHIP

RICHI KRAKDOWN: Safari Club reminded me of when I first started going to shows at the Anthrax in Connecticut, because when you're leaving New York City in the early eighties, you're leaving a tough fucking area. Just walking around in the Lower East Side, you're looking over your back and you're just saying, "What the fuck is in front of me and behind me and beside me." And then you go over to Connecticut and it's the friendliest hardcore kids on Earth and they all just love hardcore. The kids in NYC also loved hardcore, but they're also watching their back! When you see a lot of kids in the NYHC scene back then, especially skinheads, you don't say hello. You don't look at them at all. It's like you're walking into a jail cell. In DC, it was like, "Hey, what's up? You gotta Krakdown shirt?" I think we sold or gave out all our shirts at that show before we even played.

KURT UBERSAX: I remember pulling in front of the Safari Club the first time and seeing about thirty people hanging out. I felt excited to meet new people. At a night show, like at the 9:30 Club, you went in, maybe saw a few friends or familiar faces, then the show started. But the matinée was a chance to *hang*. Really spend some time talking to people between bands. It was a different vibe, more like a community.

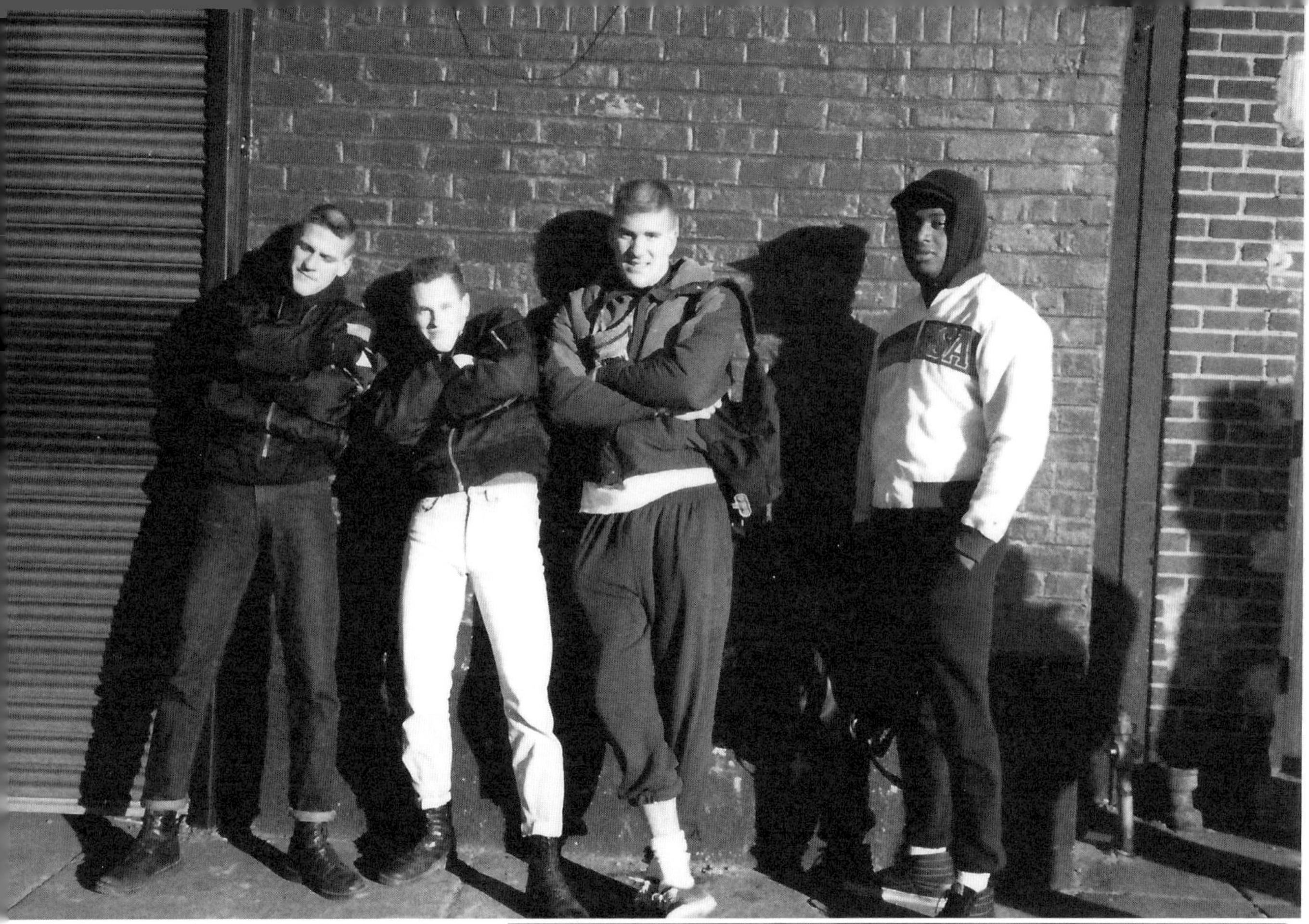

Left to right: Tyler Carper, Mike Smith, Adam Helfer, Big Mike. Photo by Nathalie Sheinbein.

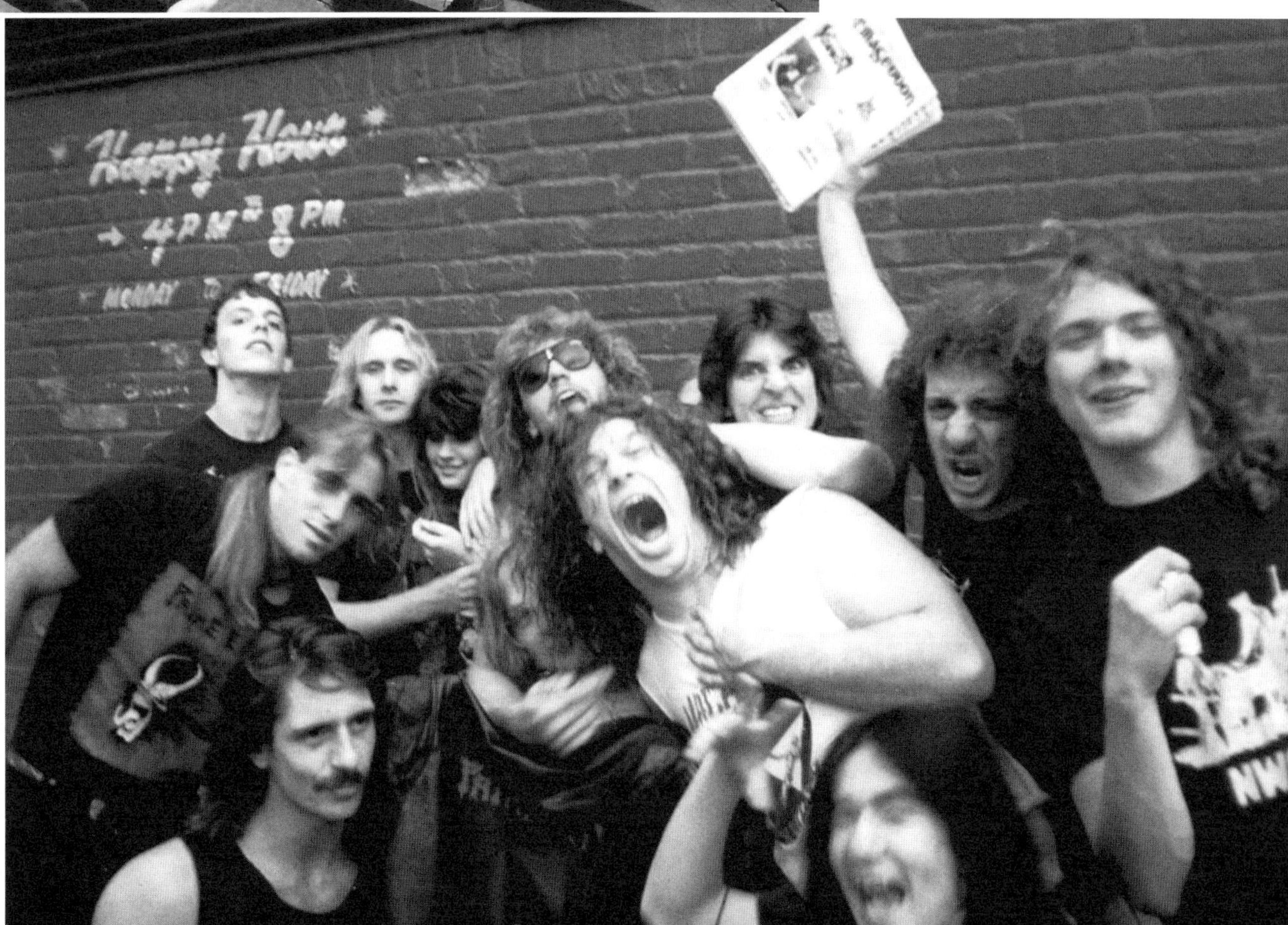

Deceased and friends in front of Safari Club, circa 1988. Photo courtesy of Mark Adams.

PHIL BAXLEY: I remember Safari being so self-contained. If you hadn't gone to a show, you couldn't find it. There was no Internet. You couldn't find out about the next show unless they gave you a flyer.

TIM OWEN: I met Chris Toliver in high school and he said "come with me to this show." It was kind of funny because I remember having to kind of pick out what I was gonna wear. He used to wear a Uniform Choice shirt over a hooded sweatshirt and he had combat boots. I was this skater kid, so I grabbed the only clothes I had. I had a Thrasher T-shirt or Powell-Peralta or something. I thought that was part of the look, I had to put a T-shirt over my hoodie. But it wasn't a band T-shirt because I hadn't been to any shows yet. Somehow we heard that shows were starting to be booked at the Safari Club. And at the first show, I met Karl Hedgepath and John Galbraith. The thing that just drew me into it was you could meet people instantly and you were friends with them instantly.

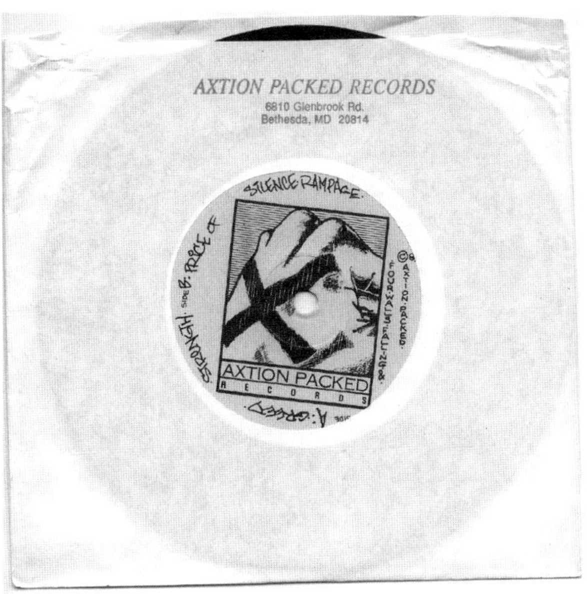

Axtion Packed was start by Tim Owen, Karl Hedgepath, and John Galbraith. That trio soon fell apart and Tim remained the sole member.

CHRIS BATTISTA: Just the idea that you could go up and talk to any these guys [the bands] after the show was over, that was the best part of it. This scene was a very small family. Could not have been more than two hundred regulars.

RICH DOLINGER: That era was so innocent and egalitarian. I loved that kids from the scene were playing the shows, booking the shows, putting out the records and zines in every aspect. I remember when the Initial Reaction's 7-inch was being released on John Galbraith's Cornerstone label, Chris Jordan had a box of the records with him at a show but wouldn't sell them to us because the covers weren't finished yet. That really hit home for me. The scene really felt like a DIY cooperative. Everyone here is participating.

PHIL BAXLEY: You used to see the same faces at shows all the time. One time I was at Ft. Myer with my mom and I was wearing a Mouthpiece shirt. Jon Hennessee was there and I had never really talked to him before. He came up to me and we started talking for like twenty minutes just because I had that shirt on. I don't think that happens these days. You don't go up and talk to somebody and have a kinship with them. I was at Disney World with my parents once and the same thing happened.

JR GLASS: We used to come down from Baltimore with Gut Instinct all the time. I loved seeing them play with Initial Reaction. I think I have a board tape of a Gorilla Biscuits show. Everybody from Baltimore used to come down because DC had such a good scene. For the most part everybody got along, before there were a lot of divisions. One show would have a tough-guy band and straight edge band and a pop band. It wasn't all divided, which was cool.

STEVE ZEITZOFF: I remember Little Dave and Derek—Derek running across the crowd and lurking on the bass cabinet or whatever.

STEVE SQUINT: That was like a fight club before a *Fight Club* ever came out. I'm sure if Edward Norton ever got any ideas for *Fight Club* it had to coming through the Safari Club. It's kind of like *Sesame Street*-gone-bad every weekend or every other weekend.

DARREN WALTERS: I was standing next to Adam and this metalhead guy was like "you man, let's fuck up some niggers" and Adam was like "really?" We looked at each other like "did he just say that to us? Who the fuck does he think we are?" So Adam goes *smack smack smack*. So this huge fight erupts and word spreads through all the kids and we chased all the rednecks away and Adam [A. C. Thompson] got on the roof of their car and screamed. It kind of resonated with us. It's the safety zone as well because you knew that you can't get away with that shit here. Everything is cool until it isn't cool.

That was like an urban legend—racist skinheads coming to DC. "The British are coming! The British are coming!" —Gabe Onrubia

ADAM THOMPSON: We chased some redneck metal guys out of there once when they were saying some racist shit.

JOHN GALBRAITH: One of my favorite things was being able to beat up Nazis. If they were trapped in your club… I had played football in college and still had a lot of adrenaline. Our scene compared to what was going on in Philly was pretty good.

One time some Nazis were beating up on Grant from Chucky Sluggo then Squint got involved and the kid ended up with twenty-five or thirty stitches across his face. I've seen Chuck maul some guy up and down the street after using the "n" word. I just got everyone from Baltimore and Gut Instinct to do security, which worked out well. Generally everyone got along really well.

ADAM HELFER: I know people are recounting stories, painting the Safari Club as violent, crazy, etc., but I actually felt quite the opposite. Well overall the dancing became more aggressive along with increased crowd participation, but gone was much of the bullying, violence, and elitism with the previous scene. There was much more unity and just a more overall positive vibe that was quite refreshing. There were times bullies tried to come, but we stamped it out pretty quick. Bouncing at the club was actually something I looked forward to. Although I will say I went home with the blood of others on me more then a few times!

MATT DOLAN: We were totally influenced by Washington, DC bands. We weren't as much throwing-down fighting and going crazy as New York was. I wanted to meet Brian Baker, so I was always like "in DC maybe I'll see him!" We drove down for other shows. One time we went down in the winter and there were a lot of oilcan fires outside. My brother even did a semester of college at Catholic University.

MICHAEL STRAIGHT: My last name really is Straight—it's my birth name. People were jealous of that and I got threatened in The Land of Straight Edge—someone said "you shouldn't call yourself straight if you're not straight edge." I told them and then they felt kind of dumb.

JOHN GALBRAITH: Compared to a lot of scenes back then, the skinheads and straight edge kids got along well. The Baltimore and DC straight edge people… I think a lot of it

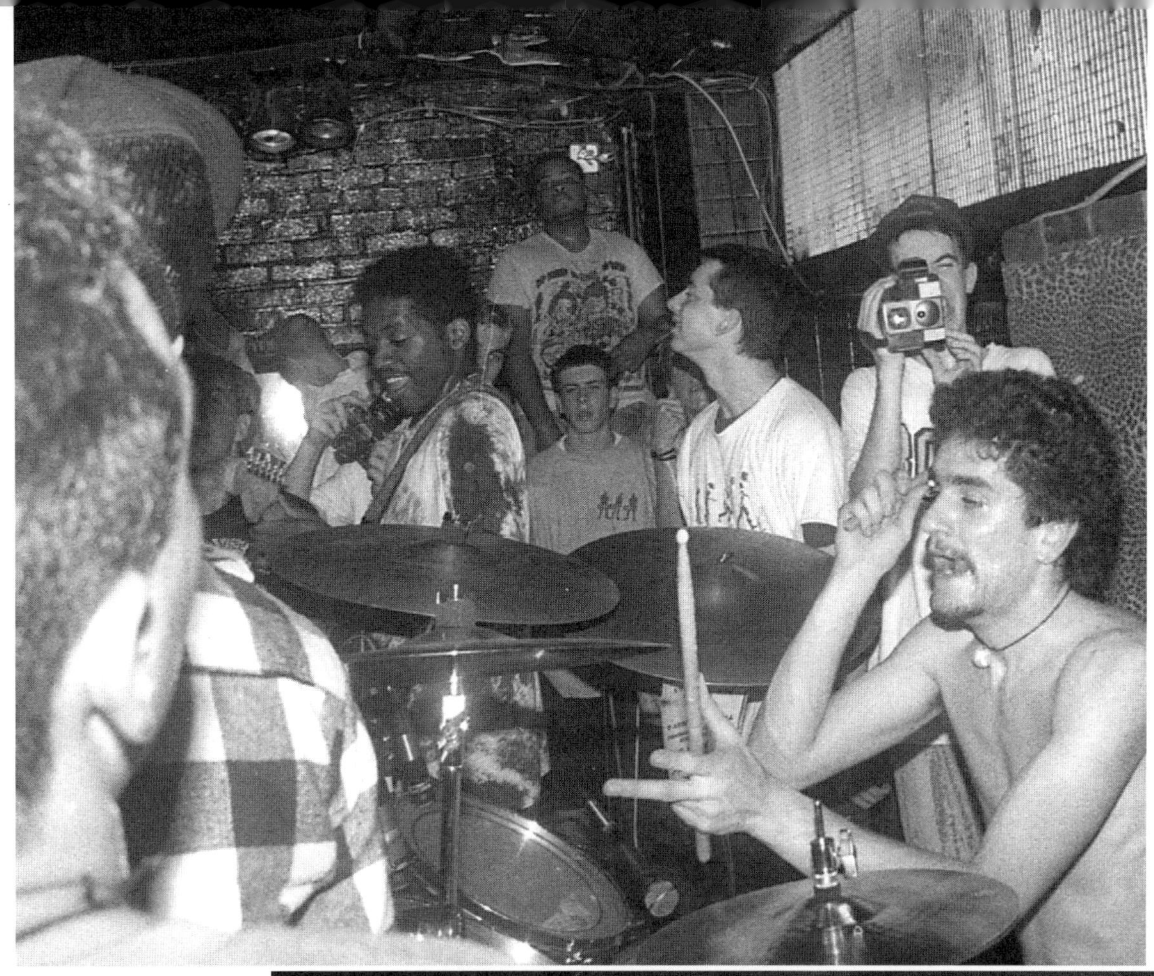

Tim Owen films Token Entry, 1989.
Photos by Joe Wongananda.

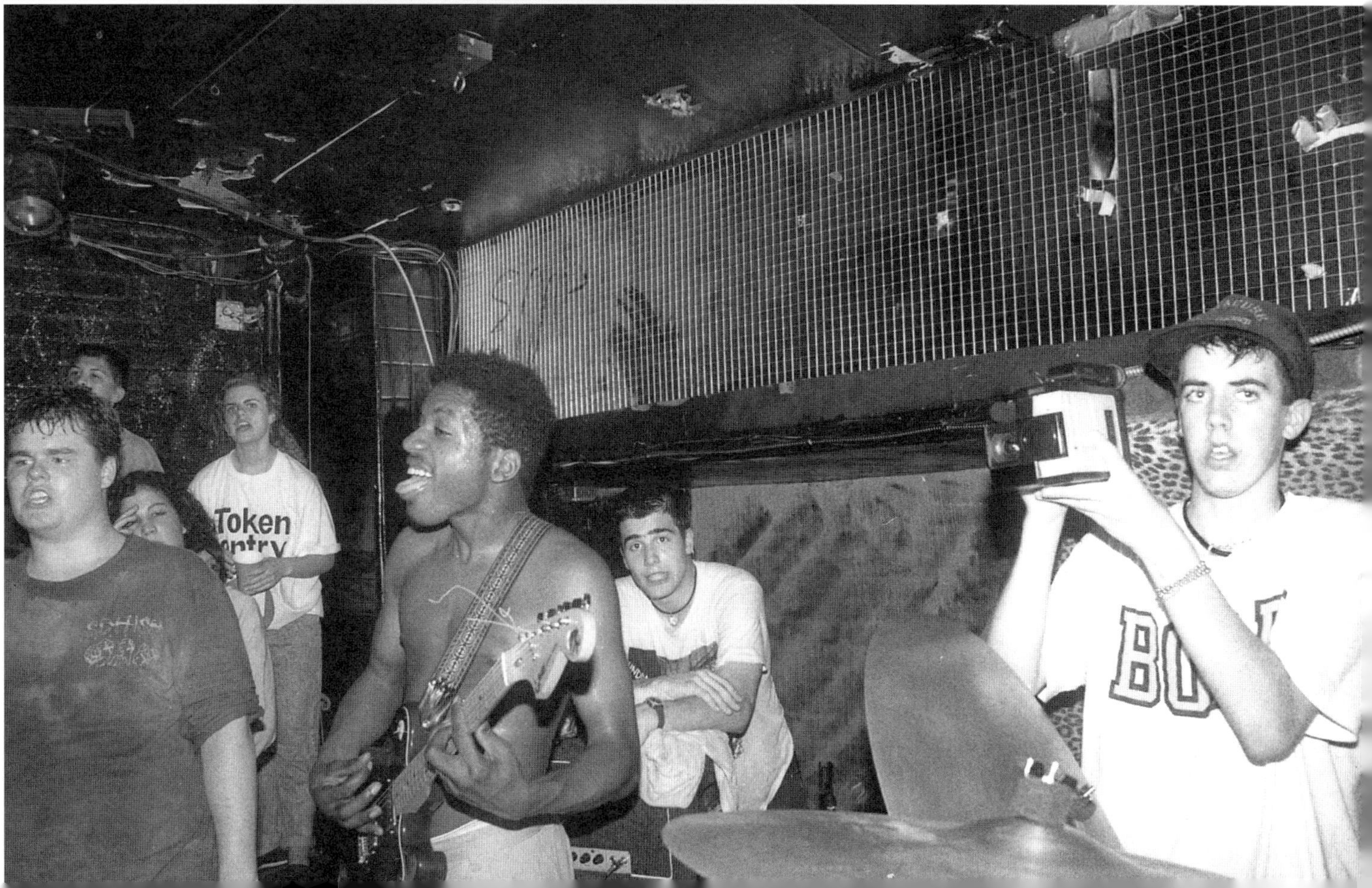

was stuff going on in California and Nazis were taking over. Every racist got chased out of here.

GABE ONRUBIA: That was like an urban legend—racist skinheads coming to DC. "The British are coming! The British are coming!"

TIM OWEN: It brought all these people from so many areas in DC. It was kind of like this beacon, like the lighthouse. You knew where to go. It was just so innocent. That's the exciting thing about all of it. Each show you can have a vivid memory, but as a whole just the times that you had there. Being older, I reflect on a lot of that stuff now. I used to get so excited about all the bands I got to meet by being there, like Insted and Youth of Today staying at my house. Each show was kind of a new adventure. Who are you gonna meet this week? What's gonna happen?

JOE SONGCO: DC had a real good vibe to their scene. To this day, whenever I think of Safari Club, I think of this Asian girl Latifah—a definite scenester—who was at a lot of the shows. I don't remember if we nicknamed her that or if that was her real name. Needless to say a couple of the guys in the band took a fancy to her, and from what I can remember she was actually pretty cool and friendly. Somehow, one of our friends got their hands on a promo poster for Queen Latifah's *All Hail The Queen* record and we brought it to one of our shows at the Safari and taped it to the wall behind the stage. I'm pretty sure Brian even dedicated a song to her during his in-between songs banter. After that show, a few of the guys stayed in DC an extra day to hang with her and her friends while some of us headed back to NYC that night. All the times we took the stage, we never made an Outburst banner to hang…but we once hung a poster of Queen Latifah to impress a girl at the Safari.

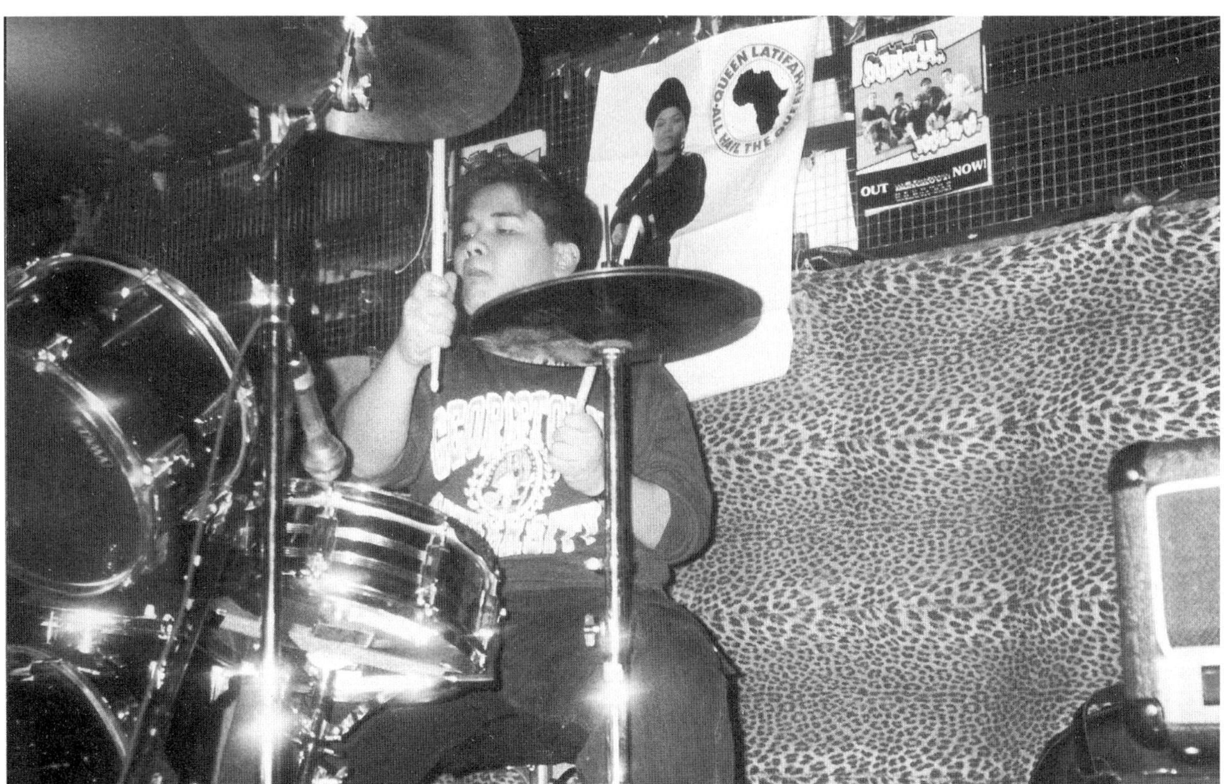

Joe Songco of Outburst. Photo courtesy of Joe Songco.

Even though we couldn't find a mic, Brian screamed himself hoarse and conducted sing-alongs with the crowd so it sounded like gang vocals on every song.
—Joe Songco

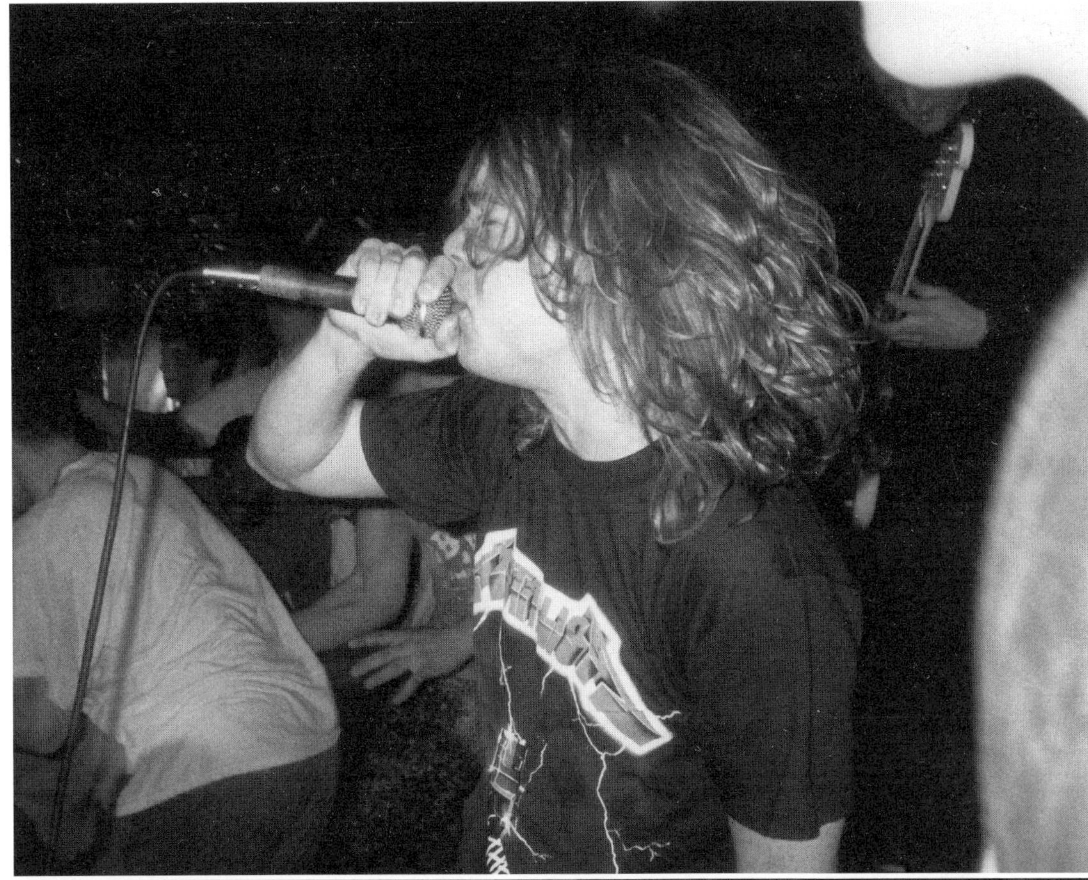

Outburst singer Brian Donohue. Photo by Eric Hochberg.

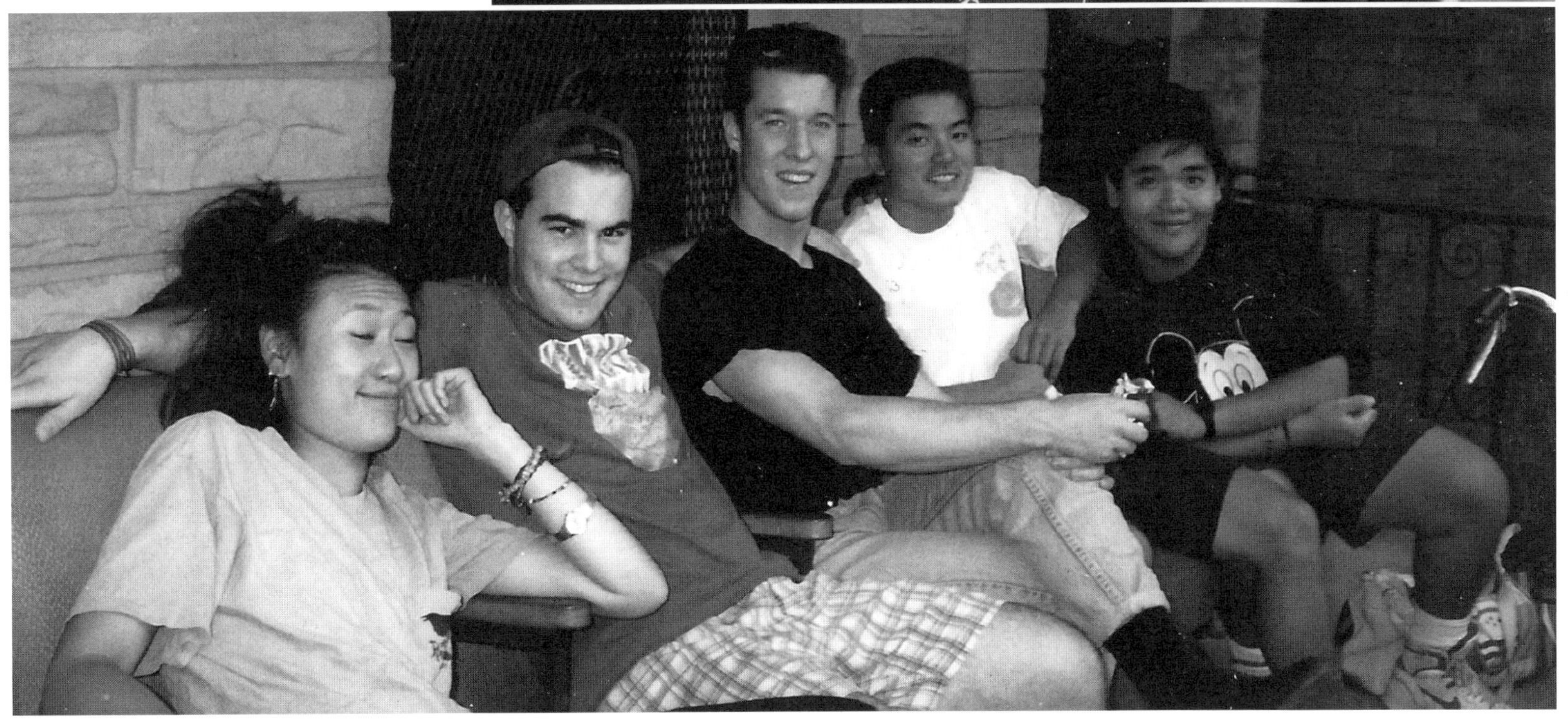

Outburst with Linda Hsu. Photo courtesy of Joe Songco.

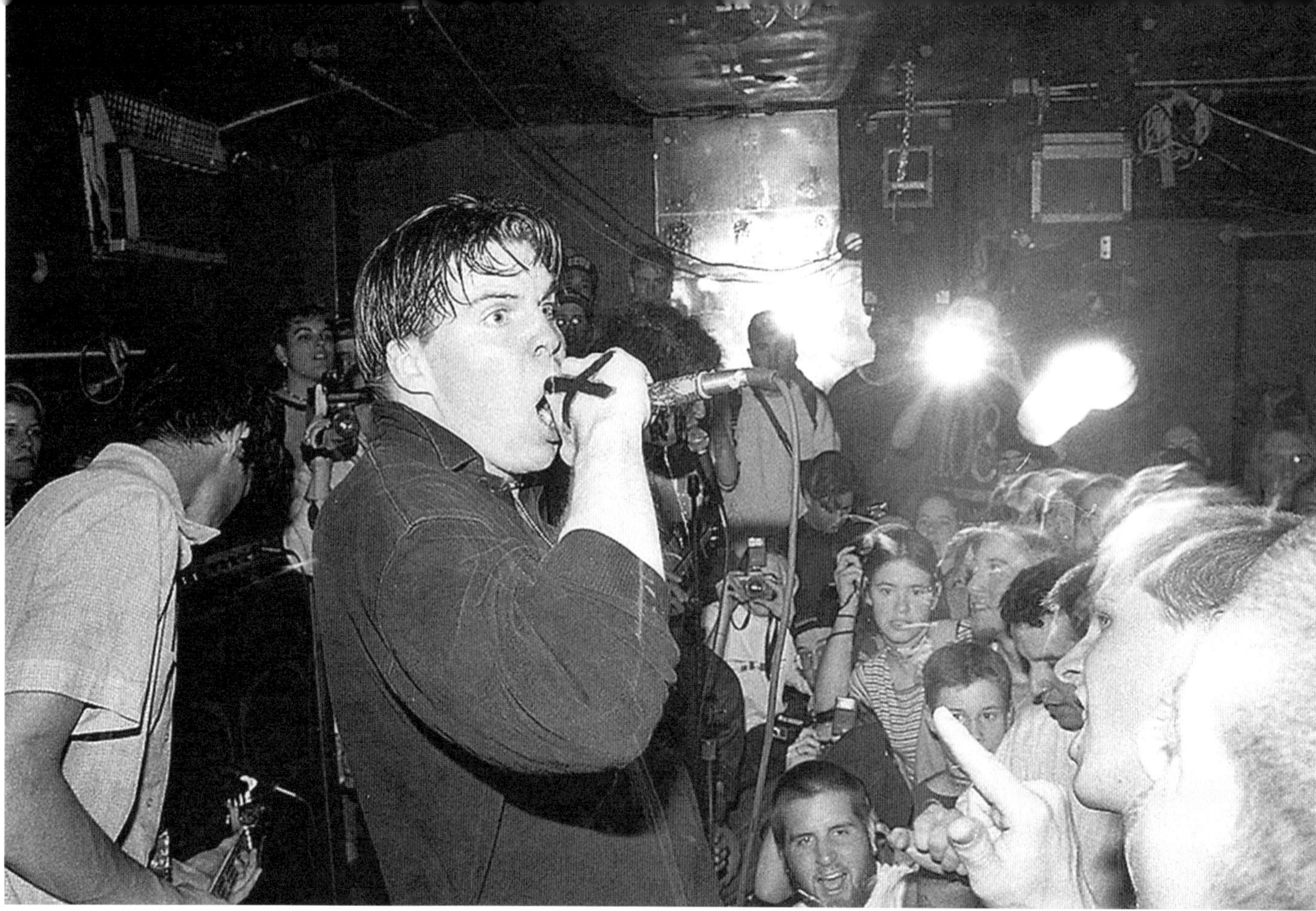

KATYA ODDIO: Once witnessed DC loyalty outside the Safari. Somebody was selling all his records for two dollars a pop on the sidewalk. A former Dischord House resident and I were flipping through them, and he insisted that the guy take five dollars each for the Scream records out of respect to the band. I was so impressed with the DC scene at that moment.

TRU PREY: Once we saw a girl get hit by a car crossing the street. I don't think she was at the show but nobody knew what to do.

JON HENNESSEE: Someone came and told me a girl got hit by a car. I wasn't in medical school yet—I only had my nursing degree, but I went and waited with her until the ambulance came.

STEVE ZEITZOFF: I know Martin through graffiti but not hardcore. I got more into hip-hop. When that Sick of it All record came out and KRS-1 was on it, someone played it at Safari Club and I stopped in my tracks, like "holy shit!" It was like peanut butter and chocolate.

MICHAEL STRAIGHT: I did a comp tape called DC Today in '89. From there I knew a bunch of different bands. John would call me to get in touch with bands that weren't necessarily hardcore. Then one day he called me and asked "do you want to start booking shows?" I said sure. I'd been doing shows in my parents' basement with bands like Agent 86. I was more into the punk side of things so it was kind of perfect for me.

JASON FARRELL: For one of our records we were like "we should put Xs on our hands and wear dresses and smoke cigarettes," and we did this whole photo shoot where we're just like in drag with big Xs trying to look as tough and hard and youth crew as possible, which was right in the middle of our tenure at the Safari Club, just because we were mad at that music.

Above: Damnation's first show. Photo by Mark Beemer.
Facing page: Earth Crisis. Photo by Brendan Bobzien.

TIM OWEN: Going to the 9:30 Club was like a business. It was a whole organization. But when you went to Safari, it was a whole different mindset. You'd get so excited. You'd spend the whole afternoon there then go to someone's house and go swimming or go to a Ft. Reno show afterward.

JASON FARRELL: Swiz went on its first US tour in '88 with Soulside, and we had already played with Youth of Today at the 9:30 Club in late '87, and I remember that was sort of the first exposure to the New York thing, and not really liking it. Then we went out on tour and started to see it popping up all over the country. Every question we'd get in interviews was "so are you straight edge? What do you think of Revelation?" You could see the momentum of this scene building. From where we were, it felt a little plug-in. I didn't really like the NY bands—it sounded too easy at the time. Touring was hard and there was a lot of whining on our parts and then you see who's doing well and you don't think they're good or play well and you're like "that sucks!" So by the time Safari Club came around and pretty much turned into this conduit for New York—bringing all these NY bands and tons of people coming out—at first it was like "what are we doing in the kiddie pool? This isn't where we wanted to be or what we wanted to do." It was dismissive and it was not right, but it's something that we did. It was this weird thing where we're stuck in-between scenes and being a bit whiny about it instead of accepting at the moment "this is where you are." There was a very youthful thing about it, like a moon bounce where everyone's going crazy and you're like "fuck, moon bounces are fun!" And then you get in the moon bounce. It took a couple of shows playing there to realize "these people are accepting us and our music fits. We

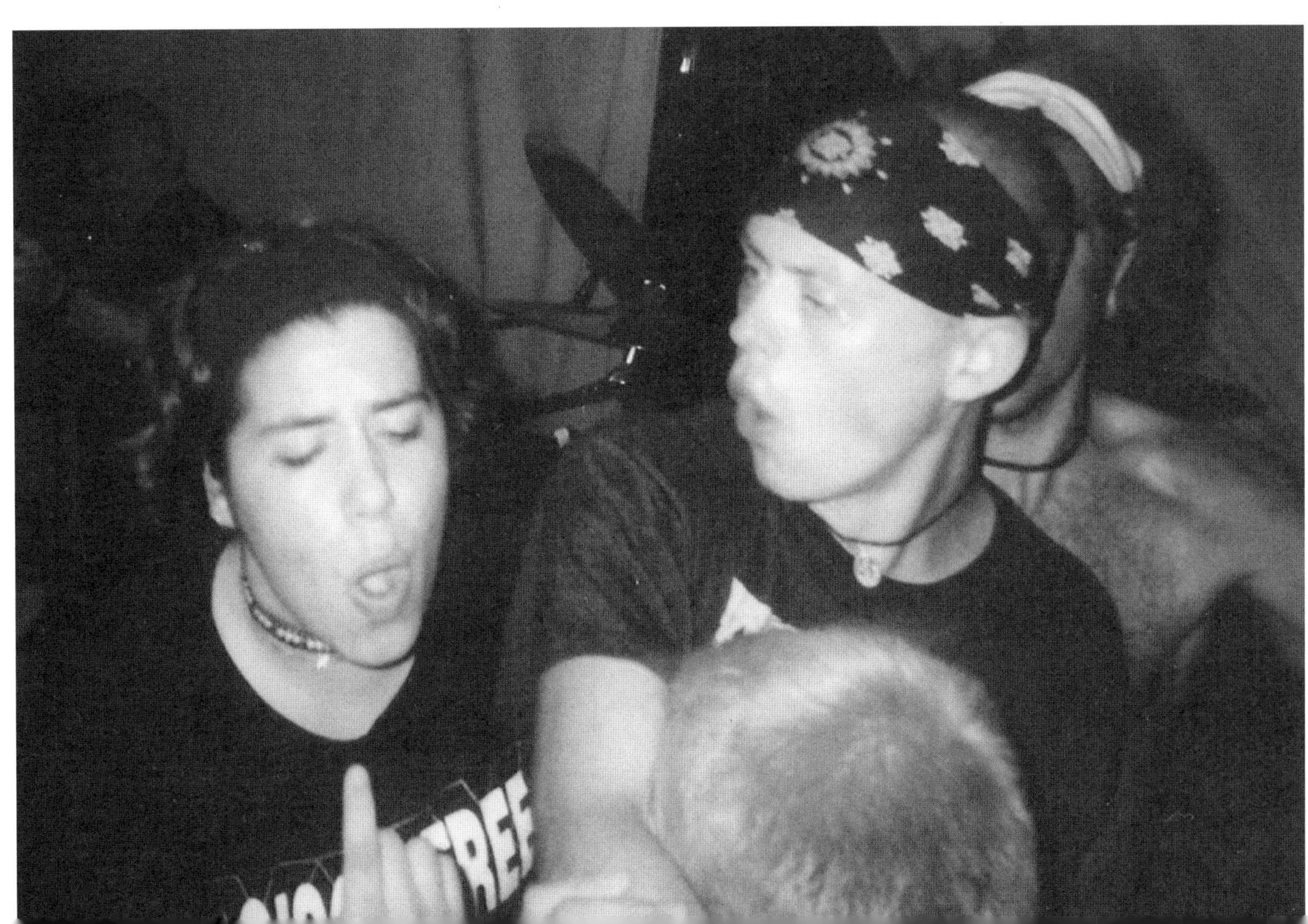

should be happy people are slam-dancing and doing stuff." We weren't high art. Eventually we realized "this is where we're supposed to be."

BEN CHUSED: Graffiti was a big part of the DC hardcore scene's identity, just like it was for the surrounding scenes on the east coast like Philly and NY. Most of my friends who went to hardcore shows were writers, it was just what everyone did during that time. Graffiti was all over the place—flyers, zines, records—all around downtown DC. I remember when I got the Initial Reaction 7-inch just staring at the cover and trying to draw letters the same way. The late eighties were also particularly significant for DC because that was when the first big wave of writers started doing their thing.

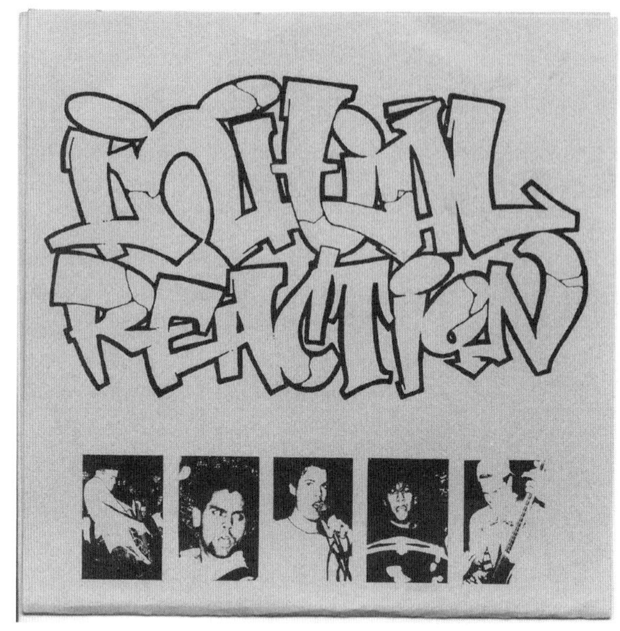

KEVIN YOUNG: I recorded a lot of shows on cassettes and I would go home right after these shows and type up the info about the shows (on a real typewriter no less).

CHRIS LYMAN: I had always loved punk rock but there was a refreshing lack of nihilism about the hardcore scene. Being an only child that had moved many, many times before arriving to the DC area, there was an overwhelming sense of brotherhood, positivity and toughness that drew me both to the music and the kids that were making it. Even though it seemed as though there was a constant battle for the soul of hardcore music between the straight edge kids and those that weren't, for that one brief shining time, we all just got along like family, which of course has many interpretations I guess.

THANX TO NO SCENE ZINE FOR MAKING THIS
SHOW POSSIBLE AT SAFARI CLUB-7/01/89
side a:
GOOD HUMOR-TONITE,SPEEDO,SAY WHAT,BED
WETTER,BUDDY,HUMOR,HE-SHE--DRY,SUICIDE,
CRANK,TIME
side b:

THANX TO PAM AND SHAWNA OF NO SCENE
ZINE FOR THIS SHOW AT SAFARI-7/07/89
side a:
GORILLA BISCUITS-FORGOTTEN--NEW DIREC-
TION,BREAKING FREE, BETTER THAN YOU,
DEGREDATION,BIG MOUTH,NO REASON WHY,
TWO SIDES,HOLD YOUR GROUND,HIGH HOPES
side b:
BOLD(LAST D.C. SHOW EVER)-YOU'RE THE
FRIEND,CHANGE WITHIN--SEARCH,HATEFUL,
TALK IS CHEAP, ACCEPT THE BLAME,
RUNNING LIKE THIEVES,CLEAR,WISE UP.

Cassette covers courtesy of Kevin Young.

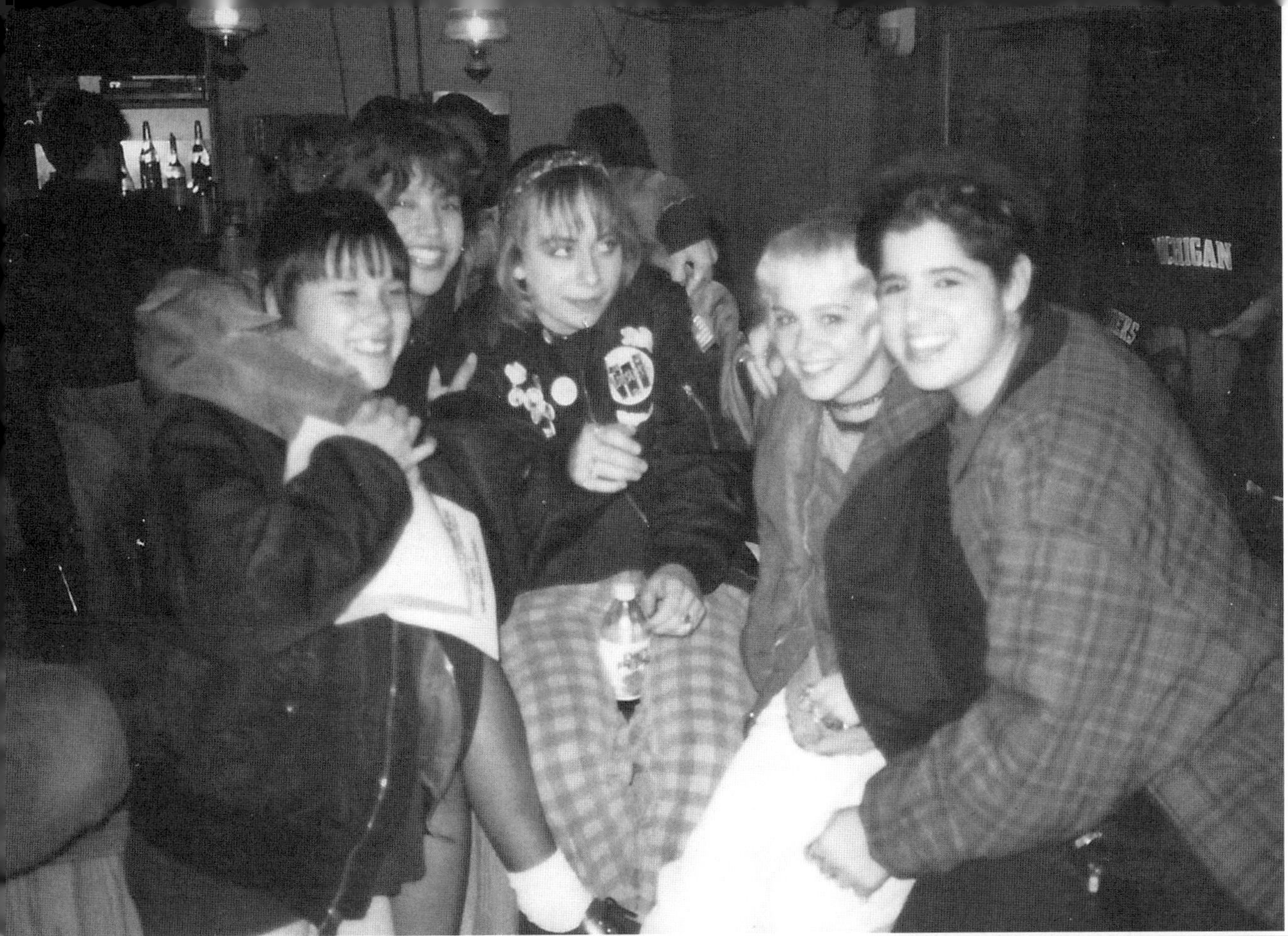

Tara Fogelman, Patti Becera, Anne Rickert, Erica (Long) Dillingham, Nathalie Sheinbein. Photo courtesy of Nathalie Sheinbein.

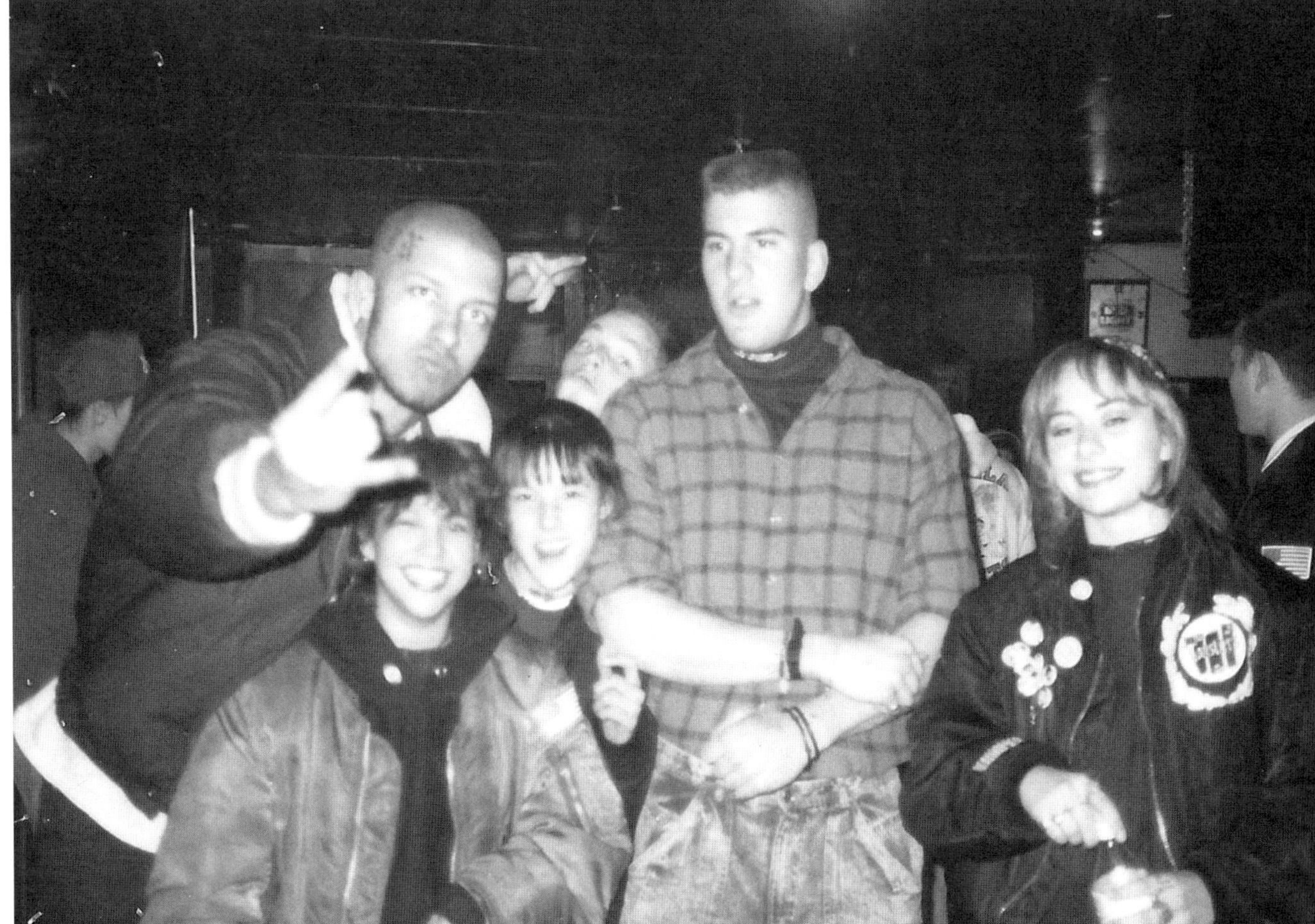

Leo Felton, Patti Becera, Tara Fogelman, Mike Smith, Adam Hefler, Anne Rickert. Photo courtesy of Nathalie Sheinbein.

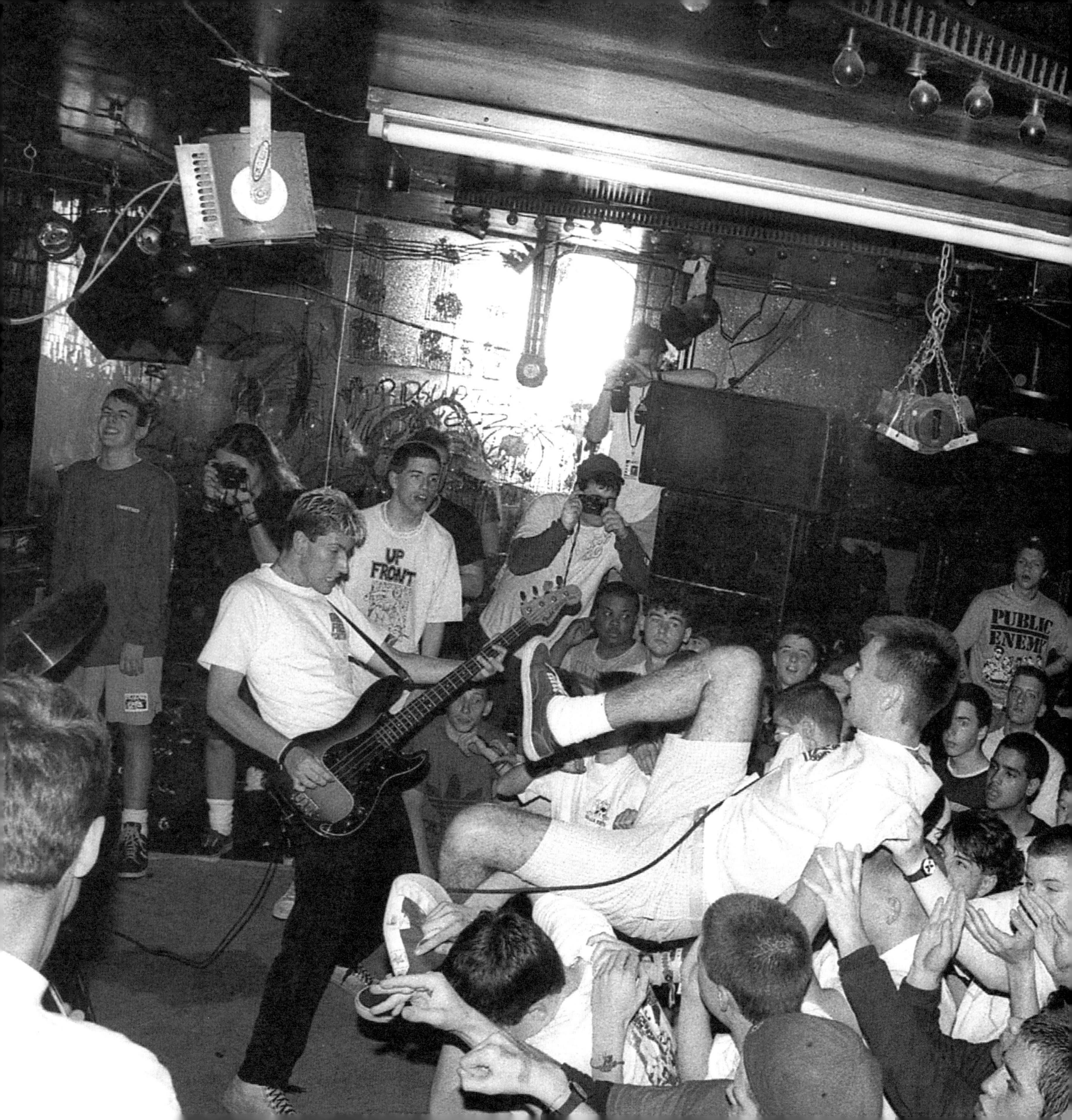
UP
FRONT
PUBLIC
ENEMY

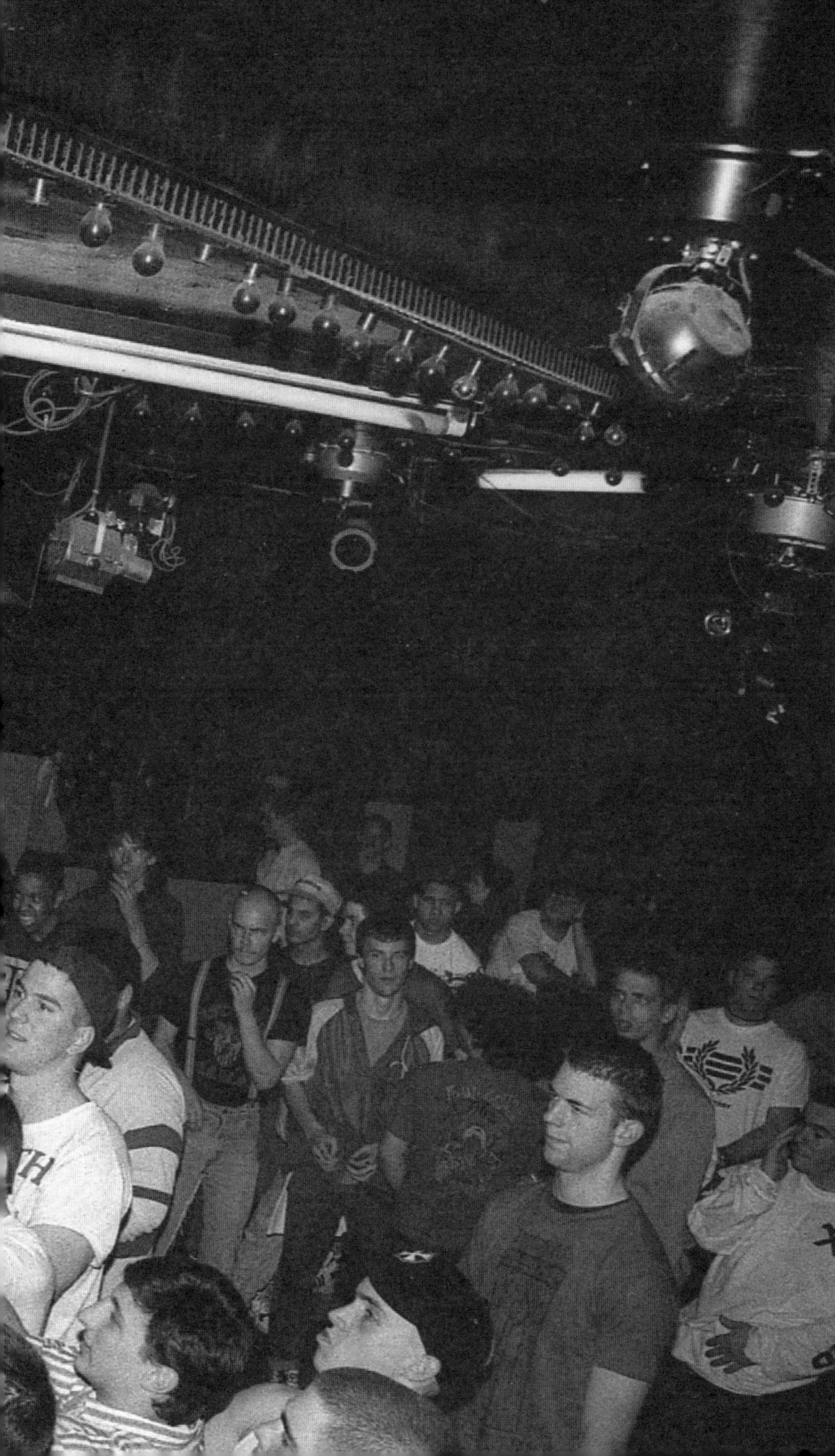

I used to get so excited about all the bands I got to meet by being there, like Insted and Youth of Today, staying at my house.
—Tim Owen

Insted. Photo by Joe Wongananda.

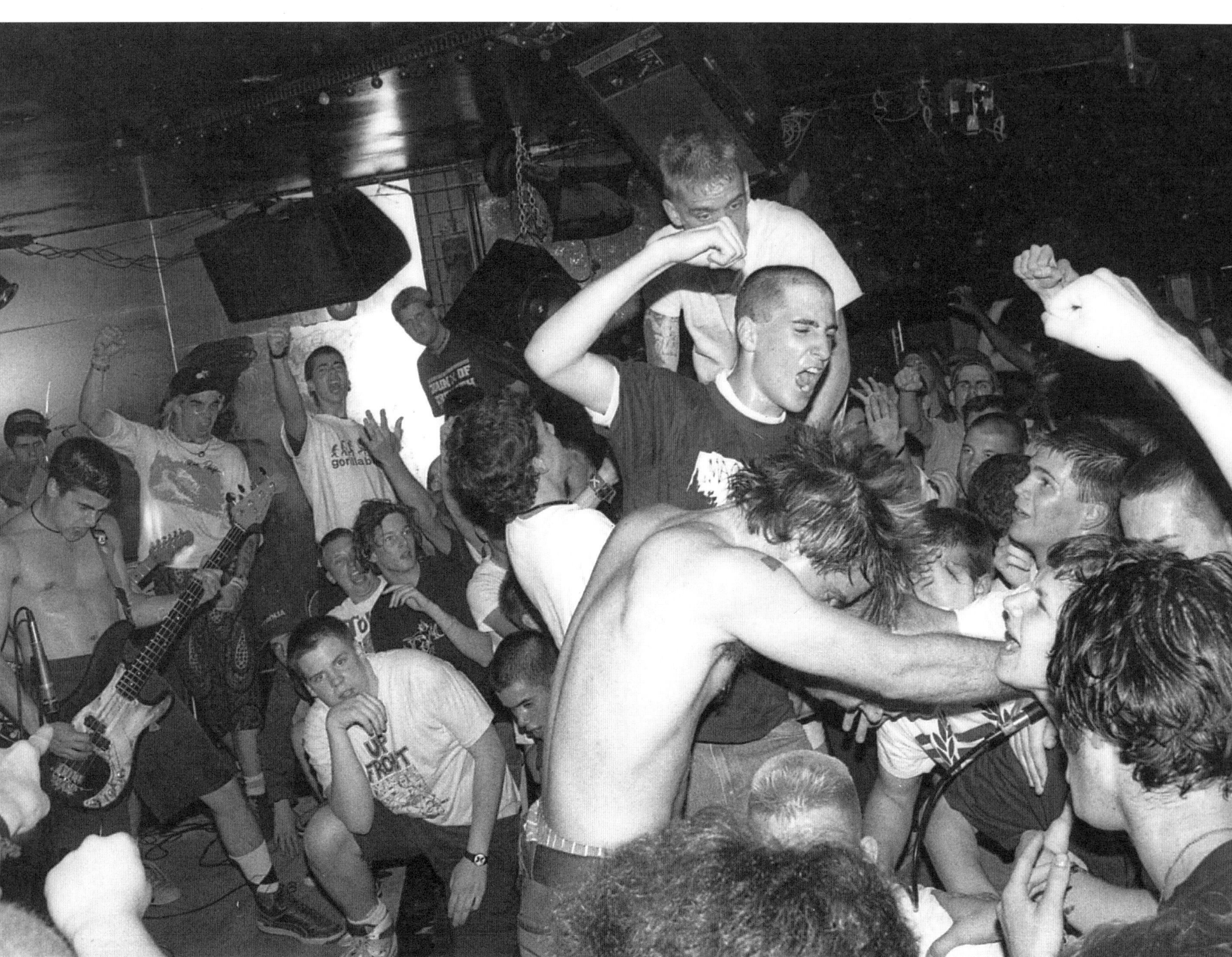

In Your Face, 1989. Photo by Joe Wongananda.

CHAPTER 4: WHERE THE WILD THINGS ARE

ALEC MACKAYE: Ignition played at Safari Club a couple of times. Once with Knife Dance and Nation of Ulysses in September of 1988 and again in February of 1989 with Electric Love Muffin and Scram. What I remember most about the show was that the day before there had been a fire at the old Ford dealership building at Fifth and K. It was a massive concrete structure like a parking garage. Homeless people camped out in there, and one of them was killed in the fire. While we were doing a song of ours called "Lucky 13," I was struck by the reality of it all. It was a song addressing the craziness of the world, the amazing progress in some areas—and the poverty that seems never to be abated.

CF BEST: The Safari Club show was probably one of the better Ignition shows I ever saw. I think it was one of the few shows where they brought out a saxophone. I think I got the flyer at Smash.

BRYAN WASSOM: I saw Ignition play a Sunday matinée at the Safari, which drew an entirely different crowd…one of the best live performances I have ever seen. During a song addressing the homeless situation in DC, Alec MacKaye ran off the stage with the mic and sang the rest of the song from a vacant lot across the street, which was pretty crazy.

KATYA ODDIO: Think Ignition may have been the draw for the first Safari show I caught. There were at least two wonderful Ignition shows at the Safari. We laughed ourselves silly at one at an opening act's name—Electric Love Muffin! ELM was punk, Scram was ska, and Ignition was hardcore. A fun lineup mix!

DAVE CHELSEA-SEIFERT: I remember one great show when Ignition played and either Chris Bald or Alec got naked. I seem to recall him leaning into the crowd or maybe even crowd surfing, and a few people who didn't relish the

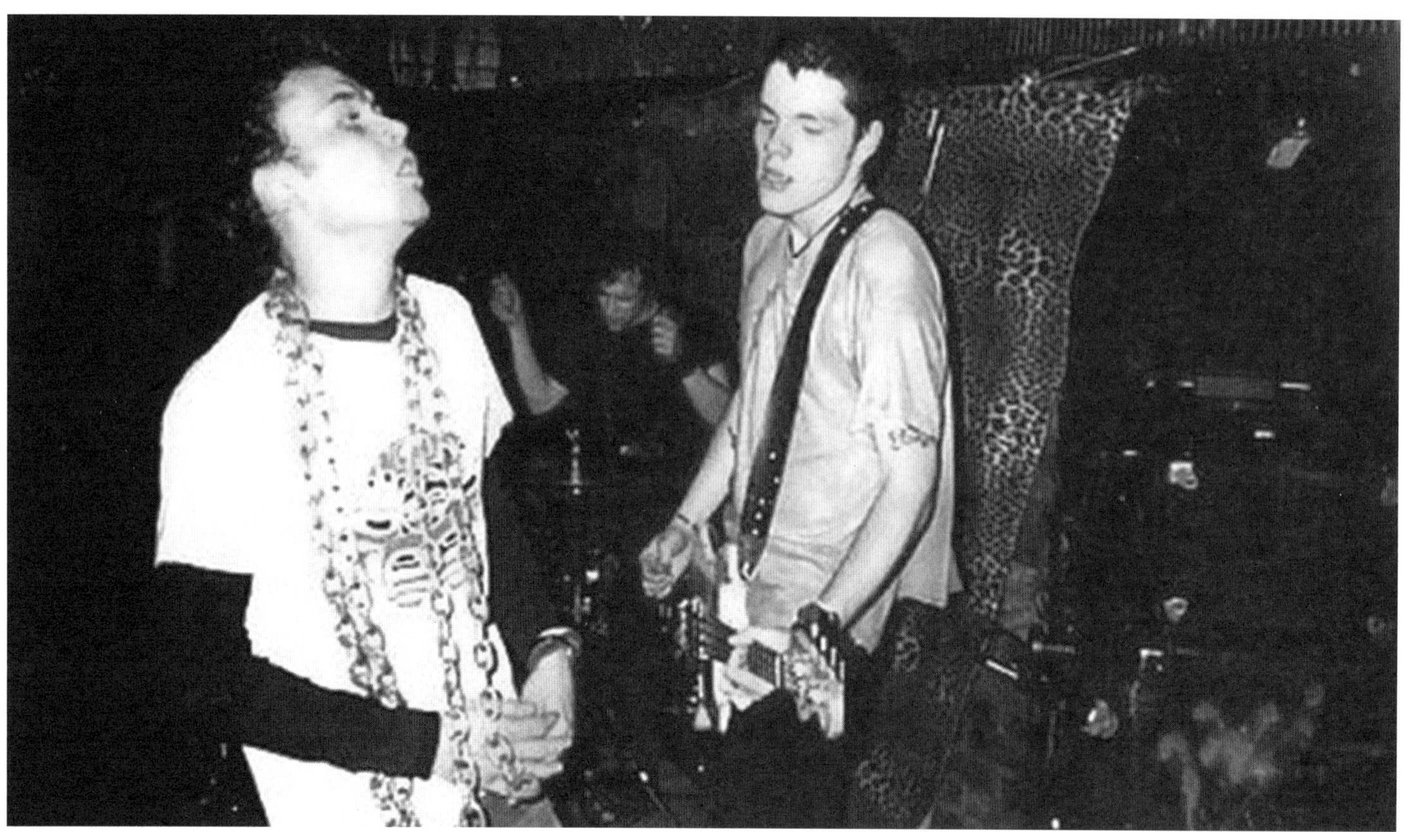

Alec MacKaye and Chris Thomson of Ignition. February 25, 1989. Photo by Joseph P. McRedmond.

thought of a schlong across their forehead freaked out and headed for the back of the club.

MICHAEL STRAIGHT: I was really excited for the Ignition show because when I was fourteen and fifteen, Ignition was my favorite band, but I didn't drive and had never seen them. The Safari show is the only time I saw them before they broke up. I remember Alec talking about the homeless guy who got killed and thinking that was so brutal—DC at that time was like that.

MARK ANDERSEN: I have some powerful memories of shows there, a diverse mix of images and emotions—Jenny Toomey with her early band Geek, the power of Swiz at their "monster sound creative peak," Alec MacKaye dedicating a wrenching version of "Lucky 13" to two homeless men who had died in a fire in an abandoned building across the street, trying to stay warm on a frigid night.

JASON KOOKEN: I loved Scram from Philadelphia. They came down with Electric Love Muffin and played with Ignition. I think Chris Bald wrote some of the best lyrics. It

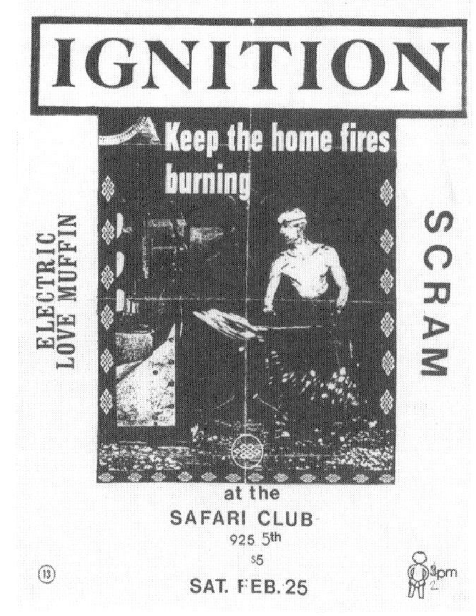

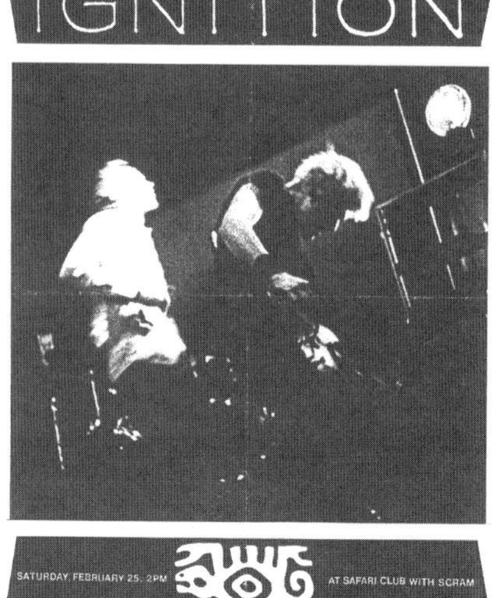

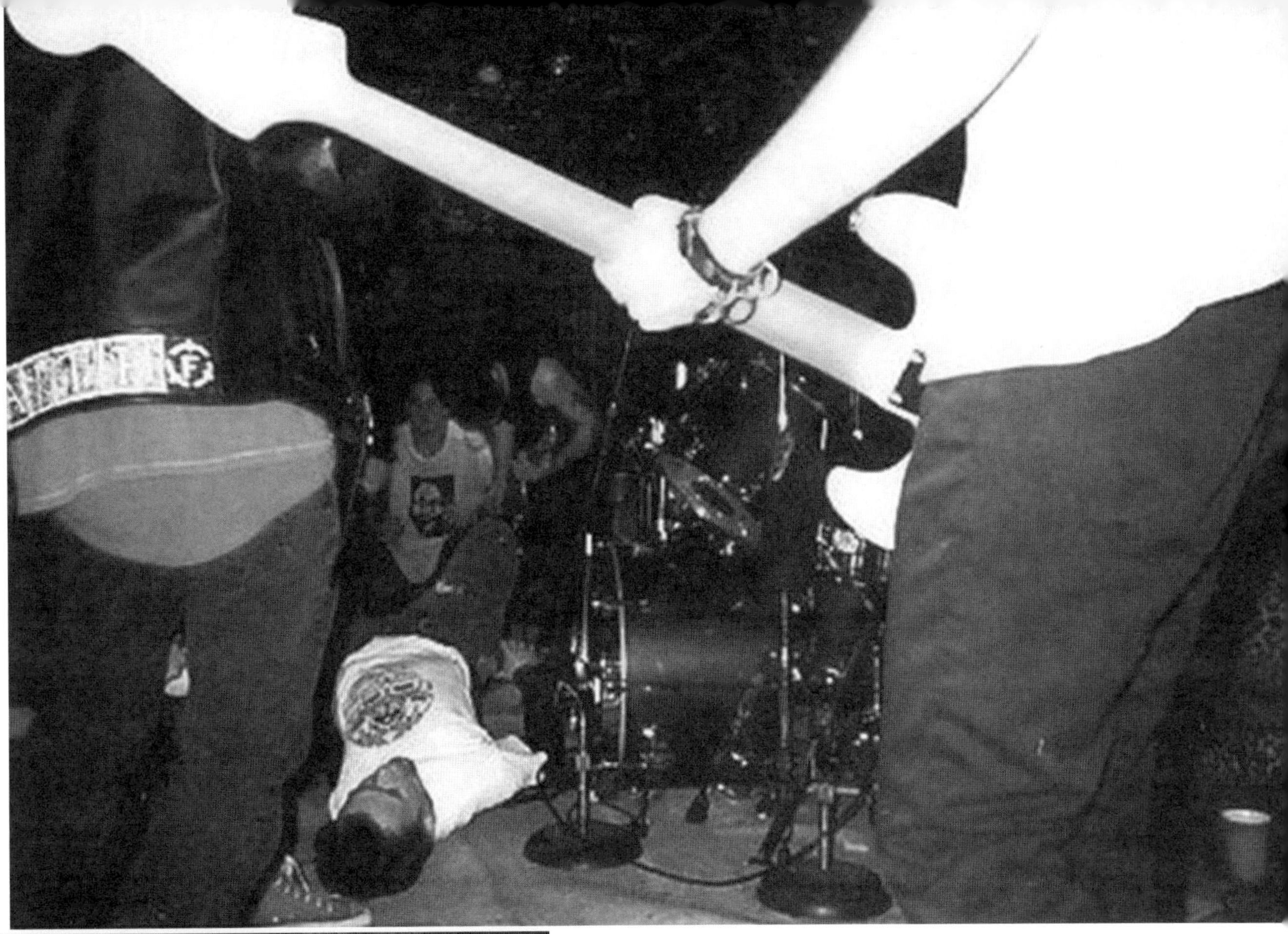

Ignition, 1989.
Photos by Joseph P. McRedmond.

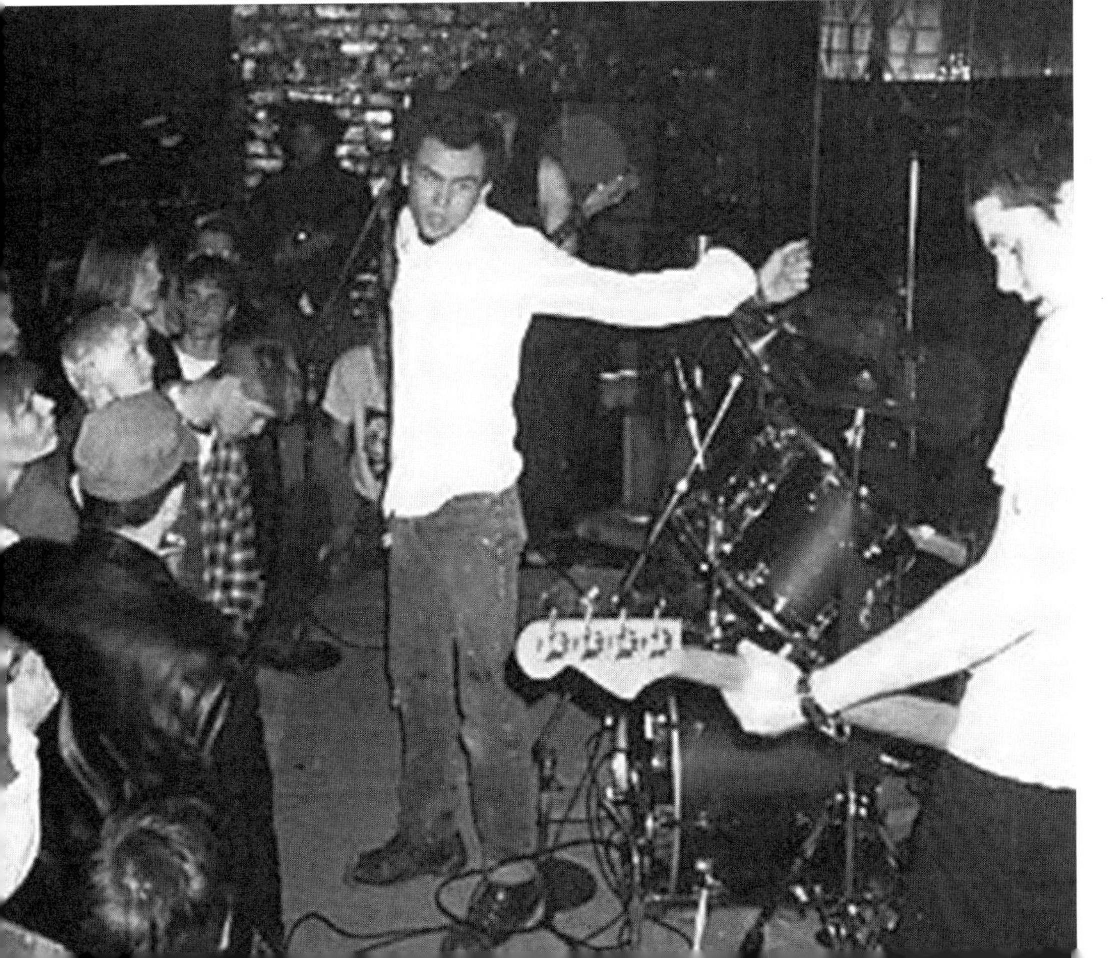

While we were doing a song of ours called "Lucky 13" I was struck by the reality of it all. It was a song addressing the craziness of the world, the amazing progress in some areas—and the poverty that seems never to be abated.
—Alec Mackaye

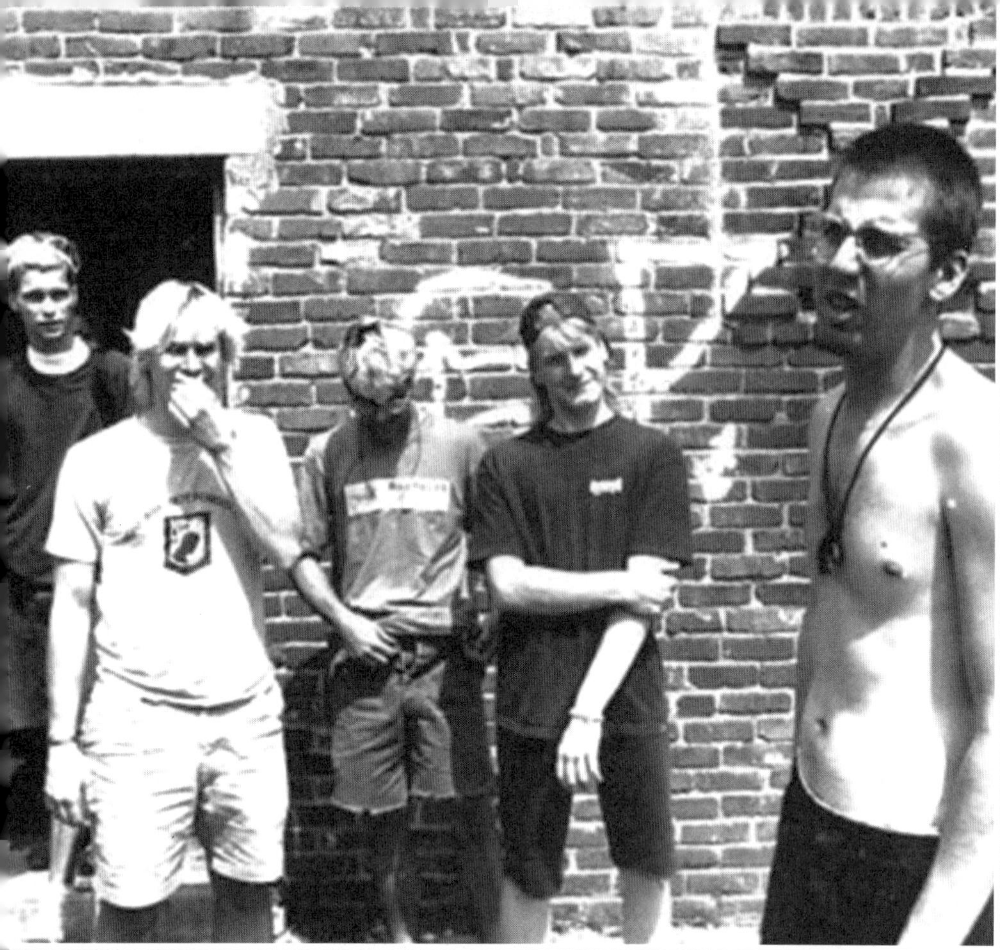

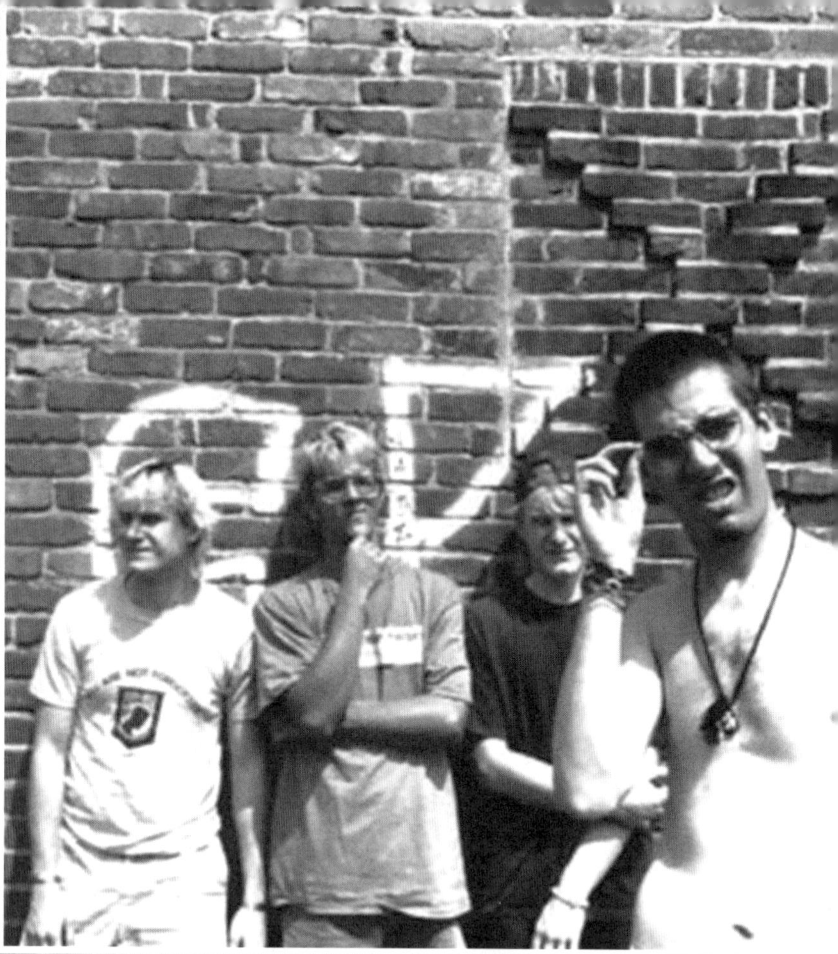

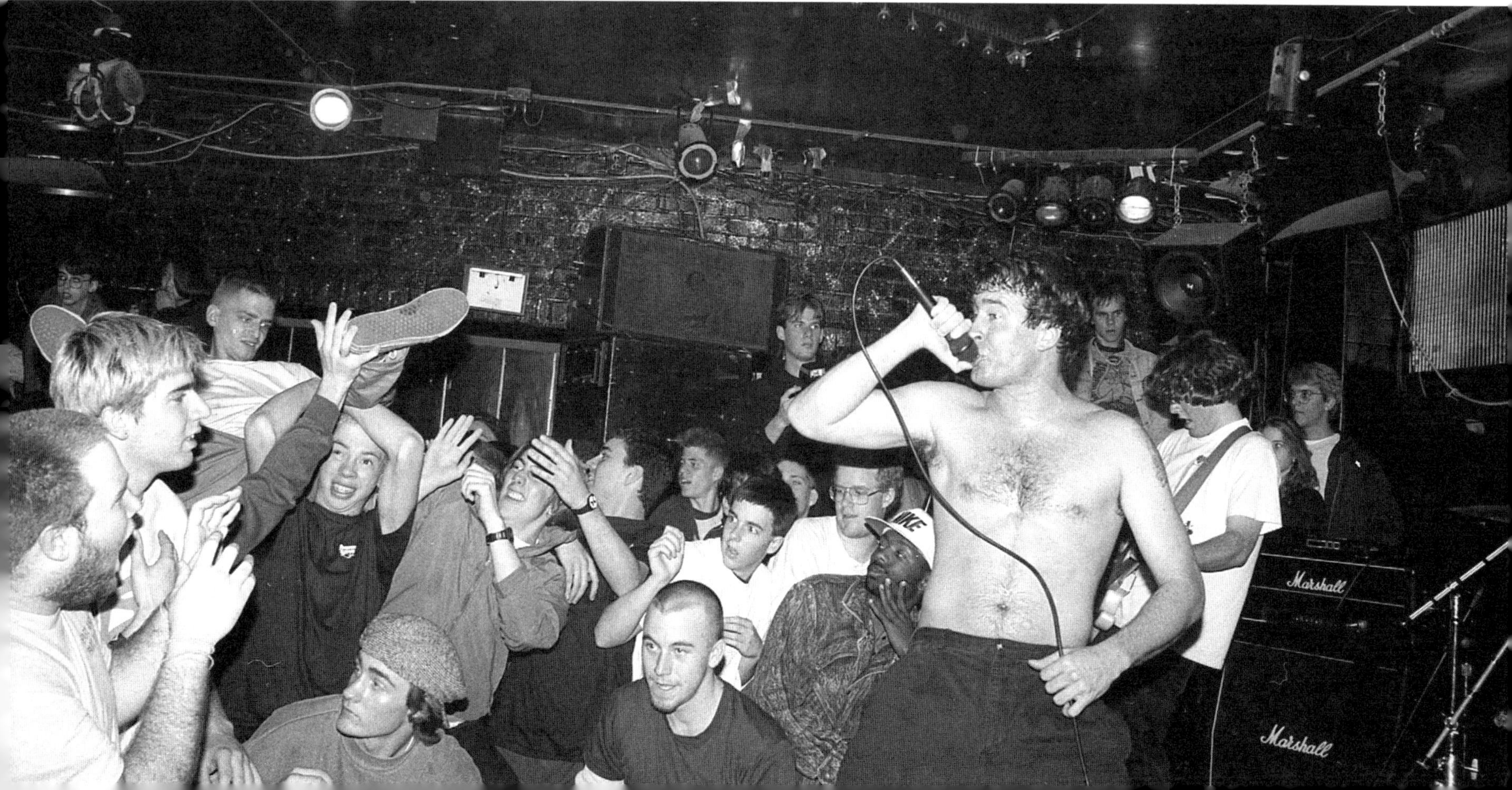

was a shame there weren't a lot of people there for that show, but I liked it because I could watch the bands without the usual intensity.

JOSEPH MCREDMOND: Playing there when I was in Admiral the first time opening for GI, and there was barely anybody in the room while we played. Played there again with Admiral at a show with Wind of Change earlier on a Sunday, again nobody was there, maybe like five people. The Ignition show was my favorite. Also met Henry Rollins outside of the show in his longer hair days.

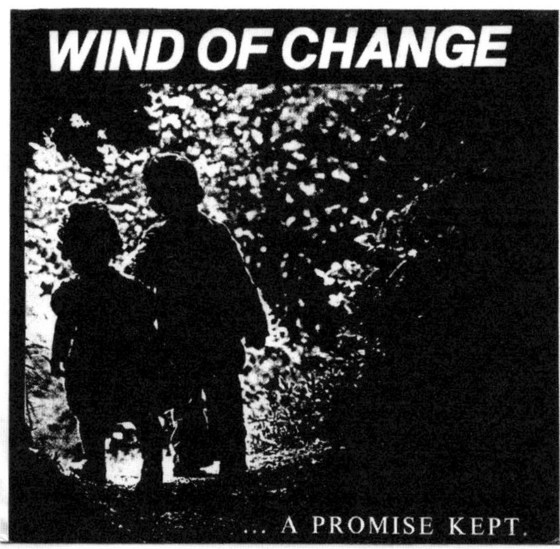

MATT DOLAN: American Standard played with Underdog in '88 or '89. Before that we had played the 9:30 Club with Dag Nasty and the Circle Jerks and some others. Safari was our first experience with a real inner city club in Washington, DC. It reminded me of playing in New York City. It was a little more dangerous and that was cool. Our show with Underdog was one of my favorite shows at Safari. Fury played and a band from upstate NY played. It was perfect. A great show, I loved it. We did a tour with Swiz and Soulside in 1989—the Swaside Tour.

JASON FARRELL: We ended up meeting the Chain of Strength guys through that and to this day I'm friends with those guys. Musically I had put them into "I'm not gonna listen," but when they played the Safari Club they killed it. I remember thinking about Chris Bratton: "a drummer with stage presence. What?" It was amazing to watch. They were very entertaining.

RICHI KRAKDOWN: Getting out to DC was a lifelong dream. Somehow we got booked with Swiz. We stayed with them that night. The neighborhood was pretty ghetto. We were worried about the truck. But the show was awesome. The kids were really into hardcore. They wanted to talk and know everything you can tell them. We made a lot of good friends and it was really cool.

CHRIS HARTNETT: There was a skinhead guy from Virginia who stood on the stage and acted like a frog while tripping on acid at a Swiz gig.

ANTHONY COMMUNALE: It was our first time in DC. It was Raw Deal with SOIA. We played a lot of shows together back then. We were great friends and I was part of the alleyway crew. I was psyched to play there, the land of Dischord, besides I was straight edge then. Started drinking in my twenties when I started on Wall Street. Still have proudly never tried a drug. The crowd was great.

JOHN GALBRAITH: Karl from Jinxproof and I were in military school together. The first show I went to there was that Sick of it All and Raw Deal show, where it was just like "welcome to the real world." Karl and I went on tour with Insted, all over.

Facing page, top: Admiral outside of the club after playing with Wind of Change, 1989.
Photos by Alex Dunham, courtesy of Joseph McRedmond.
Facing page, bottom: American Standard. Photo by Joe Wongananda.

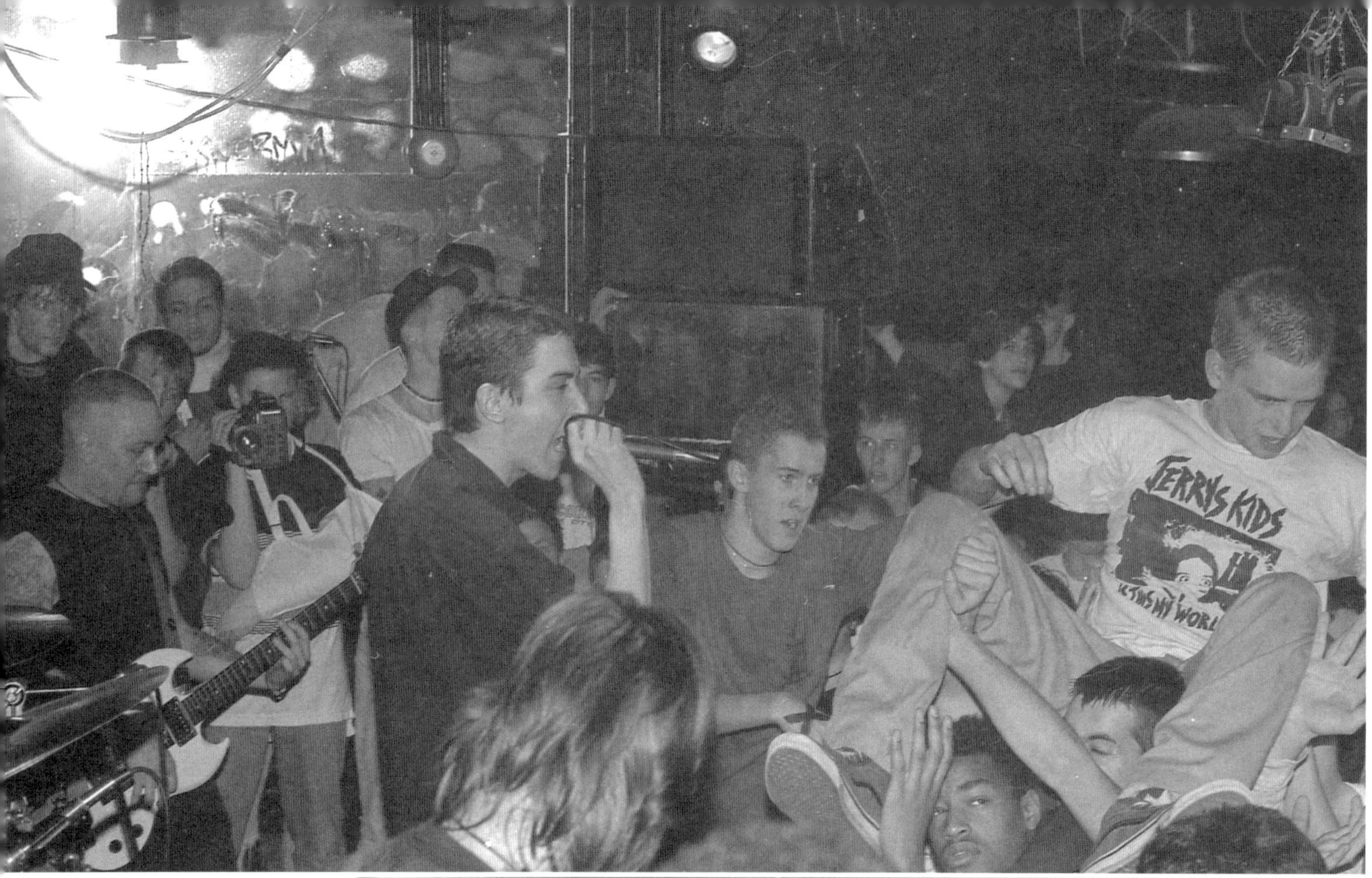

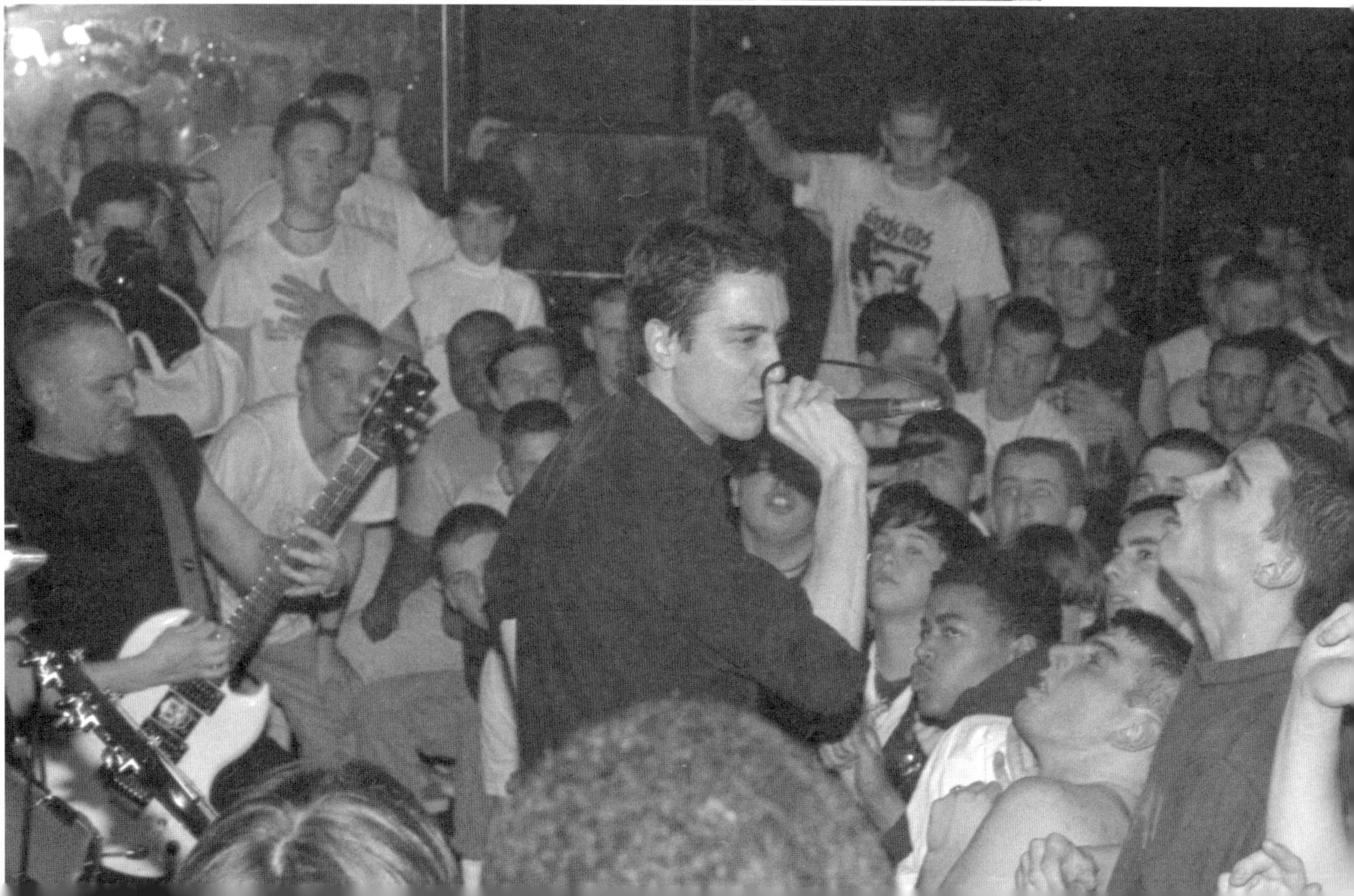

CHUCK COPELAND: The first time Sick of it All and Raw Deal played Safari! That show was insane. My girlfriend at the time, Carrie, got in a fight with Deirdre, I'm really good friends with Deirdre, Sick of it All is raging, I'm trying to walk Carrie to the metro to go home, and not get beat down, by Deirdre, and still run back to the club to see Raw Deal.

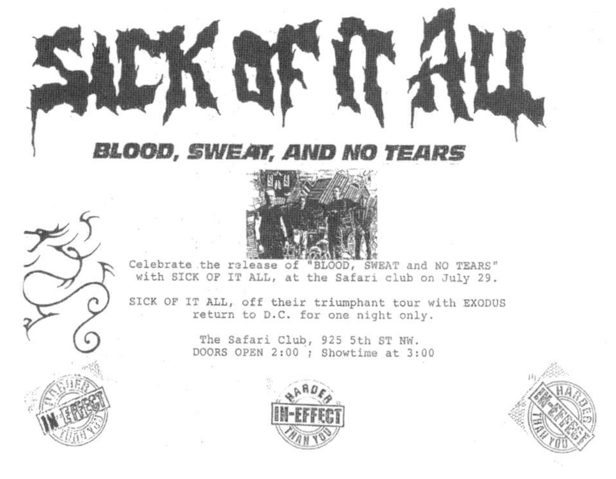

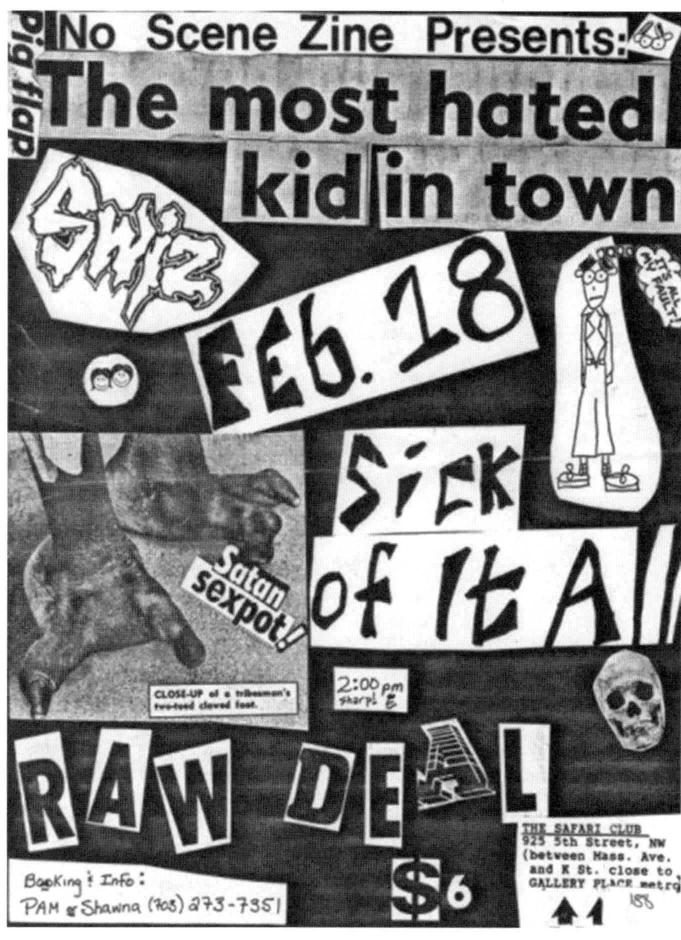

RANDY MOLER: My first show at Safari was Sick of it All. I was hooked instantly when they opened with "It's Clobbering Time." Up to that point I had been listening to mostly thrash metal—Nuclear Assault, Slayer, Metallica. The slower, heavy mosh rifts and lyrics about everyday things really resonated with me.

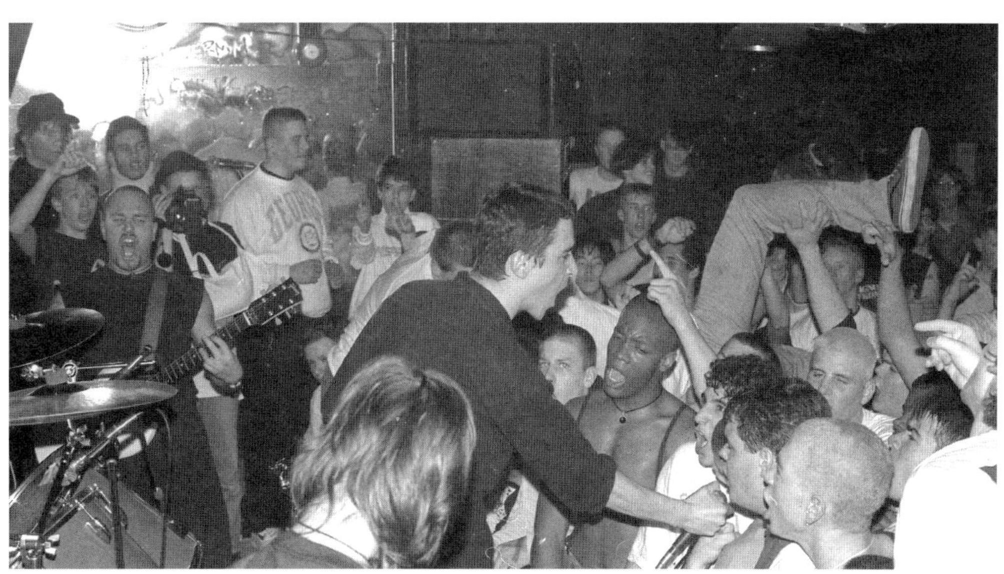

Sick of it All, 1989.
Photos by Joe Wongananda.

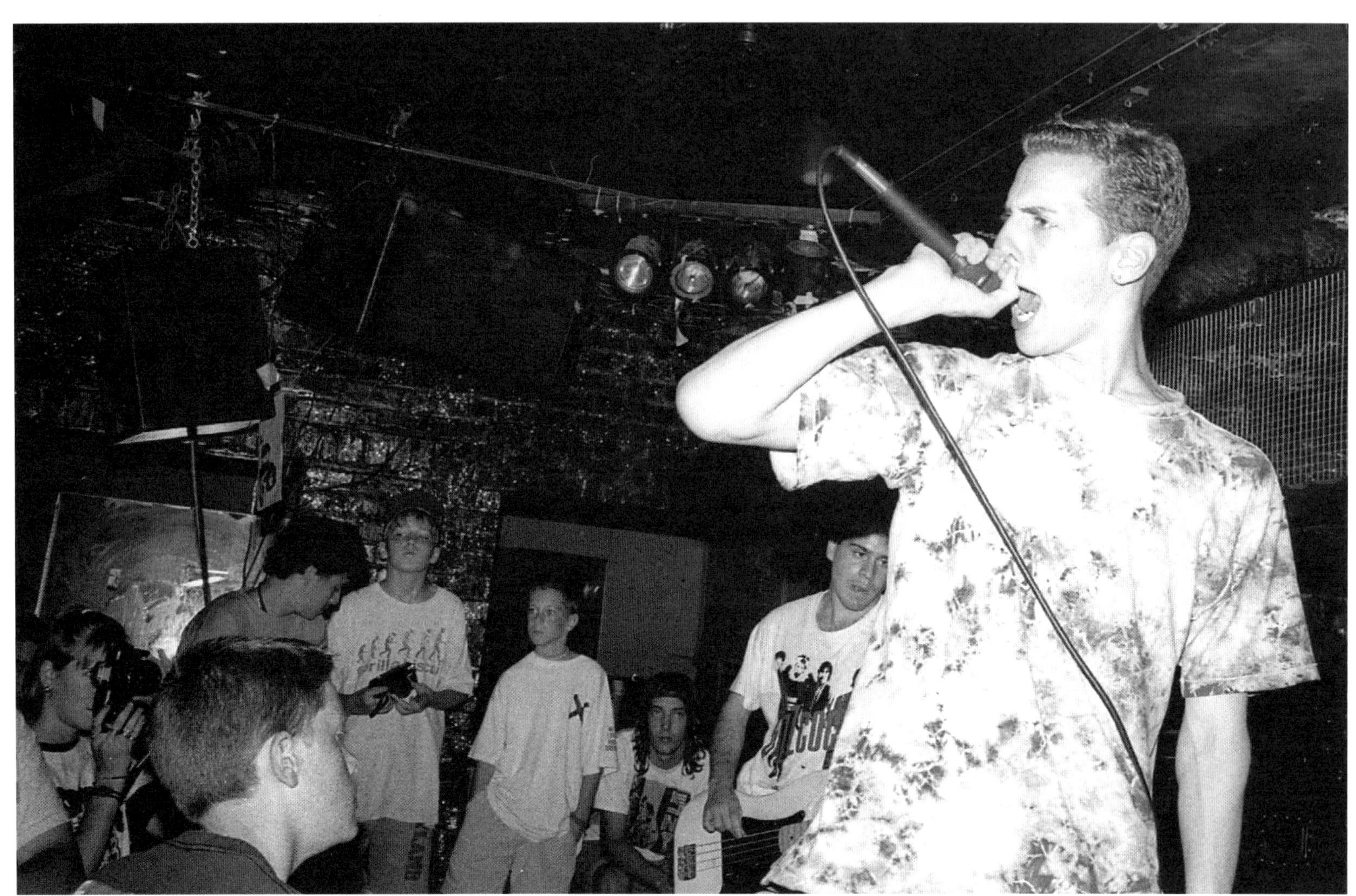

Supertouch, 1989. Photo by Joe Wongananda.

ANDY GUIDA: I wrote on the cassette after we played: "Supertouch at the Safari Club." I wanted to see the Watergate Hotel, so we went there after and I was running around it at like one in the morning and getting chased by the guards.

STEVE ZEITZOFF: I remember a Supertouch show where Chaka was the roadie and got beat up by a bunch of skinheads. Supertouch played and it wasn't that crowded but Chaka was jumping around and bumping into people just trying to hype it up and these redneck skinhead-type dudes just started stomping him. I was young so I was kind of scared, and then Mark Ryan asked, "what the fuck is going on?" Later, when Burn came out, I recognized him as the guy who was with the Supertouch guys.

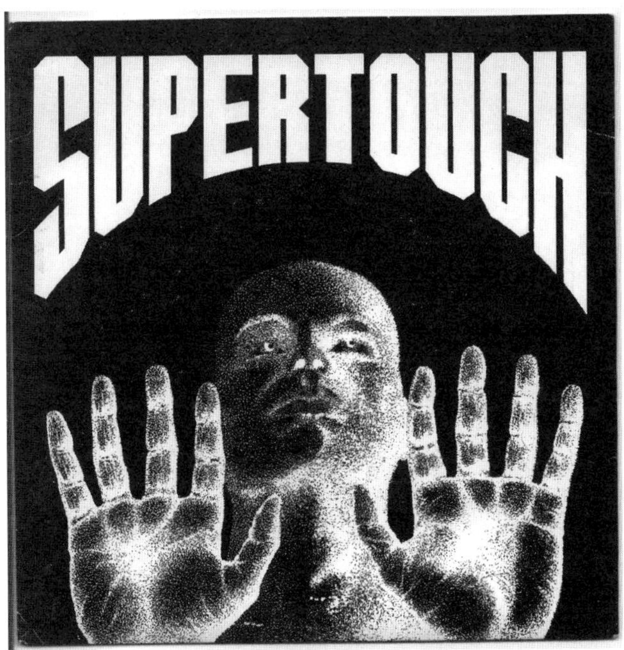

SHAWNA KENNEY: I was there for every show we did except for The Dwarves. I went to New York that weekend for some reason and left poor Pam to deal with them.

RODNEY BUTINELLI: I didn't know who the Dwarves were at the time. I'd heard the name and I think I saw a 7-inch cover. Then we were on the bill with them and I was like "this could be interesting." It was Parasite, the Mopagans and the Dwarves. The show was going fine and all the bands were getting on well and then it just did a u-turn. I guess the singer's idea was "let's antagonize the crowd," which he did from the start. He was saying, "DC is this lame fucking place to play, we hate it here, blah blah blah," and in between every single song he would just rip on either the bands that played, DC, or the scene in general. He'd go on these little tirades to piss everybody off. He started ragging on people there. He made some disparaging comment about Spyche who was a singer and the bass player in Parasite, as she was walking across. We were like, "No, that's not gonna happen," so you had guys in the Mopagans and us saying "we need to talk to you outside." The guy was just like, "No, we do this, we do that. We're not really that kind of band!" We were like, "Dude, you don't disrespect women in DC, especially another musician." And look around, man. Most of the people here are friends with the band. If that's your whole schtick, that's fine, but it doesn't play well in DC because with most of DC, Virginia, and Maryland bands it was all about unity, whether we knew each other or not. That's just not how we do it. If you're gonna play a DC show, you've gotta realize DC bands are loyal to each other.

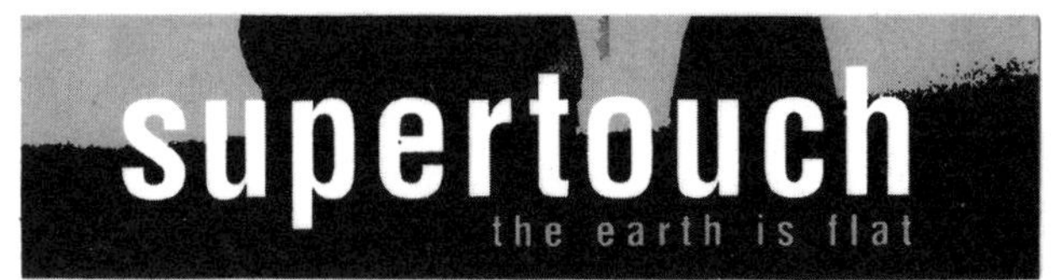

JAY MARTIN: The Dwarves show...they were just the antithesis of what I think Shawna and Pam were trying to promote there, and that show just made such an impression on everyone. HA! I don't think they got paid by Shawna/Pam for playing, and I don't think I've ever told Pam or Shawna this, but I gave them ten dollars out of my own pocket because

Aove: Supertouch 7-inch and sticker.

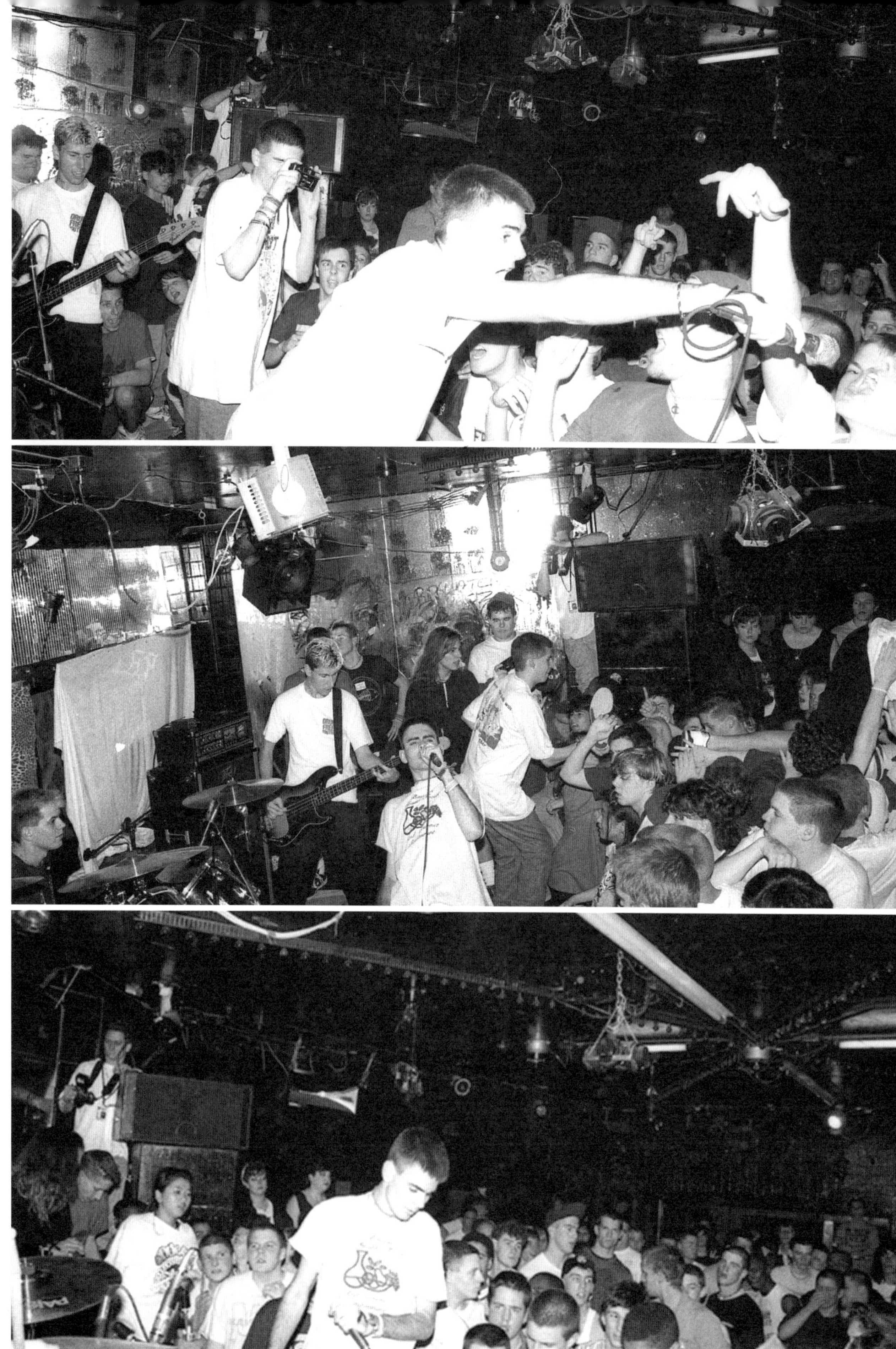

I thought they were pretty entertaining. Just enough for them to get gas to get out of town and on to their next show.

PAM GENDELL: We used their record, *Toolin' For A Warm Teabag*, as a dustpan for sweeping our apartment after that.

SHAWNA KENNEY: When I was booking literary events in LA years later, I booked Blag Dahlia on his book tour. I told him my version of what happened back in '88 and he said, "That sounds like us," and apologized.

BILL ANDERSON: Token Entry was my favorite show. I looked and saw this guy running around in his boxers and it was Toby. I think he just had his boxers on and I don't think he had shoes on—just running around in the pit. It was funny as hell and I was like "this guy has it going on" because he wasn't trying to be tough and he was having fun. To me that's what it's about.

DAVE HOOSER: One time Blast! showed up late and the club owner wouldn't allow them to use the PA system for some unknown reason, maybe because they wanted us out of there? It was a weekday show if I remember correctly. So the band played and the singer was unable to sing.

MICHAEL STRAIGHT: We had a band called Youth With Hair—me and Chris Best—and we played at the Safari Club. We played with Murphy's Law. We thought they were going to rush the stage and beat us up. Most people got a kick out of it but I was scared. It was pretty packed. I remember eating fried shrimp with Jimmy Gestapo and he was really friendly.

HEIDI MINX: Murphy's Law played there one day. We were sitting in the side room and there were all these huge stuffed animals. Jimmy had built a pyramid of Budweiser that was as tall as me. Video cameras weren't too common back then because they were pretty damn expensive. So this kid came into the backstage area and said, "I need to do an interview. I've got a video camera. It's for *DC Underground TV*." This poor kid kept saying, "Tell me about your band." Jimmy's like, "Well, we're kind of like an iguana. We keep changing." And I'm like, "No, Jimmy, you mean a chameleon." He's like, "Oh yeah…retake… Well, Murphy's Law is kind of like an iguana." Throughout the interview, Jimmy keeps grabbing a Bud and shaking it and popping the metal can open. So there's beer flying everywhere. So I guess this kid couldn't go to the show unattended, so the kid's father comes into the room and is standing behind the kid who is trying to do the poor interview as Jimmy is cracking Buds in his face.

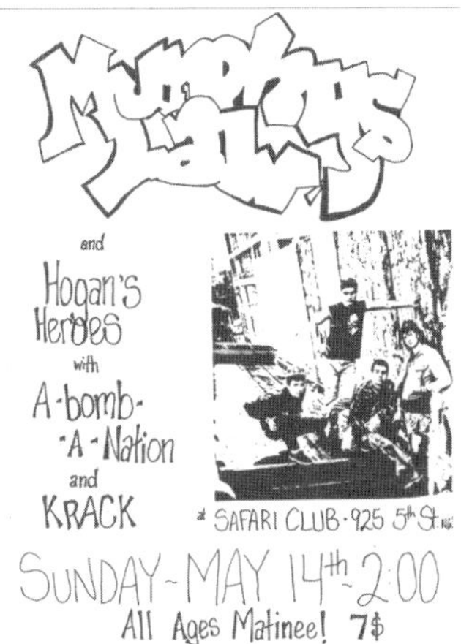

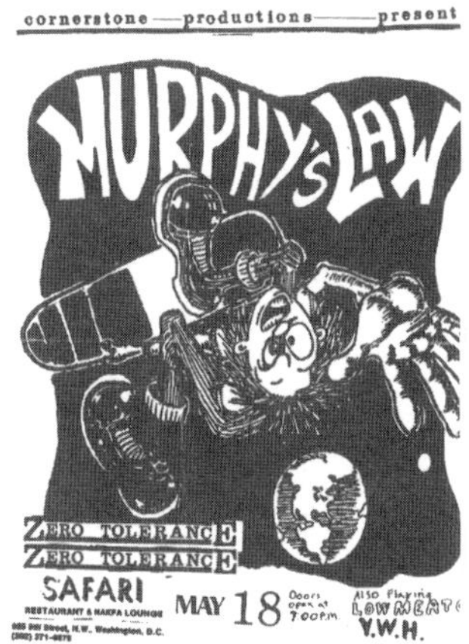

CF BEST: My first band's second show was opening for Murphy's Law (at the Safari Club). We were called Youth With Hair. We were horrible! The fact that John Cornerstone gave us a show says volumes about the fact that he either has the most amazing sense of humor on the planet or he is the sweetest human being ever

BRYAN WASSOM: We had played other venues like DC Space and the 9:30 Club with other similar joke bands, but the Safari matinée was not our scene as a band. Personally

Facing page: Insted.
Photos by Joe Wongananda.

it was for me though. I mean this was pretty much at the height of the burgeoning straight edge scene from NY during the summer of '89 and a straight edge joke band was not really well received…either the kids didn't get the joke, were offended, or just didn't understand it. So yeah, nobody really turned out, and honestly I don't think Crucial Youth was a strong enough band to hold their own show. It was fun, though. They brought the giant "youth brush" with them and were pretty funny. The highlight though: Pete Cortner who was singing for Dag Nasty at the time was their roadie and they played a spot-on cover of "Right Brigade" by Bad Brains with Pete on vocals which made the whole thing worthwhile.

SHAWNA KENNEY: We booked Crucial Youth twice—once with Murphy's Law, which we thought was hilarious but others didn't seem to get it.

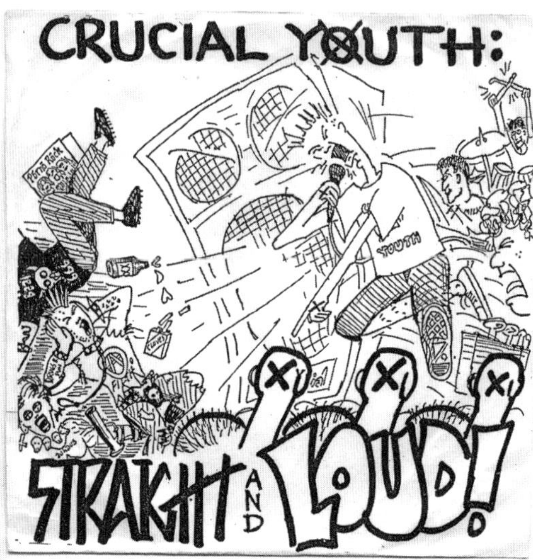

CHRIS HARTNETT: I managed a band who played there called Elegant Mess—they opened for Crucial Youth. No one showed and Shawna paid me seven dollars. Our biggest mistake was hanging flyers all over Washington, DC with the band's picture because these skinhead girls I talked to thought the guys were in their fifties. But they were one of the best bands who ever played there and I am not just saying that because I put out their record.

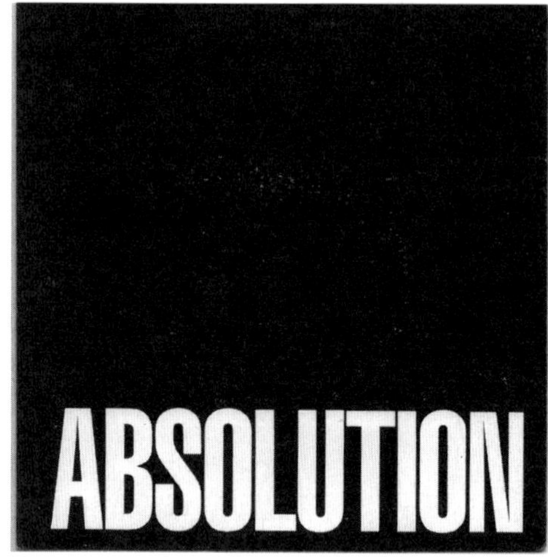

CHRIS BATTISTA: Absolution and Underdog played together. The energy in that show was unbelievable. When Absolution played, the lead singer got in the pit and started clipping people. That dude had to have been hopped up on something. First show I was ever at I was fifteen. Had very little idea what to expect. Bold was playing. The slow buildup started to "Talk is Cheap." Song went fast, and I got mercilessly pummeled in the pit. A year and a half later, I was at another matinée and they played the video of the Bold show. I got to watch myself being pummeled at my first show!

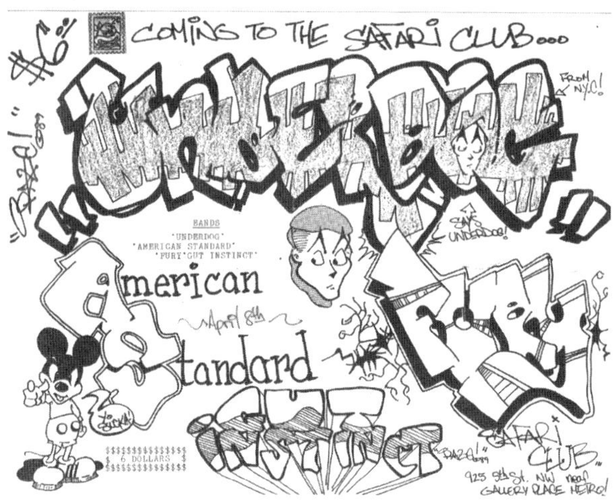

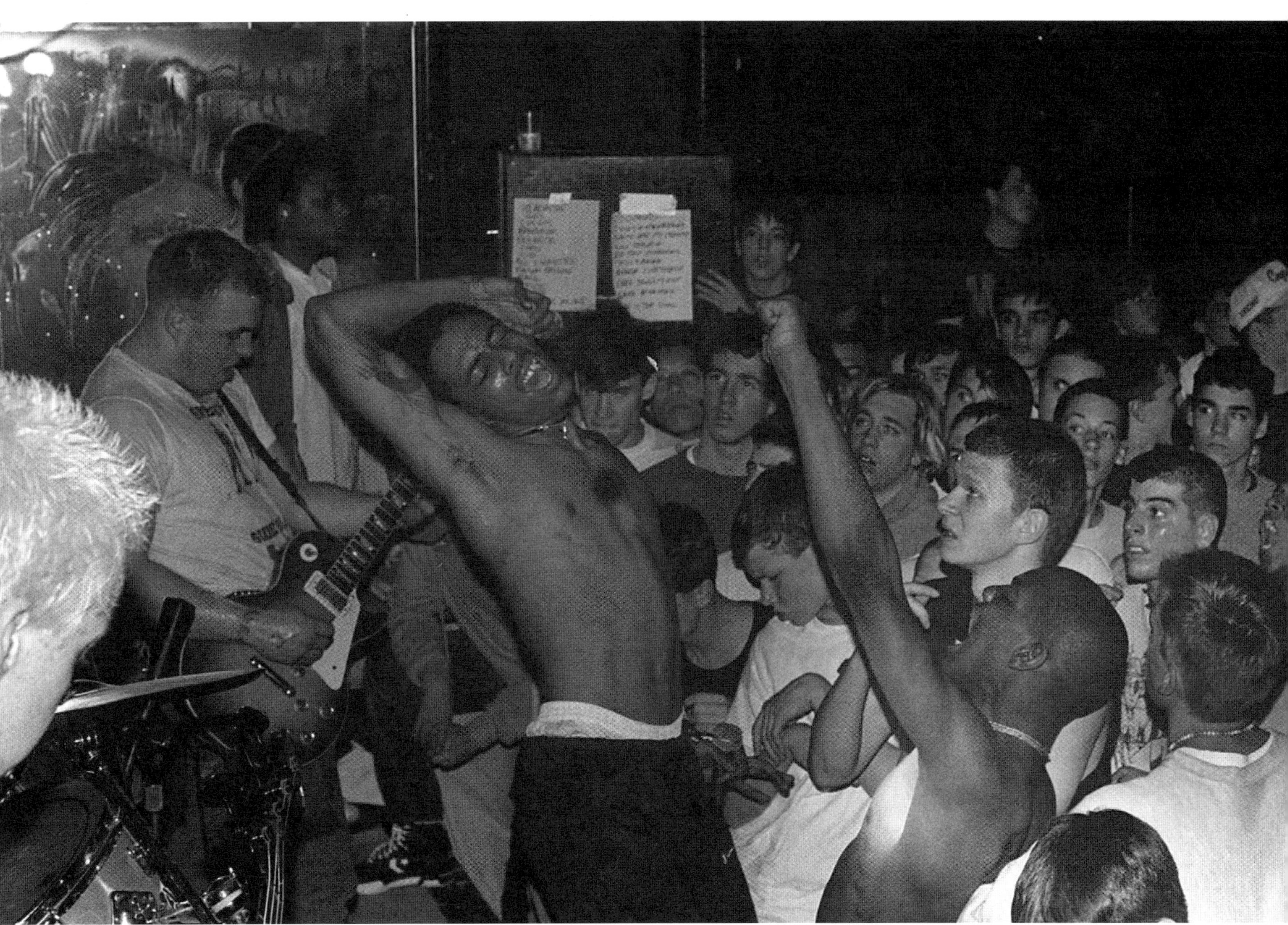

Absolution, 1989. Photo by Joe Wongananda.

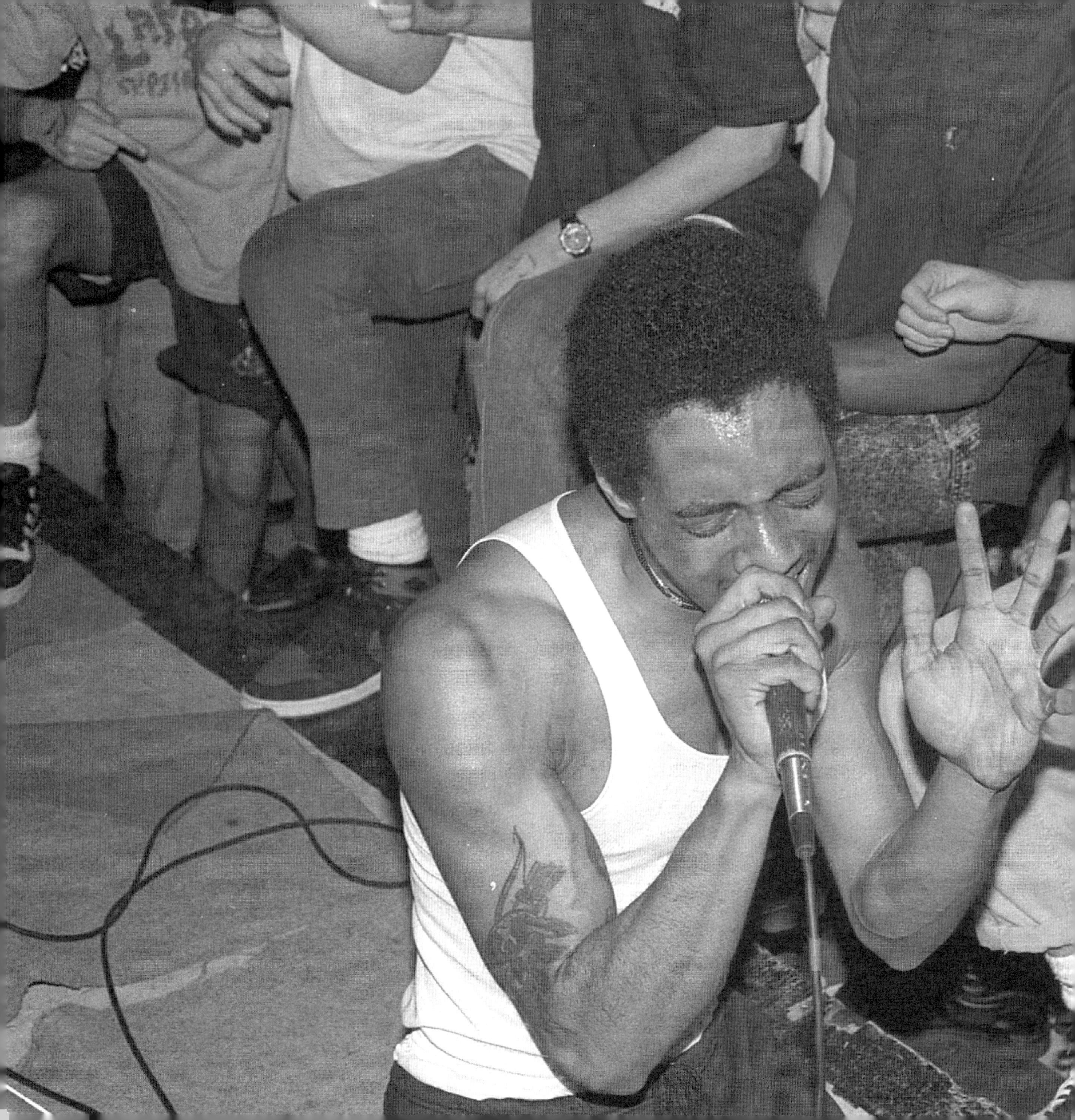

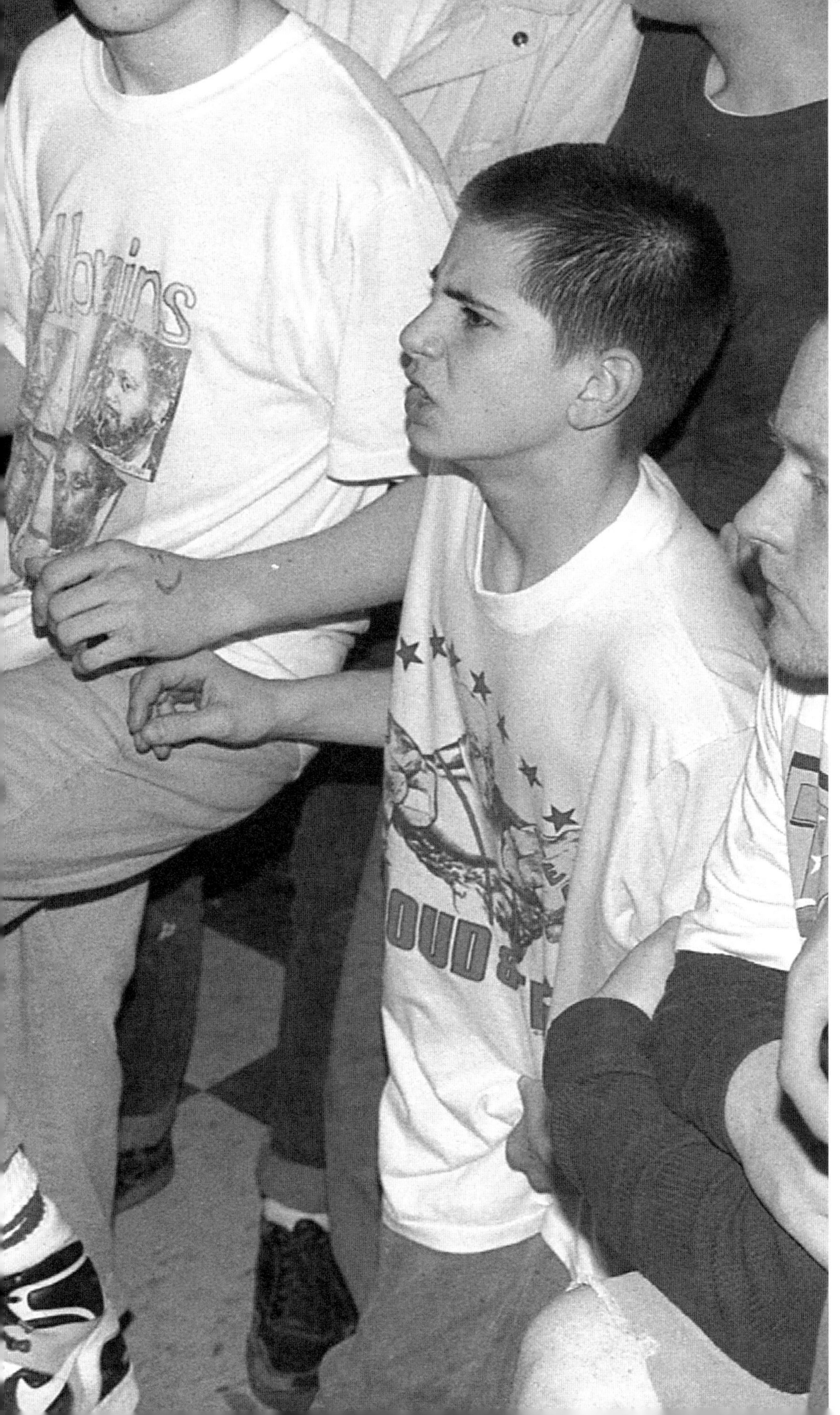

Absolution and Underdog played together. The energy in that show was unbelievable.
—Chris Battista

Djingi of Absolution.
Photo by Joe Wongananda.

Safari Club was a place where the kids were involved, versus a club owner. The scene was already there, the crowd was already there.
—Chuck Treece

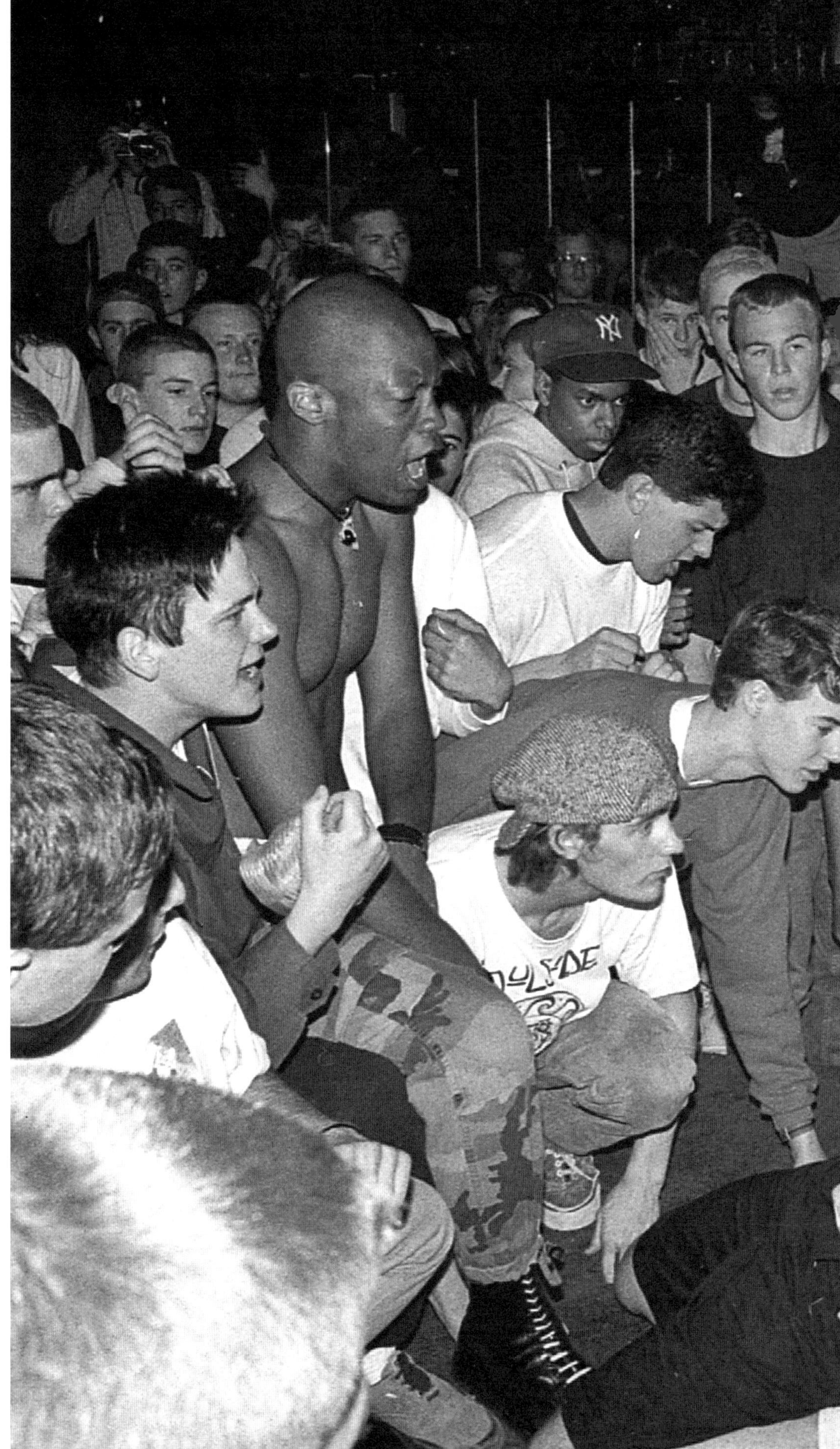

Underdog, April 8, 1989.
Photo by Joe Wongananda.

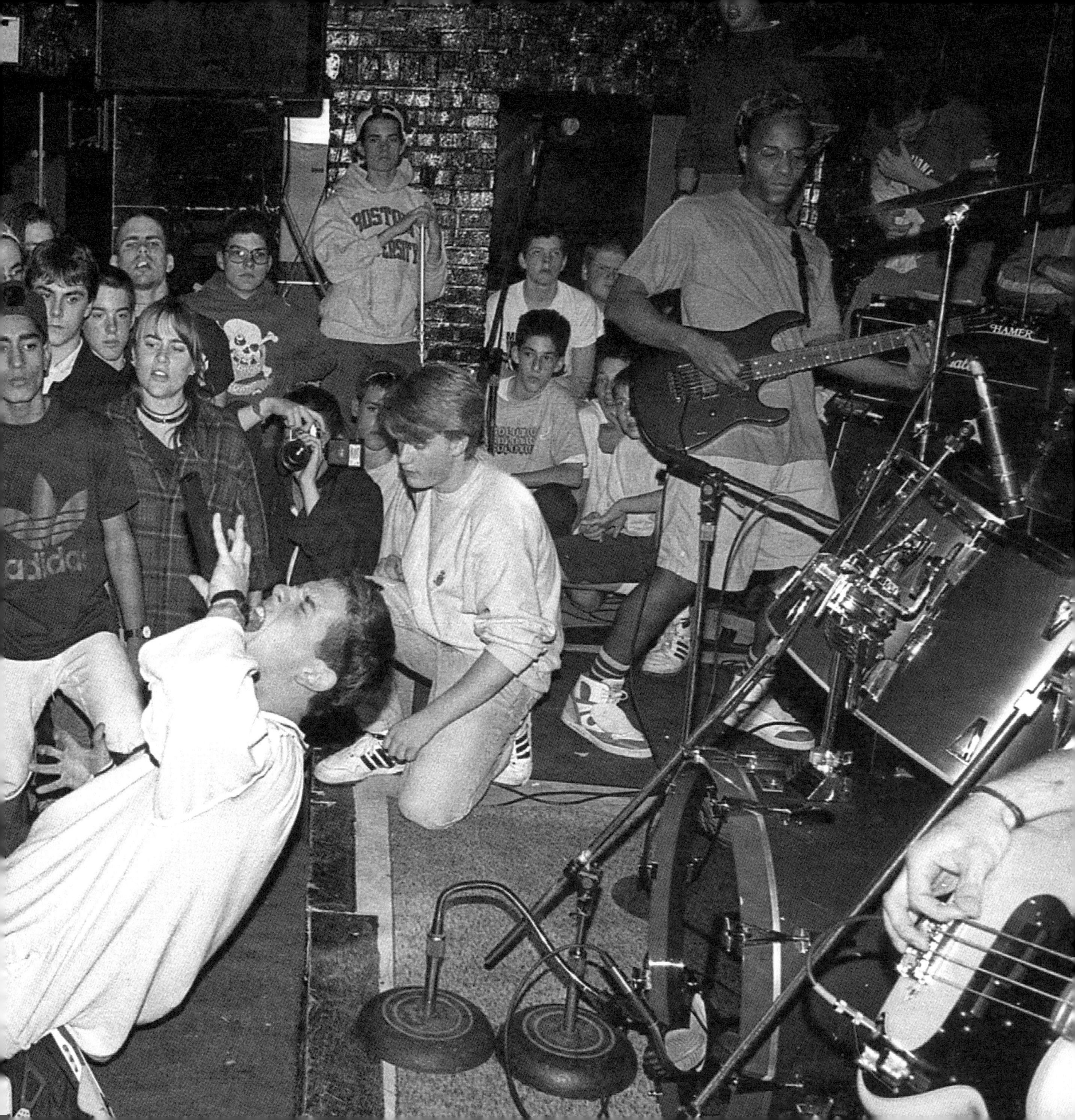
adidas
HAMER

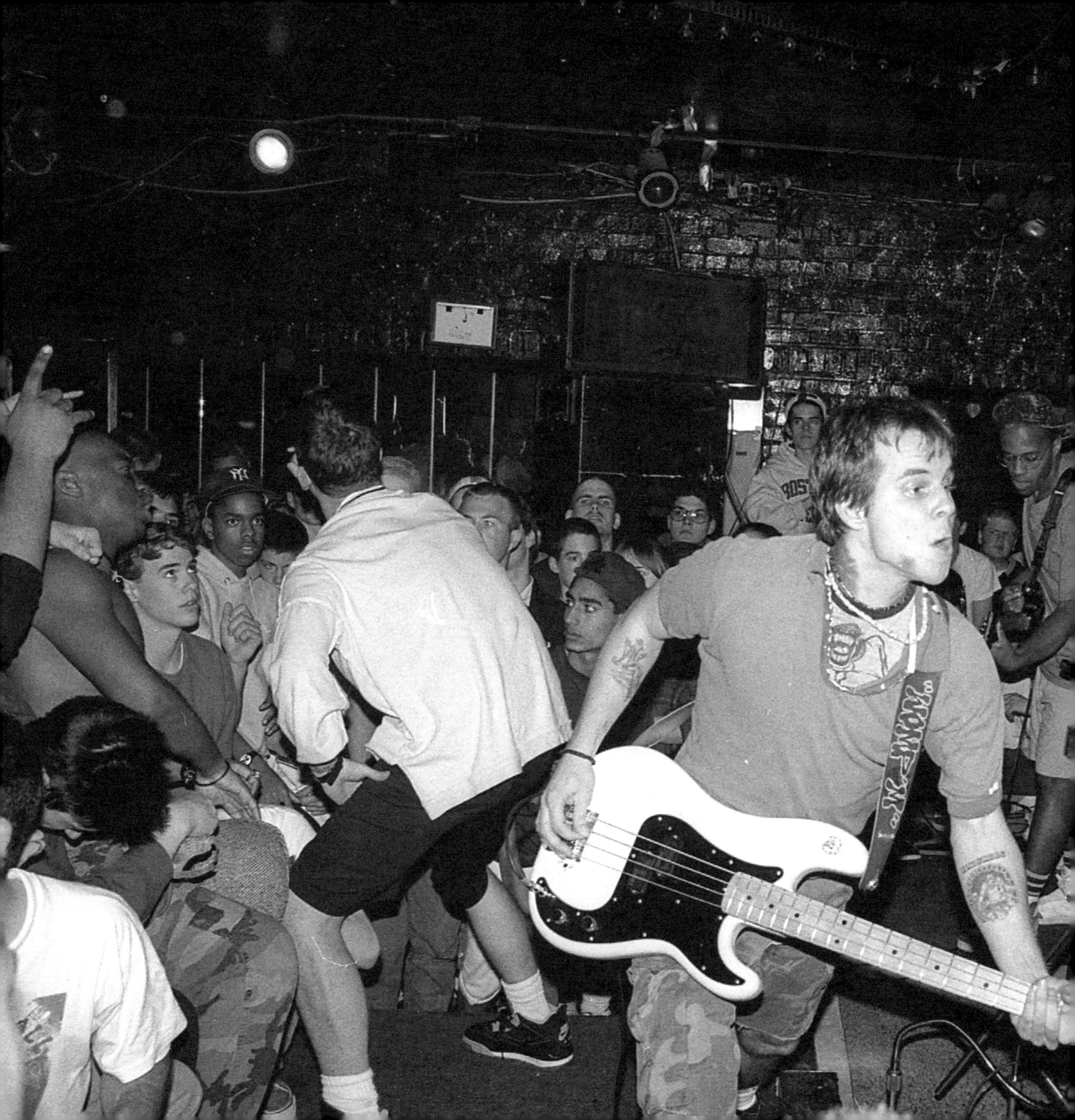

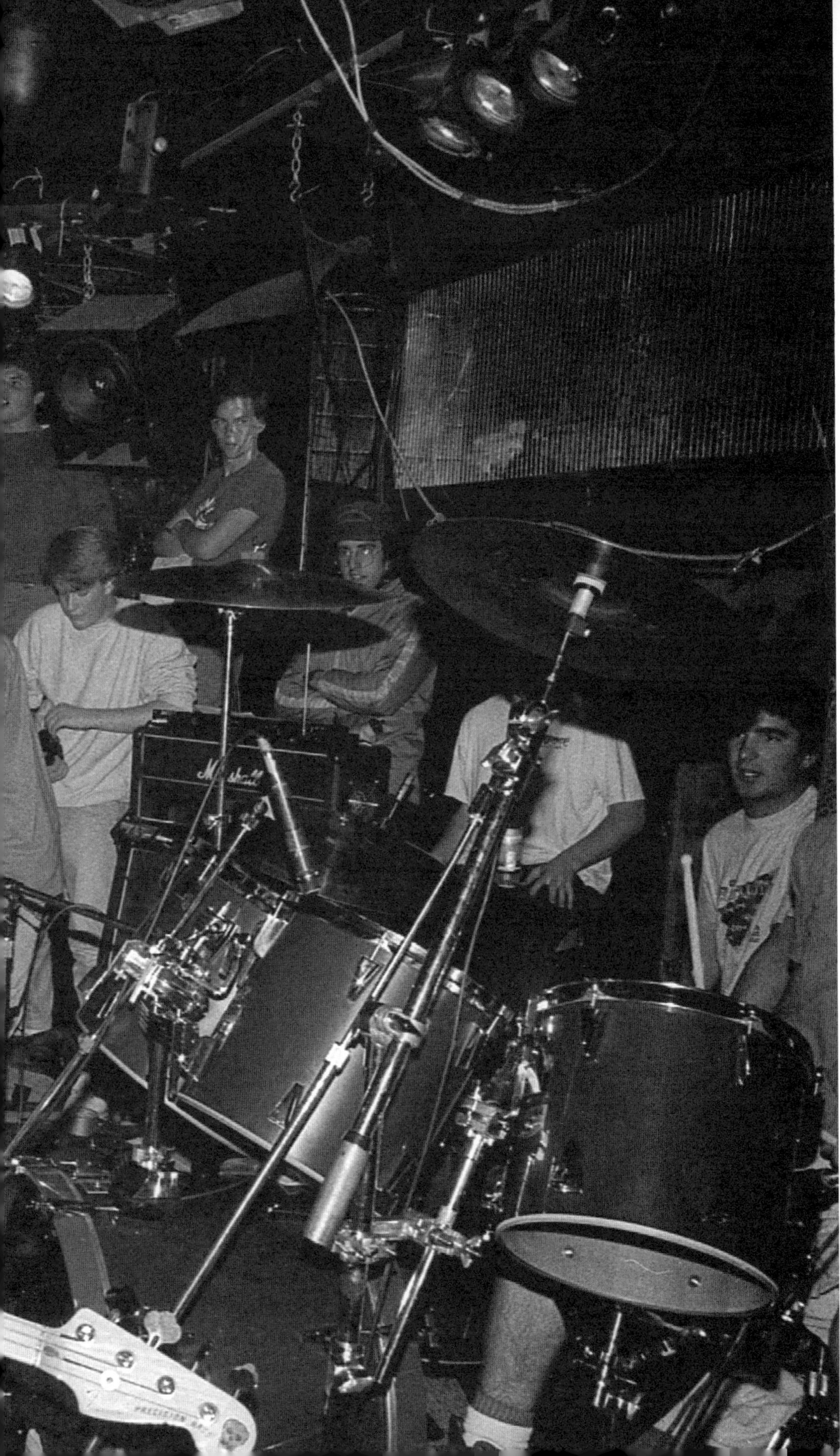

It always felt good rolling into DC, where some of my favorite bands were born. Later my mind was blown when the guys from Clutch told me they met at an Underdog show at Safari.
—Russell Iglay

Underdog, April 8, 1989.
Photo by Joe Wongananda.

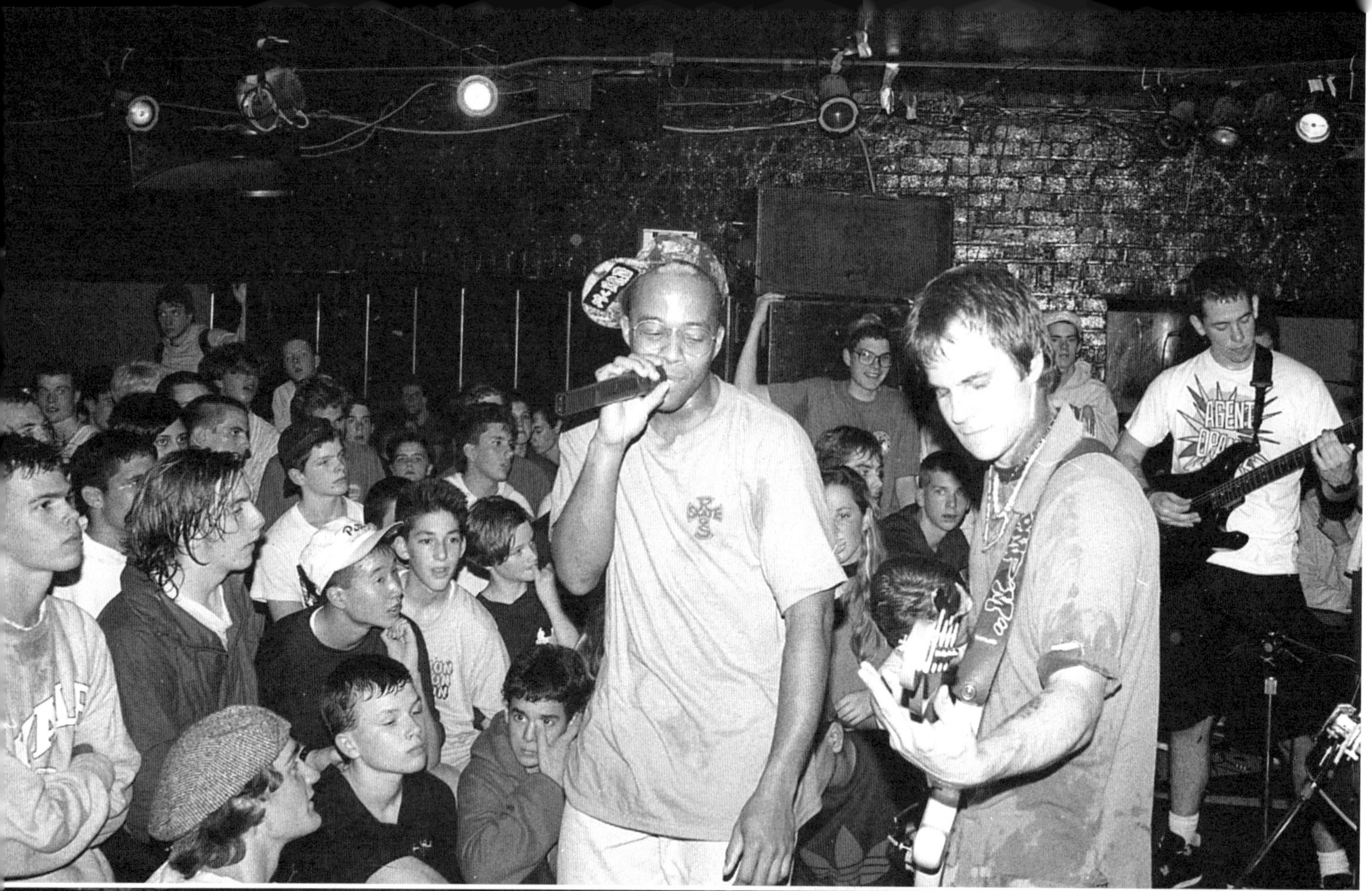

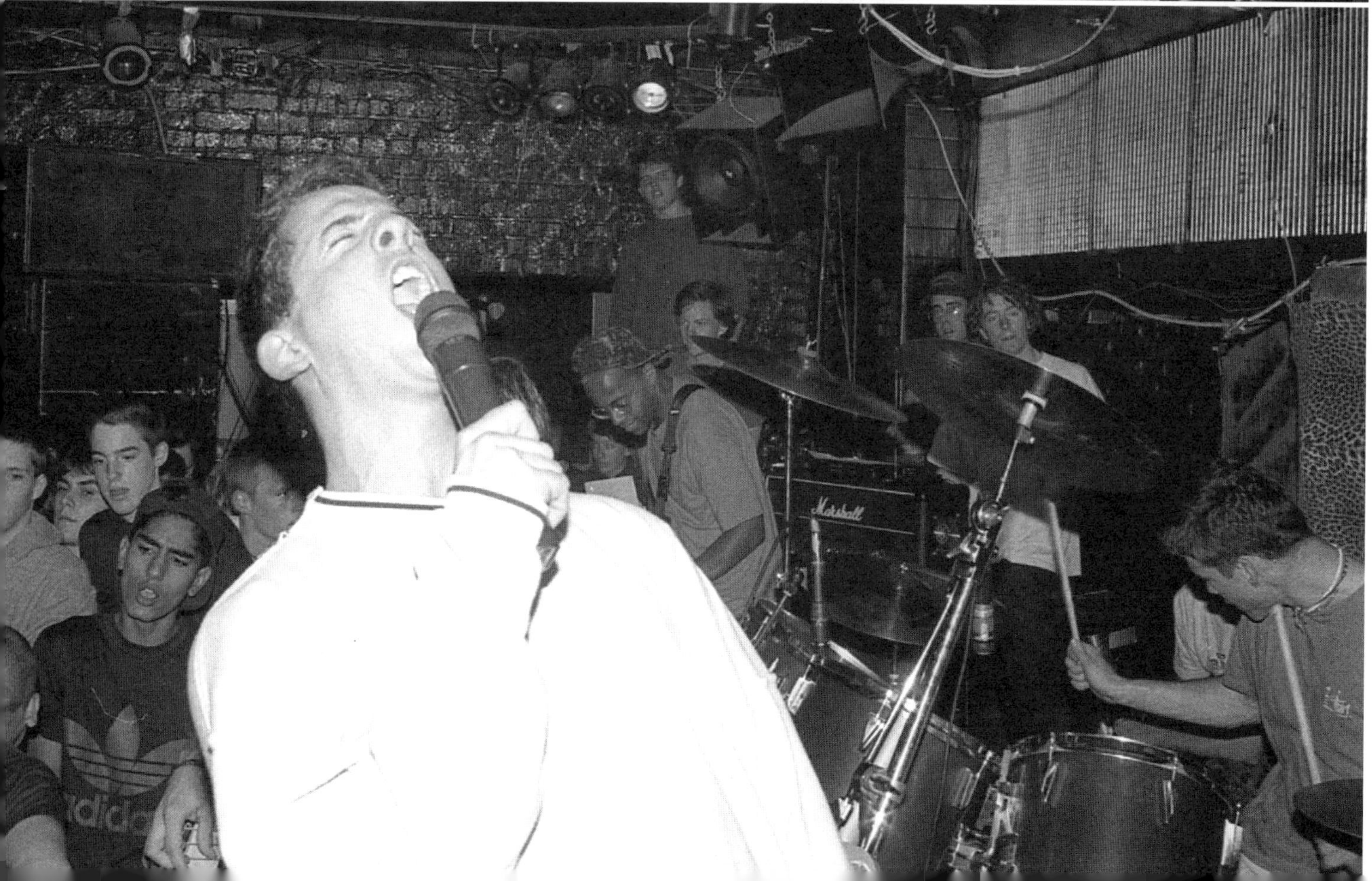

Underdog, April 8, 1989.
Photos by Joe Wongananda.

JOHN GALBRAITH: It was so cool to be hanging out and just breaking bread in Chinatown with Gavin and Absolution.

NAM DONG: I've seen the most random bands there. I saw KRS-1 there one time. I think Martin put that show on. It was at night. KRS-1 ripped it.

MARTIN CASTRO: We didn't have the money to do the KRS-1 show by ourselves because hardcore bands are on a different level, so we kind of made the contact and passed it on to the people who ended up booking him. The show was great. I'd seen a lot of hip-hop bands and the only one worth seeing was KRS. Coming from a hardcore background, I'm used to getting on stage and diving and being part of the show. Any hip-hop group was boring, it was something different. It wasn't like a go-go, you weren't there to dance. He played also at the Zulu Cave.

JOHN GALBRAITH: I did a Poor Righteous Teachers show that lost money, but it was fun.

MATT BURGER: I flew out here in January 1990, specifically for Judge, Outburst, and Turning Point, which Judge did not show up for, but I met Gabe [Onrubia] that night, and we're still great friends, and Matt Knapf, who owns Tattoo Paradise, I met him at the Burger King two blocks down the street. We were kind of lost.

BEN CHUSED: When the Judge LP came out it was a huge deal and everyone really loved that album—skinheads, straight edge kids, metalheads, skaters, whoever. After almost two years of going to shows in the DC area and seeing mostly Dischord bands in the late eighties, one of my straight edge friends mentioned that Judge was coming to DC to play at the Safari Club. Four of us just got together and took the metro to the show—it was Step Aside, Transmission, Four Walls Falling, and Judge in February 1990.

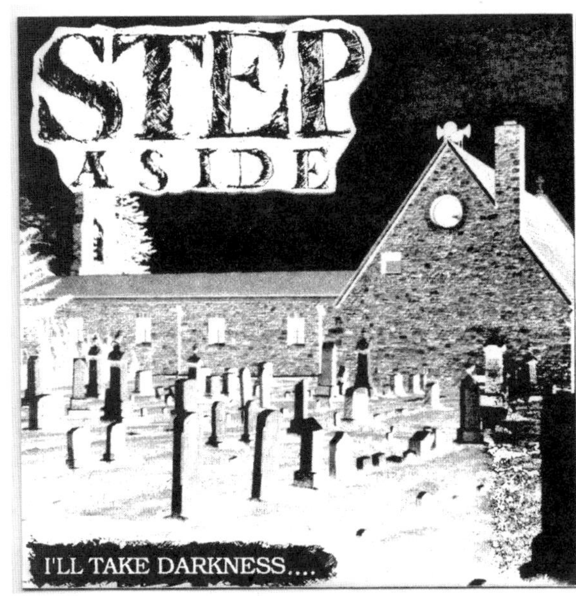

RICH DOLINGER: After living in LA for so many years, I hate using the word "networking," but the Safari Club was great for that. At the Judge show, I asked Taylor from Four Walls Falling if he knew any good bass players. He introduced me to Hillel. Him, Nam, and Rich Green were the line up in my first band No Excuse. We played once at the Safari Club with Up Front. We weren't on the bill, but we hopped on stage and played a few songs. Rich Green later started Grip with Jon Field from Up Front.

CHRIS LYMAN: The shows that I played there with my bands Color Blind, Step Aside, and MayDay were some of the most satisfying moments of my musical career. It's not to say that it was perfect: there were fights, there was bitchiness, many of us were just high school kids. It was tough, it was physical, and you had to watch your step, but it really helped some of us to improve our lives.

Gut Instinct opened almost every set with "Disturbing the Peace."—Ben Chused

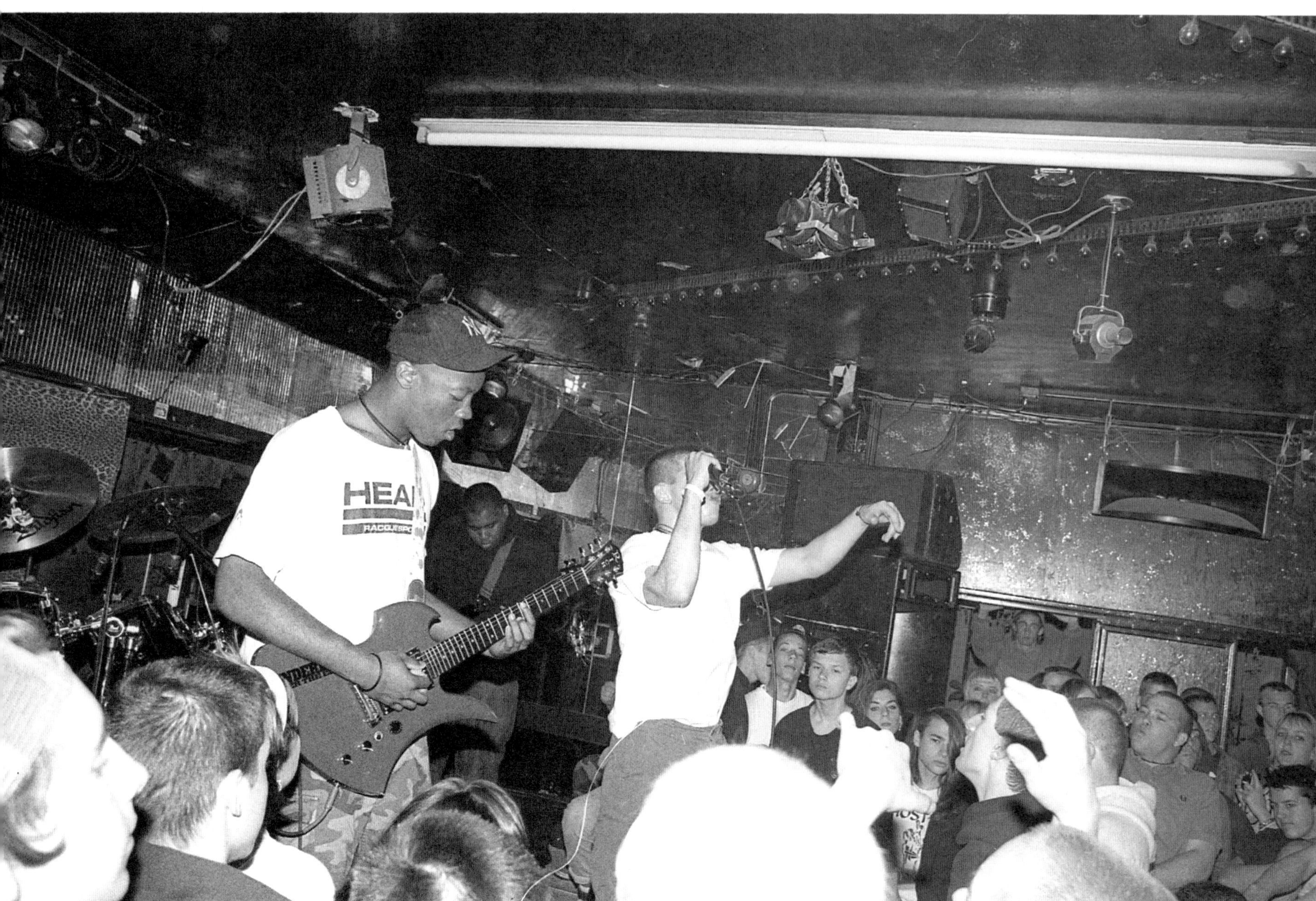

Gut Instinct, 1989. Photo by Joe Wongananda.

KURT UBERSAX: My first show at the Safari was Immoral Discipline. I tried to come most weekends for those first few months. I was a big NY hardcore fan, so a chance to see those bands was always on my mind. Later, when we formed Just Cause and got to play there, our first show was with Chain of Strength. COS finished their set with Minor Threat's "Betray" and all hell broke loose. The stage was trashed with everyone flying up on stage to sing along, then flying off the stage into a mass of mayhem—it was beautiful. Looking back now, I think there was a lot of pent up energy from kids who maybe got a chance to see that first wave of harDCore and were looking for the second wave, or (like me) never got to see those early bands live, but had all the tapes/records. Seeing it live was like a flashpoint.

hardcore show!
UNBROKEN
(from san diego on new age records)
mouthpiece
(new jersey XXX)
BROTHER'S KEEPER
(former members of sumthin' to prove)
indivision
(ex members of bon jovi)
monday, july 10th. 5:00 p.m. $
at the chamber of sound. 925 5th street. nw.
washington, d.c.
for a real good time, call:
jon: 301.239.1685 or XmartinX: 202.393.5336

KURT POWERS: I missed Token Entry, Gorilla Biscuits, and Turning Point at the Safari Club. I missed all the shows where people were like, "Oh, but you had to be there!" Some people looked at us like we were the young ones. And we were young. But I still look back and I remember Mouthpiece playing there what seemed like every month or two. The best memory I have is seeing Mouthpiece playing "What Remains" and the whole crowd singing along every time.

PHIL BAXLEY: Hatebreed played and nobody knew who they were. I had to ask Jamie a few times what the name of his band was. I think the guitarist from 25 ta Life was playing for them.

SEAN DORSEY: You can't mention Safari without Mouthpiece, who really became almost a hometown band there.

CF BEST: Token Entry was one of my favorite shows that happened there. I remember getting black and blue at that one.

DAVID BYRD: I'm pretty sure my first show there was a Damnation show. There's one YouTube video online where it's completely dark because the lights were turned off except for two blue lights on stage. It was different than where I was used to going to shows. Florida was not as participatory, as far as people jumping on each other. I thought that was kind of cool. It felt friendlier.

RICH WARWICK: I used to have to go away with my parents on vacation and I'd be like "fuck, I'm gonna miss this show and this show and this show." I think Chorus of Disapproval got back together and was coming out and I was friends with Martin, who booked the shows, and he tells me the date and I'm like you've got to be fucking kidding—I'm going on vacation. I was so pissed.

MICHAEL STRAIGHT: I wasn't into a lot of the straight edge hardcore stuff but that was what was going on at the time, but I was more into the emo-ish stuff. I booked Econochrist the next summer after Shawna booked them.

JOE SONGCO: We did a show originally booked at the Safari that ended in Woodbridge. There was a massive accident on

95 South and we were going to be super late. The hope was to get out of the traffic and haul ass to the Safari and maybe we'd be able to show up and just go on without any sound check. By the time we got to the club, it was already too late to go on. We were totally embarrassed that we didn't make it there on time. We also felt pretty bad that people came down to the club and didn't get to see us play. So we just hung around and were like "what now?" I forget who did the brainstorming, but this one guy offered up his house in Northern Virginia to have a party and maybe if they could find a microphone and a PA, we could do a set at their house. We drove all this way and it was still kind of early so we agreed. It was a scene straight out of an eighties teen comedy. Word of this party got out within an hour or two, the guy's house was full of people. We set up in the basement and did our full set. Even though we couldn't find a mic, Brian screamed himself hoarse and conducted sing-alongs with the crowd, so it sounded like gang vocals on every song. It was awesome. After the set, we hung around at the party and had a great time meeting some of the kids who lived in and around the DC/NoVa area.

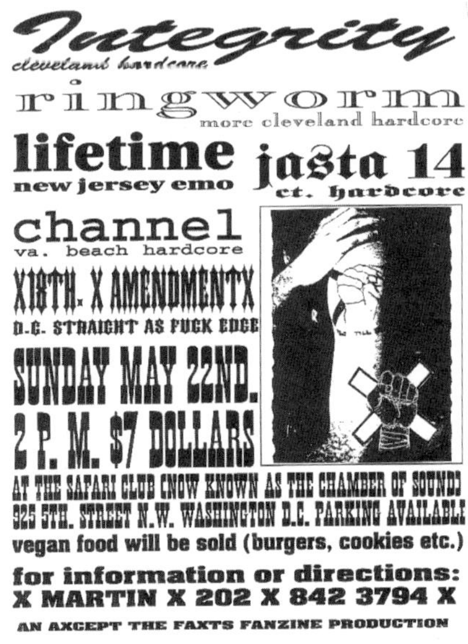

MICHAEL STRAIGHT: Bad Religion called me to book, but I gave it to John because I was going out of town that weekend with my parents. I missed it but they played.

JOHN DUGAN: I saw some other shows at Safari Club, Bad Religion for one, and spent a night or two just hanging outside on the sidewalk, but I skipped most of the heavy-duty NYHC and NY-style HC that was booked at the club for a long time—I was more into DC punk, British stuff, etc. NYHC seemed a bit regressive—though my college buddies did their best to convert me to Token Entry. That said, I did love the Gorilla Biscuits and would loved to have seen them in their prime.

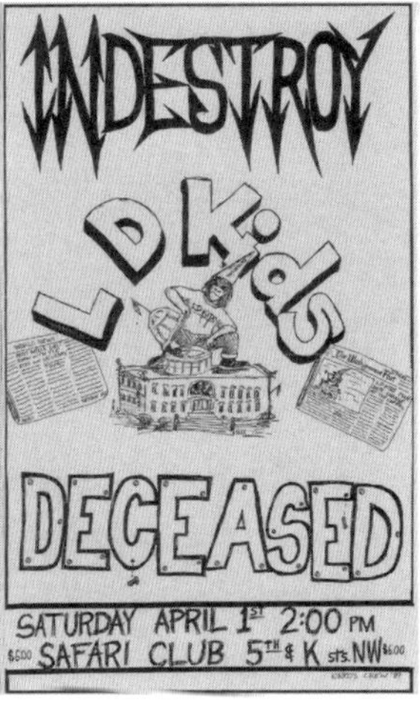

MARK ADAMS: We couldn't get booked at The Bayou or Jaxx because we weren't commercial or polished-sounding enough and didn't have an eight-by-ten glossy promo photo of us, and the only thrash stuff that the 9:30 Club was booking were national acts. The Hung Jury Pub was either shut down or wasn't booking any shows. We had heard about this place called the Safari Club that was easy to get into, but the only catch was that it was in a bad neighborhood. Our friend James Barrett whose brother Jerry played in LDKids asked us if we wanted to open up for them and Indestroy there. It was April 1989, our first club show ever there.

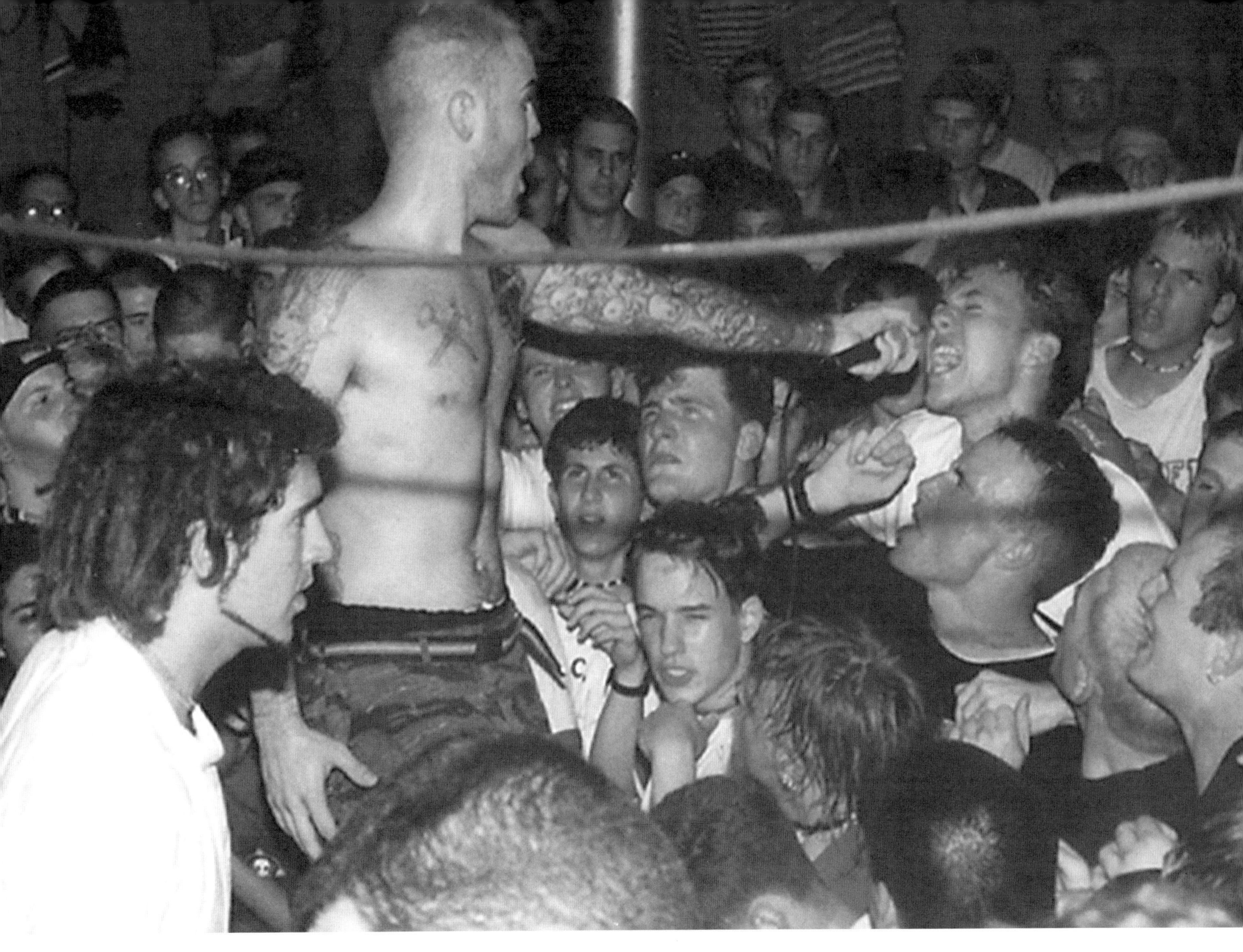

Integrity must have canceled like three shows in DC, then one time they actually finally played and that was a big deal.
—Rich Warwick

Integrity. Photo by Jim Wilson.

TOM LYLE: Government Issue played one show there. Mark Jenkins reviewed it and made snide comments on our lack of musical professionalism. Jeez, we were a hardcore band, Mark. Lighten up!

JOHN GALBRAITH: The Government Issue show was a good one, too. John Stabb was such a nice man.

PAM GENDELL: Government Issue wanted $1,000 and that was a huge deal to us. We did that show on a Friday night and it was a big debate on whether or not to charge ten dollars, which seemed like a lot in the land of five-dollar shows.

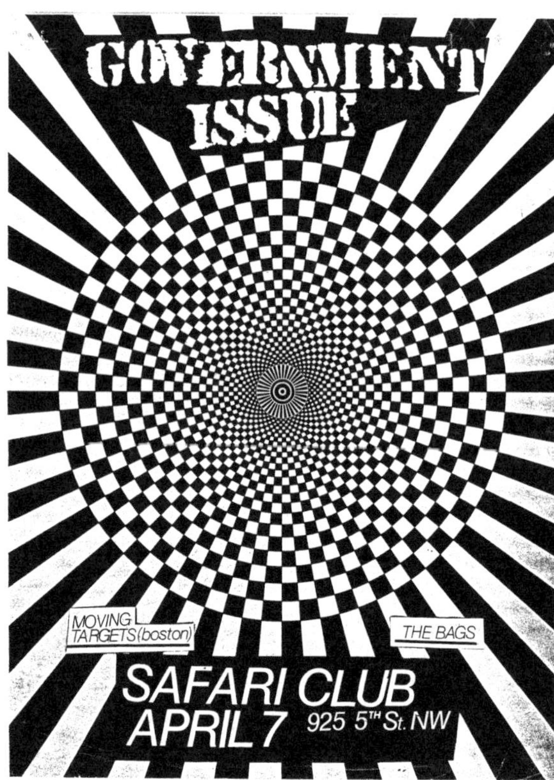

SHAWNA KENNEY: I think we handed over $750 at the end of the night after paying the traveling bands and they were fine.

SEAN DORSEY: I think the best of the many shows I went to at Safari was when Lifetime played with Integrity in '94. Neither of them are bands I still listen to now or were even my favorite bands at the time, but that show stands out for several reasons. Integrity had never played DC, although they had been scheduled to for several years in a row, and the running joke was that they would never show up. Additionally, Lifetime was in their transitional phase from the New Age band, to what they then became and popularized, and they had just released their *Tinnitus* 7-inch at the show. On one hand you had Lifetime telling people to stop dancing (like Fugazi) and then you had people killing each other for Integrity, (who surprisingly actually showed up). The dynamic of the two bands really stood out to everyone and made it an amazing show.

CHRIS HARTNETT: This guy from a hardcore band from Reston jumped up on stage and threatened to kick the guy from Ludichrist's ass for making a comment about his band. Their 7-inch had a guy with a shotgun pointed at you.

MICHAEL STRAIGHT: I was getting a lot of West Coast bands and I was psyched because I was into the Bay Area scene. One of the guys from Neurosis called and said they needed a show for July 2, and I thought, *that's my birthday!* They said there was another band coming from the south called Filth and I'd read about them in *MRR*. They played with my friend's band from Baltimore called Fifth Column. I was like "my birthday show, my birthday show!" And Excess Baggage and Love Slug from Annapolis. It was a small show on a Tuesday night, but it was fun. I had to put the bands up and they all stayed at my parents' house. I got a bunch of tents and put them all in the backyard.

RICH WARWICK: Say Outspoken was playing—they'd play DC, then Middlesex, then University of the Arts in Philadelphia. It'd be me, Tru, Martin, and Timmy and Jessica from Virginia Beach. Integrity must have canceled like three shows in DC, then one time they actually finally played and that was a big deal.

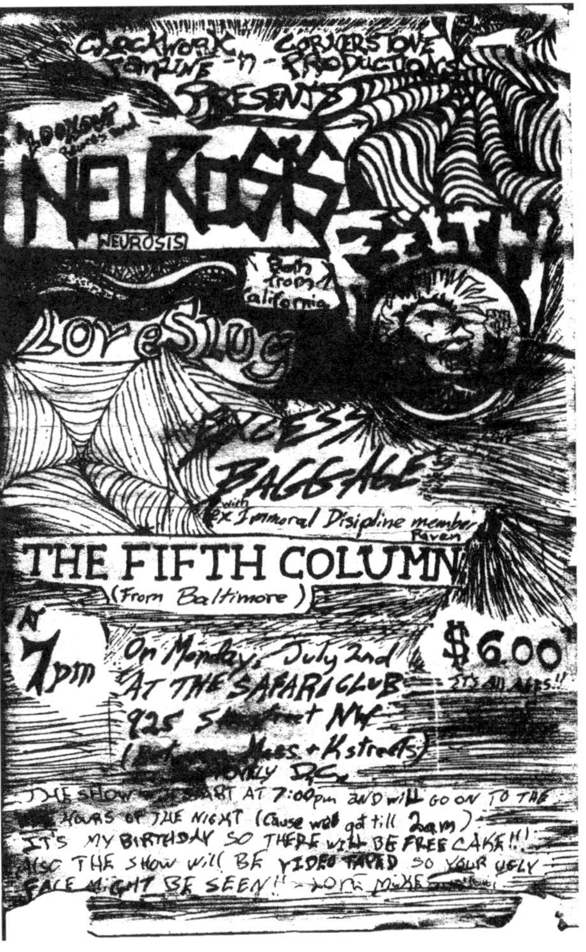

PHIL BAXLEY: I'm pretty sure the first time I went was Strife's 1994 tour, because I still have the shirt and it says Safari Club on it. On the back it's got a live picture and all the dates. I didn't realize the club went back as far as it did.

TOMMY ANTHONY: The first real show I ever saw was Swiz and Gorilla Biscuits at Safari in 1988. Inspired would be an understatement. Every weekend there was the best show of my life.

RICH DOLINGER: I first discovered the Safari Club because a friend in high school had an older brother who brought us to the first Gorilla Biscuits show. They only had a demo at the time so we were listening to it on the way to the show.

JASON KOOKEN: That GBs show was probably the first show where I saw so many kids I knew they weren't from where I was from.

PAM GENDELL: When we pulled up to the club early for soundcheck that day, there was a line already going down the street. Me and Shawna were like "who are these people and how did they all know about the show?" We made flyers, but it was a surprise how big it was. We knew maybe five of the four hundred people there.

The first time we played was when we were just on a compilation on Revelation.
—Walter Schreifels

SHAWNA KENNEY: Later we learned that kids were traveling from out of town—Delaware, Ohio, Pennsylvania, New Jersey, and New York, mostly—but at this time we had no idea. The size of our second show was a huge surprise.

WALTER SCHREIFELS: The first time we played was when we were just on a compilation on Revelation. The next time

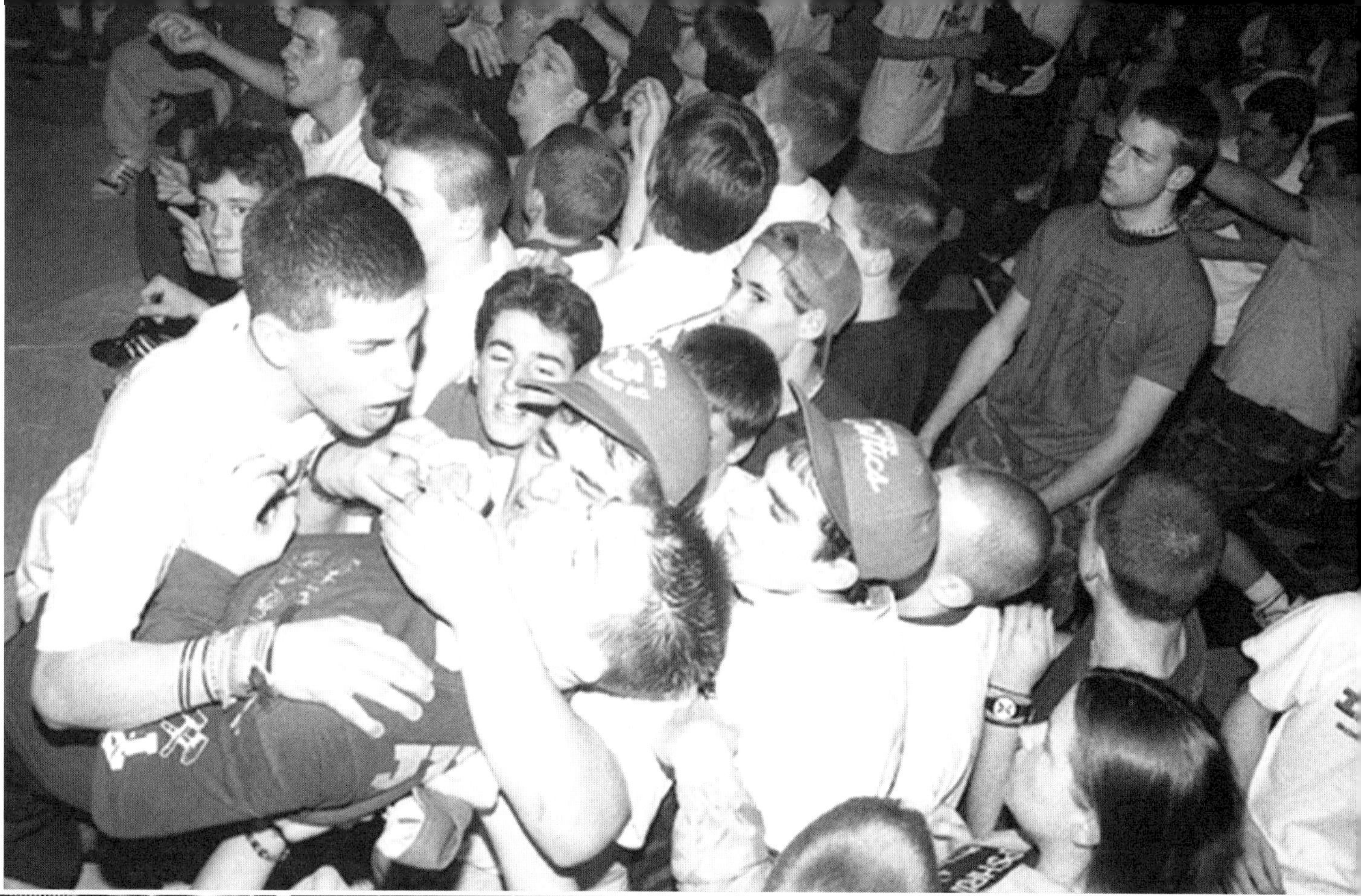

Right: Vision singer Dave Franklin. Below: Vision, 1989. Photos by Joe Wongananda.

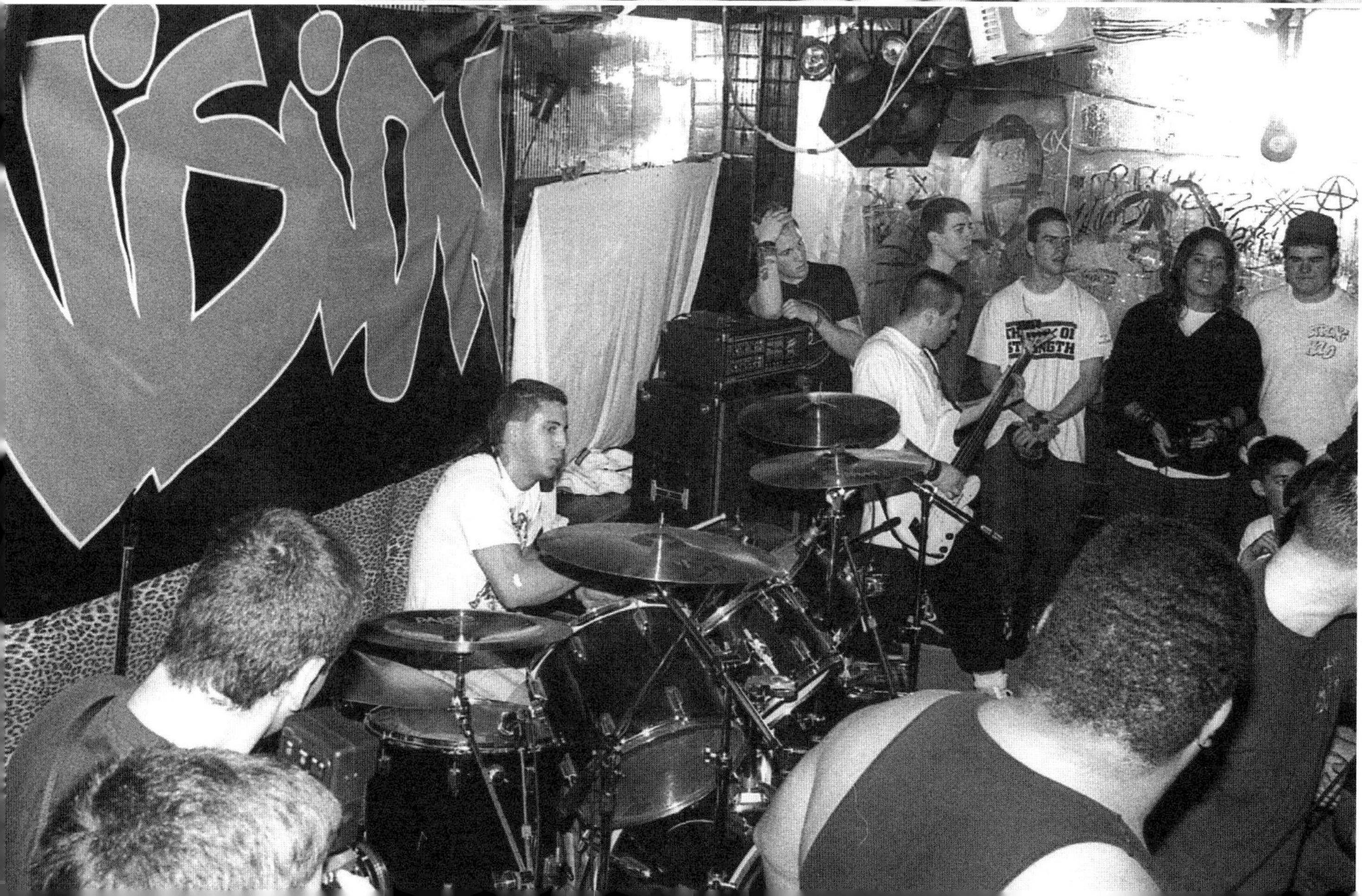

must have been when our 7-inch came out. I think we played on tour before Start Today.

ZAC ELLER: I remember seeing a flyer at Vinyl Ink for Gorilla Biscuits, Swiz, and Outcrowd. Went to that show and Gorilla Biscuits was like eight hours late but we waited and it was worth it.

BRYAN WASSOM: The first Safari show I went to was the first time Gorilla Biscuits played DC with Swiz (perhaps autumn '88?). I think Lucy Brown even played first, which seems a bit odd now.

SHAWNA KENNEY: Lucy Brown was a local band that Haile, the owner, had added to the bill, unbeknownst to us. We were annoyed. I think we paid them fifty dollars.

BRYAN WASSOM: The flyer I had for the show had In Your Face as also playing, but they didn't. I remember the city paper had it listed as "Swiss Gorilla Biscuit In Your Face" as the featured band…it was right after GB had released their 7-inch and Swiz had put out their self-titled 12-inch. Swiz went on at like 1:00 or 2:00 p.m. and completely shredded. GB was way delayed and didn't even arrive till like 7:00 p.m., but the dedicated few still hung around for them. DC was hungry, and GB didn't disappoint. It was worth the wait. The infamous Gus Pena came with them and did the whole Spanish intro thing as they kicked into "High Hopes"… To make up for the delay they played a couple covers, including YOT.

SHAWNA KENNEY: We got a call from someone in the band saying something about someone's dad having a heart attack, but they promised they'd be there. I don't know if that was true but we had to relay that to the crowd, hoping they really were on their way.

DARREN WALTERS: That first Gorilla Biscuits show, I would say they were easily four if not more hours late. It was "no, no, no, they're coming!" I don't know if kids would do that now for a hardcore band.

DAVE SIEFERT: My friend Jim and I went to the famous Gorilla Biscuits show where they showed up seventeen hours late. We were both crazy Swiz fans, and they were one of the opening bands. We also had the Revelation Records comp *New York City Hardcore: The Way It Is* that had the GB song "Better Than You" on it, so we were pretty psyched to see them, too.

When we pulled up to the club early for soundcheck that day, there was a line already going down the street. Me and Shawna were like "who are these people and how did they all know about the show?" We knew maybe five of the four hundred people there.
—Pam Gendell

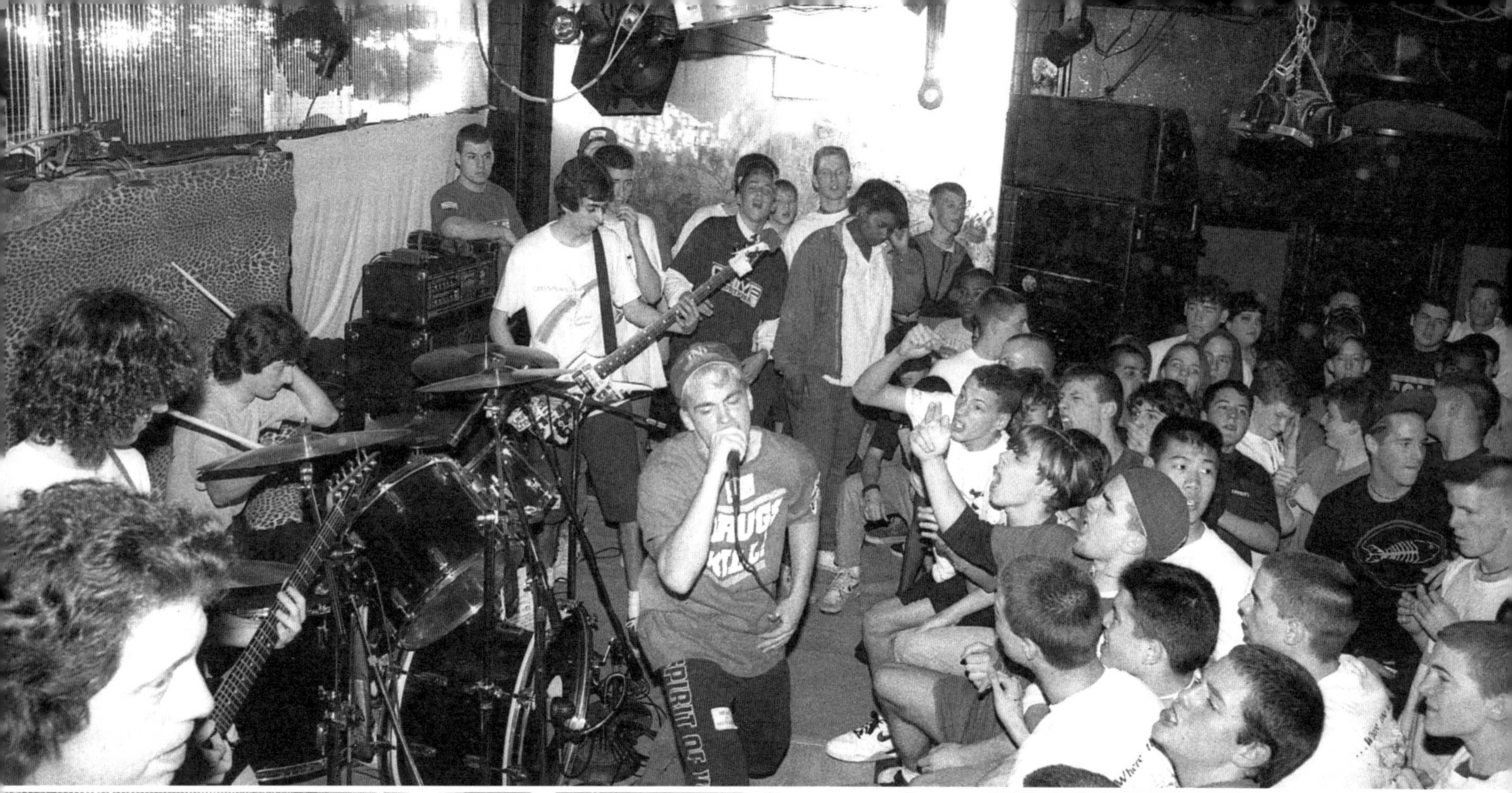

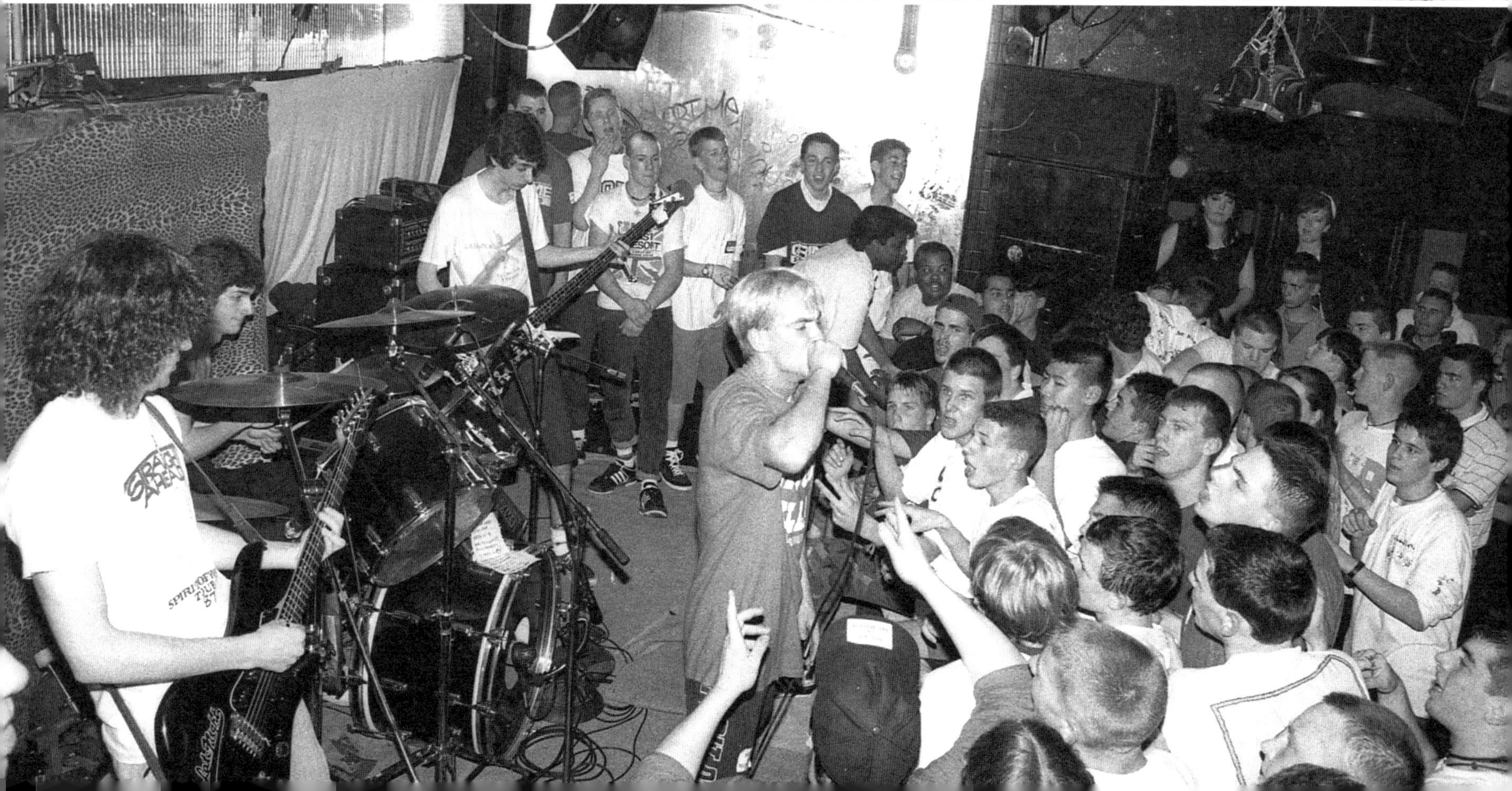

RICH DOLINGER: I thought they got there around six o'clock. I remember my friend Ravi Nair left before they played. He had to get home to do his homework!

JOHN GALBRAITH: We sat there and waited. It was fine. Time didn't matter as much as it does now.

DAVE SAULNIER: GB showed up late, and all the openers had already played, leaving everyone sitting around waiting on GB. I remember having to wait a long time, but no one would go home. One friend could no longer wait and had to go home, so another friend (Big Jim Parlett) and I walked him to the Gallery Place/Chinatown metro station. During our walk back to the club, a van pulls up and some dude with a shaved head leans out and asks us if we know how to get to the Safari Club. We told him we were heading to the club. Suddenly the side door opens to the van, and Civ is sitting inside with some pit bull. We hopped in the van, the pit bull lunges at my friend, Civ restrains him, and we all ride back to the Safari Club together. We pull up in the GB van and get out with Civ with all our friends watching.

I loved how small the stage was. The crowd was right in your face. —Jon Field

WALTER SCHREIFELS: Gorilla Biscuits was late? Haha, yeah I think our van broke down or we left late or something.

SHAWNA KENNEY: They were four hours late. It was nerve-wracking, but ended up being okay. We booked them two more times and I think John Cornerstone booked them there later.

PAM GENDELL: We gave Swiz an envelope with $250 in it after the show, not knowing if that was enough. They said the most they had ever been paid by the 9:30 Club was $100, so they were stoked.

ALEX DANIELS: I remember running into Ian MacKaye one day after we played and he asked what we'd been up to. I told him we had just played a Safari matinée and he asked if anyone was there. I said "yeah, about four hundred people" and his jaw just dropped.

MIKY SCHEER: It was summer '89 and GBs were on their tour for *Start Today*. They stopped to play at Grey's Place. There was this parking lot where all the Richmond types would congregate. They pulled up in two vans and they were playing Safari Club the next day. I think Bold decided they were gonna stay at Cain's apartment, so I called my parents and said, "There's quite a few of them" but my mom said, "Yeah, yeah, it's fine." It's back in the woods and these guys were definitely not rural types. We went out there and my mom cooked them a big vegetarian meal. It was the band plus Gus and that big German guy Stefan. My mom had bought some watermelons and Stefan kept telling my little sister to "eat ze watermelon—it makes women beautiful!"

We had a well at the house, so if you did too much laundry or people took too many showers at the same time, it would go dry for a little while. It'd take a couple of hours to fill back up. And all those guys were taking showers and damn if that thing

Facing page: Up Front, 1989. Photos by Joe Wongananda.

I quit my job—I was like "oh my god, Gorilla Biscuits are staying at my house!"
—Darren Walters

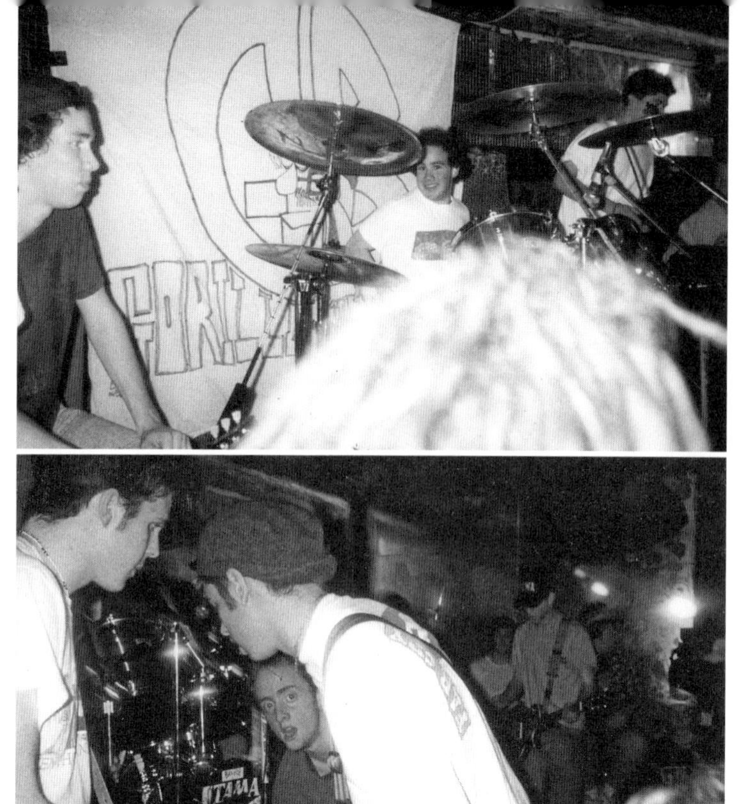

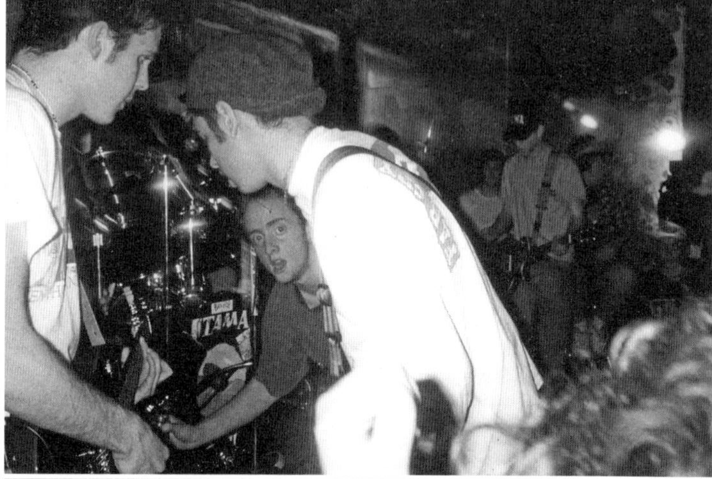

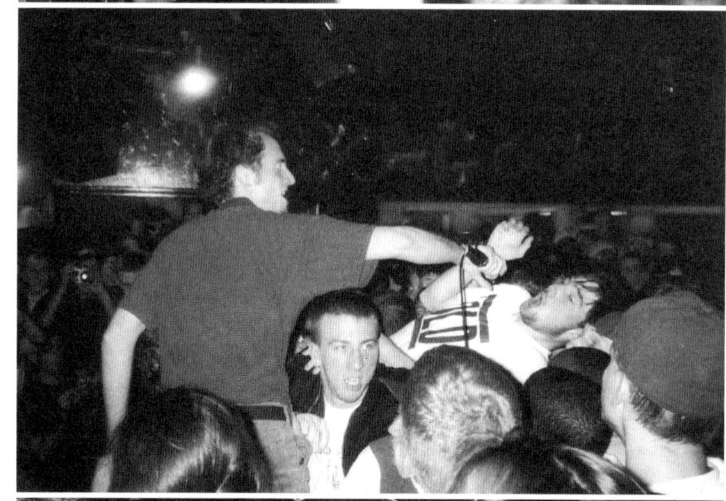

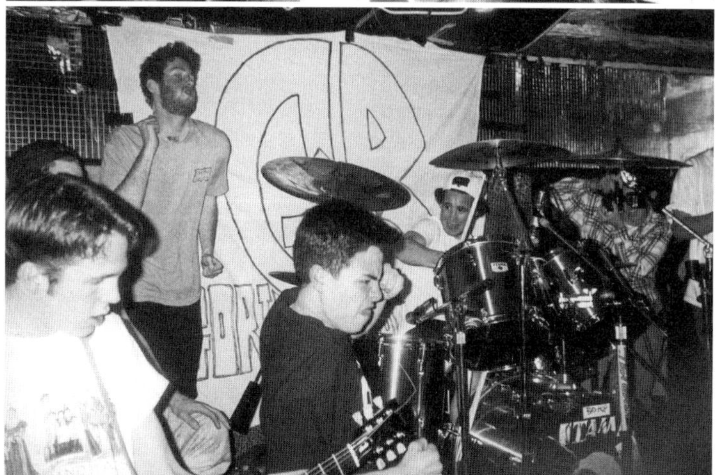

Left: Gorilla Biscuits.
Photos by Eric Hochberg.
Right: Gorilla Biscuits and Rich Dolinger
Photo by Dave Brown.

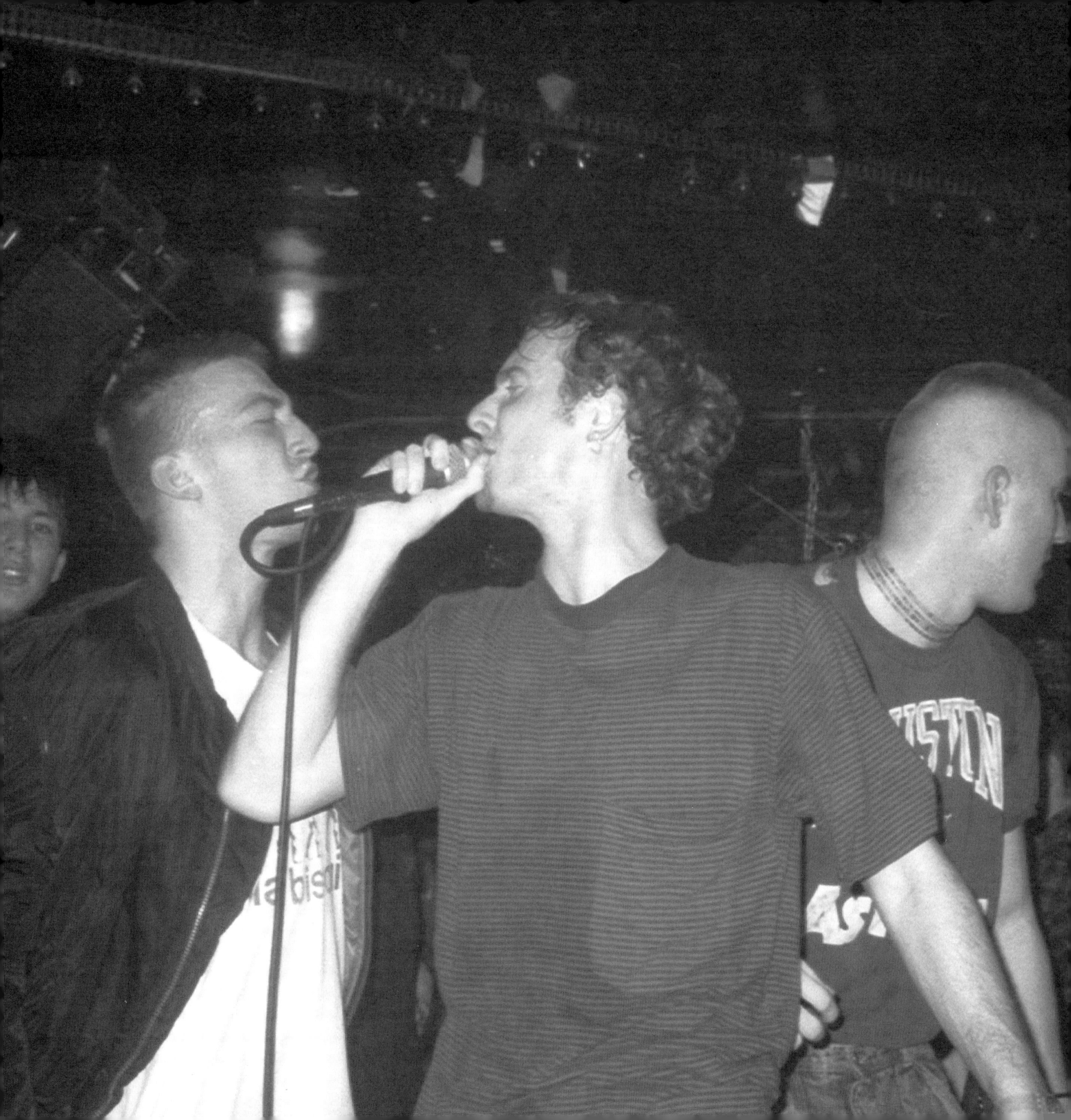

didn't go out. A couple of them had to go down to the creek and finish up their showers with soap all over them.

We stayed around the house doing shit that hardcore kids do—listening to records and telling stories. The next day we all decided we were going to Kings Dominion. We were pretty well-practiced at sneaking in there, except for Brad.

TAYLOR STEELE: Brad ran up this embankment and jumped over without looking over the wall and it dropped down on the concrete. He did the biggest belly-flop onto the conrete!

MIKY SCHEER: Then Karl Bailey jumped right into the security station. I know there was at least thirteen of us and every one of us, except for Karl, got in—Karl's the only one who got caught. So we spent the day there. I can't remember if they stayed another night or the show was later that day—it was probably the next day. We all rode up there and saw them play. That was a really good show.

I think the only time we played with them (GBs) was when we were on our way back from recording an album and they actually opened up for us. On the end of that 7-inch you can hear "stick around, Four Walls Falling is up next!"

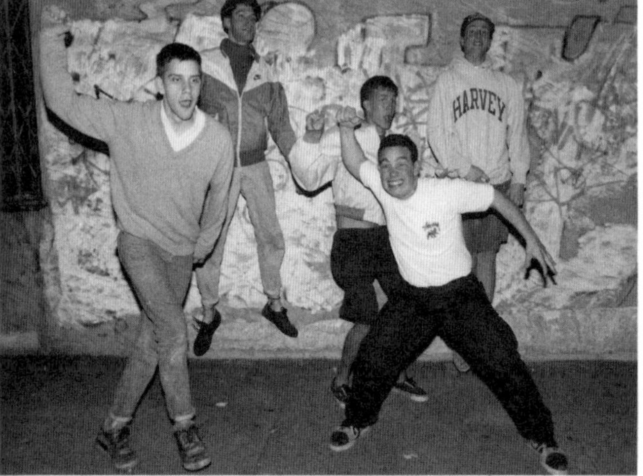

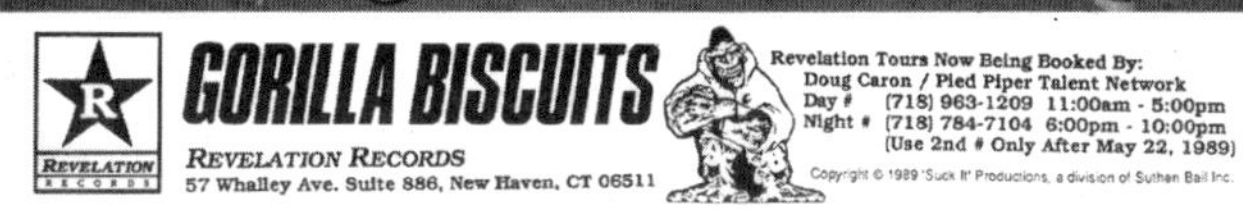

TAYLOR STEELE: [It's heard on the record] As everyone faded out of the club.

KEVIN YOUNG: I remember one time Civ telling me what a great time he and GB had with Taylor and Four Walls when they jumped over the fence at Kings Dominion to ride some roller coasters.

STEVE ZEITZOFF: I think a couple of weeks before, we had gone to an Insted show somewhere in Maryland and there were flyers for it there and we were like "oh shit—Gorilla Biscuits!" I had bought skateboards off Jason Farrell because he worked at Sunshine House in Bethesda, so then I was like "oh shit, the guy from Sunshine House is in this band." He had a rep for being a rad skater. It was all coming together.

DARREN WALTERS: One of the shows, I can't remember where Gorilla Biscuits were coming from, but they stayed at my house and went to DC from there. I quit my job—I was like oh my god, GBs are staying at my house, fuck it, I'll go to the show in DC with them. This is awesome. And that's what the *Live at the Safari Club* bootleg is from—my friend did that record.

BRYAN WASSOM: I think it was the fourth time GB played Safari (spring '90?) and the first time since their LP had been out…they had just returned from Europe and Civ had grown his hair out. The place was packed. They played with Bad Trip (NYC) and someone from the band had brought a mini-trampoline with them and put it on stage. The Safari had pretty low ceilings…and I remember the first poor sap who stage-dived from it didn't gauge the trajectory right, and rocketed straight into the ceiling head first…ouch.

Above: Gorilla Biscuits promo shot.

Facing page: Four Walls Falling, 1989. Photos by Joe Wongananda.

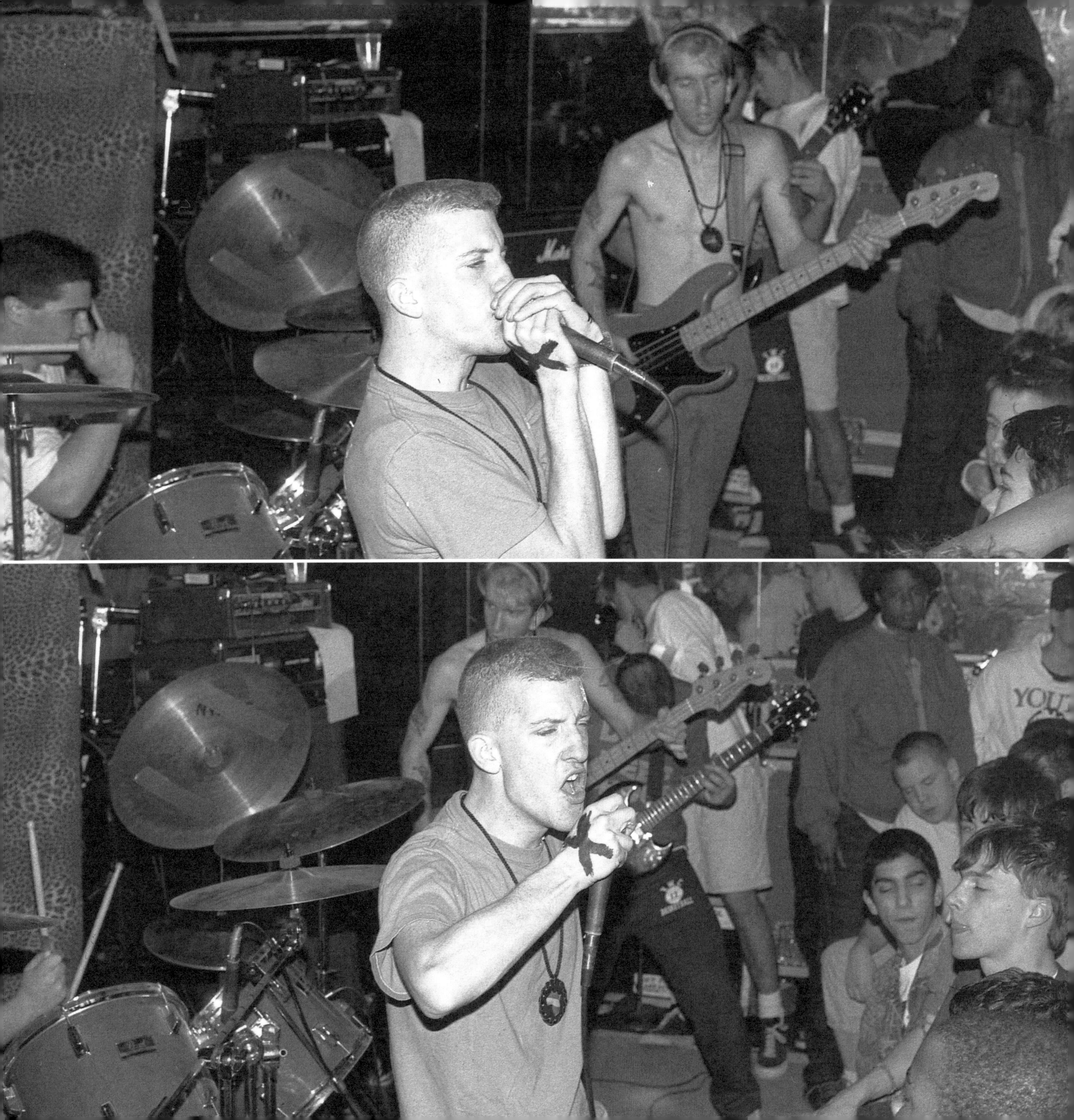

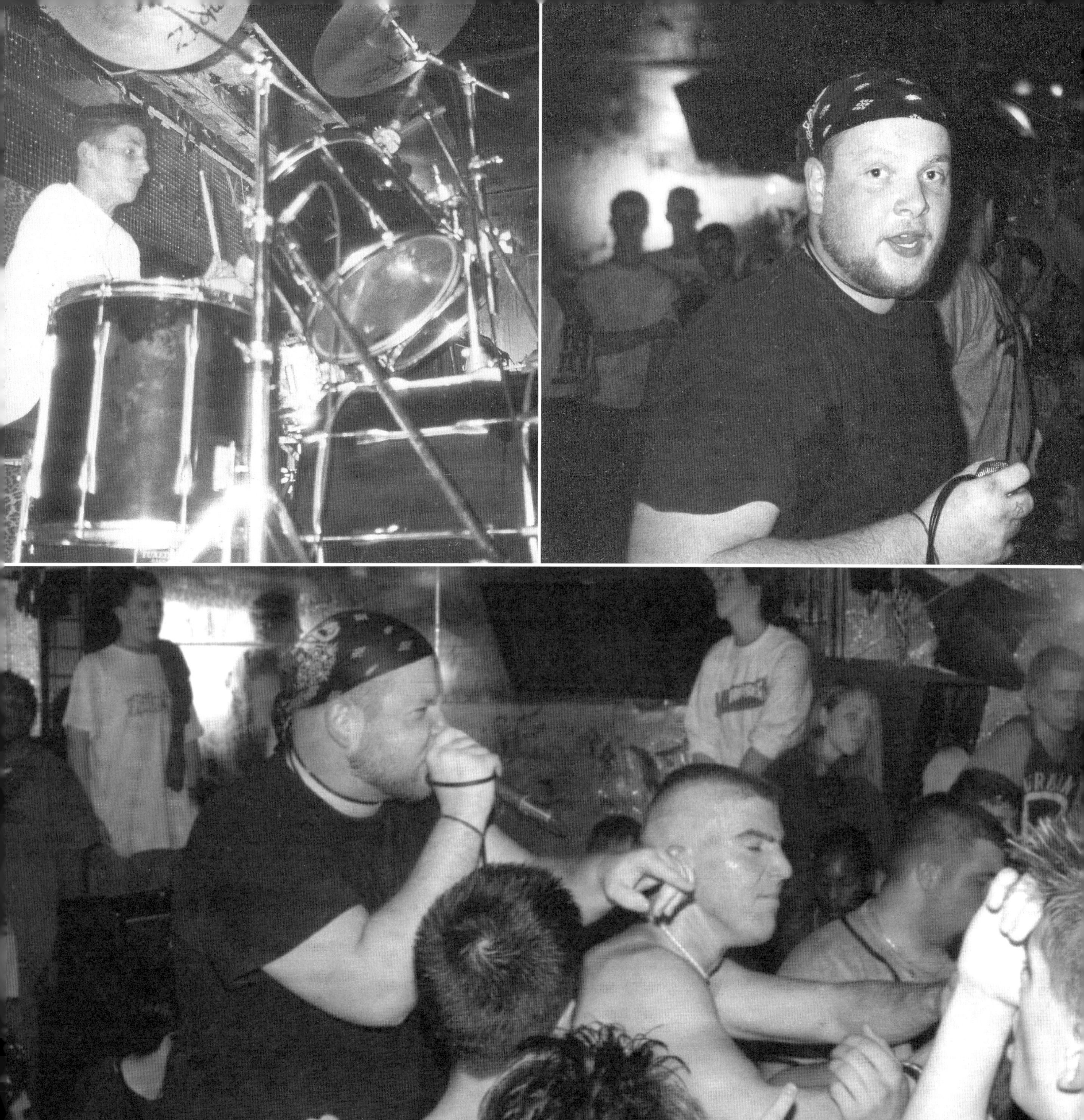

DARREN WALTERS: There was a show where we were the only ones who knew the lyrics and they were like "how come you motherfuckers know the lyrics?" It was because we had stayed at their house and taken the tape from Walter's room and Karl went out to his car and dubbed it. Then they played DC and we were all singing. I think that's the bootleg. I remember him being surprised.

JOHN GALBRAITH: Any time Gut Instinct, Four Walls, or Initial Reaction was playing, I was there. Summer Slam and Fall Brawl came from wrestling influences. One Fall Brawl paid for the driveway at the Krishna temple—we donated all the money.

RICH DOLINGER: I was there almost every weekend from the first GB show on out. I was a little younger than the kids who were regulars at the time, but by the time the club reopened under the name Chamber of Sound, I was way more invested socially. The scene was mostly new kids by then, but there were a few of us who were left over from the early days. Of course we cherished the memories of the GB, Judge, and early SOIA shows, but we also embraced the present. I had just as much fun seeing bands like Mouthpiece, 108, and Lifetime. The styles and music changed but the spirit was the same.

PHIL BAXLEY: Unbroken, Mouthpiece, and 108 was probably the best show I ever went to. When Tim broke into "Can We Win?" and jumped into the crowd, all I remember is him being down on the ground looking up at the crowd and there were piles of people all around him with everyone singing. Because of that show I broke up with my first real girlfriend. I had been dating this girl for a couple of months and we had spent every single day together. I told her I wanted to go see Unbroken and she was really upset. I went to the show by myself. Went home soaked in sweat, by myself, and over the next couple months a long, drawn-out breakup ensued. Unbroken had said something on stage because something had gone wrong. I can't remember exactly but they said something like "we're never coming to the east coast again" and I was like "score, thank the Lord I was here." I went through two years of depression over this girlfriend situation, but I got to see that show.

Facing page: Judge. Photos by Chris Yormick.

JASON POWELL: The first Better Than a Thousand show was great. The whole line-up was good—Damnation played, who are always great band to see live. A lot of the DC kids had gone to the studio to sing back-ups on the record and Ken had also leaked some of the songs—that's how I knew them. In the first song, all the kids are singing along: *I know I know I know…* and Ray is like, "How do you all know these songs?"

SHARIE POWELL: The whole place was buzzing alive and packed. Everyone was catching everybody. It was totally energetic and positive.

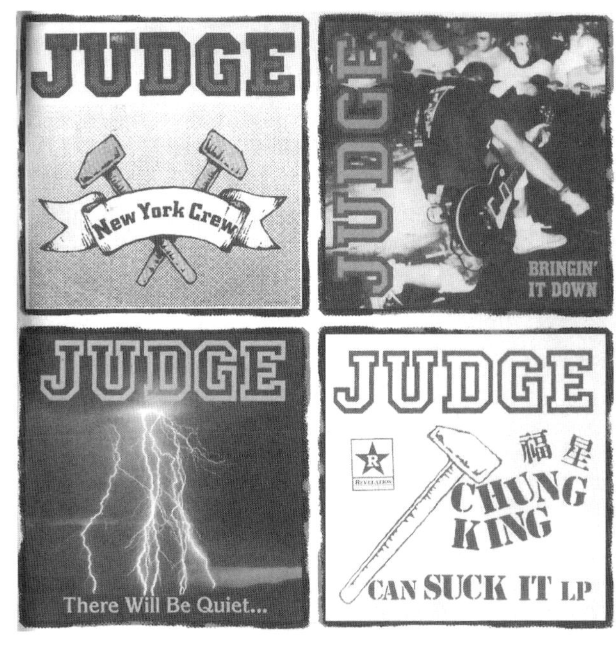

One of the first times I saw Vision at the Safari was with Insted. It was rad to see the hometown New Jersey band just kill it out of state.
—Tim Shaw

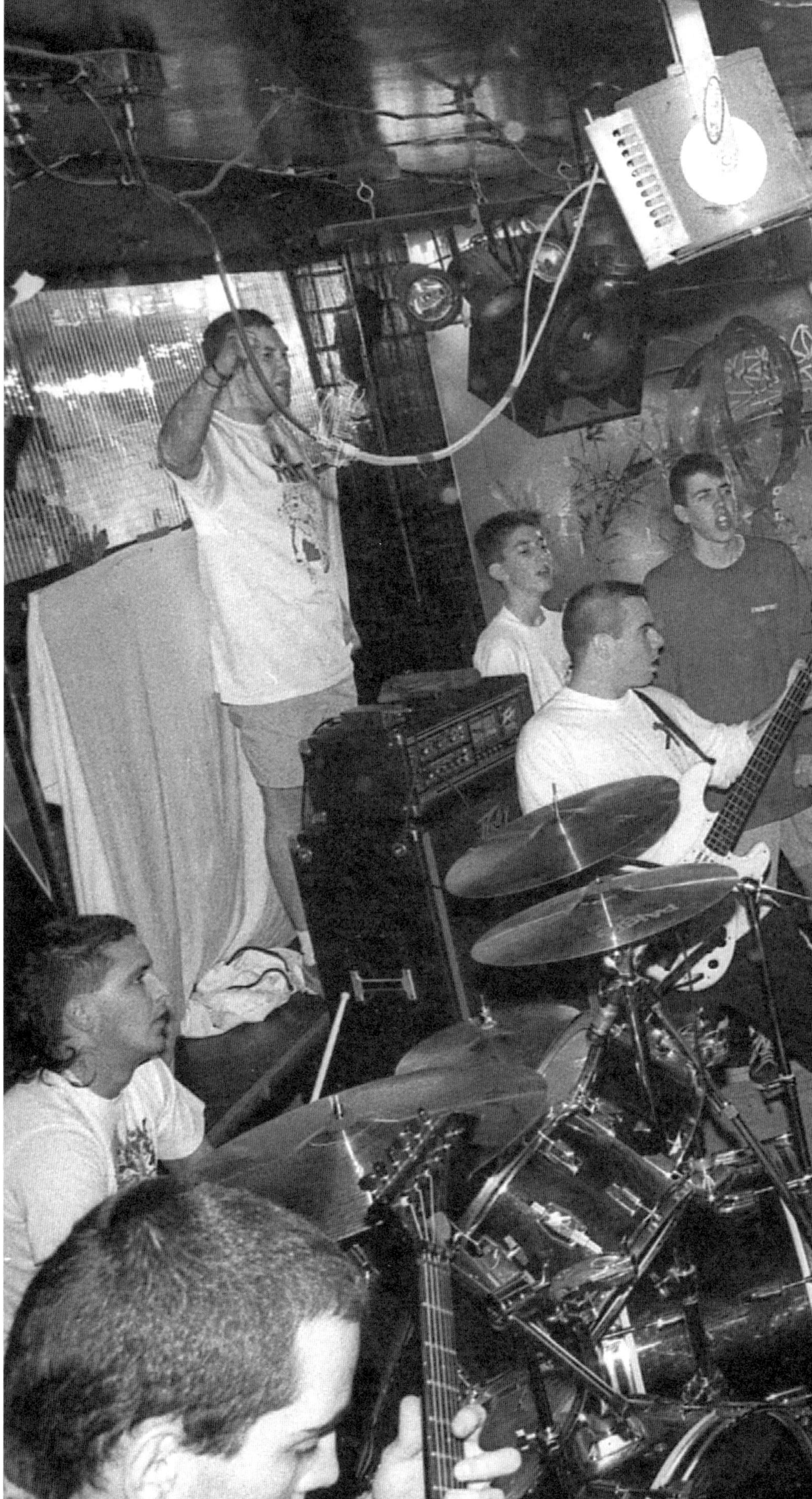

Vision, 1989.
Photo by Joe Wongananda.

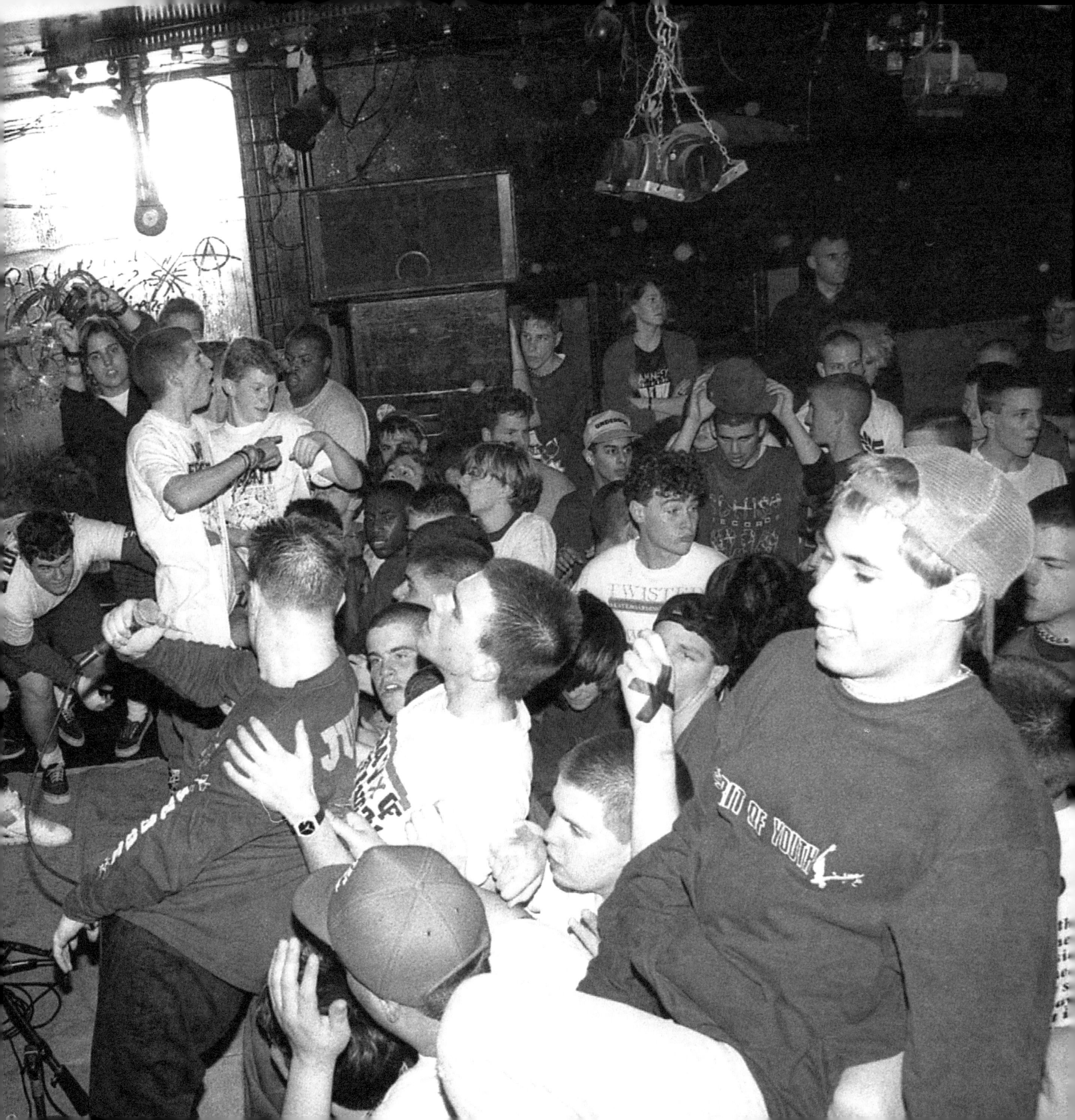
OF YOUTH

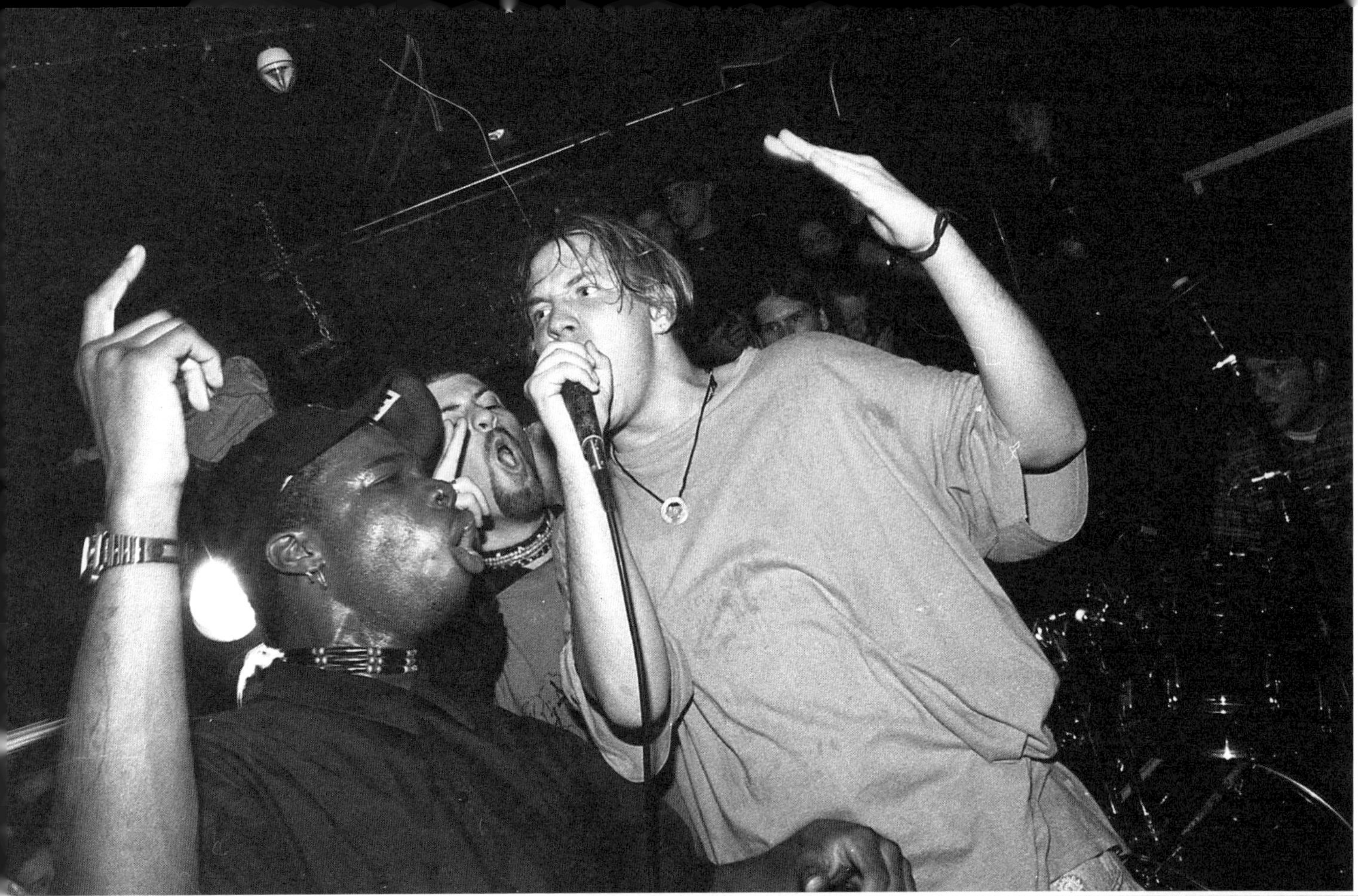

Battery. March 5, 1994.
Photos by Mark Beemer.

We gave a demo to John Cornerstorne and he put us on the Sick of it All/ Integrity show. It was our first show and it was pretty badass. —Brian McTernan

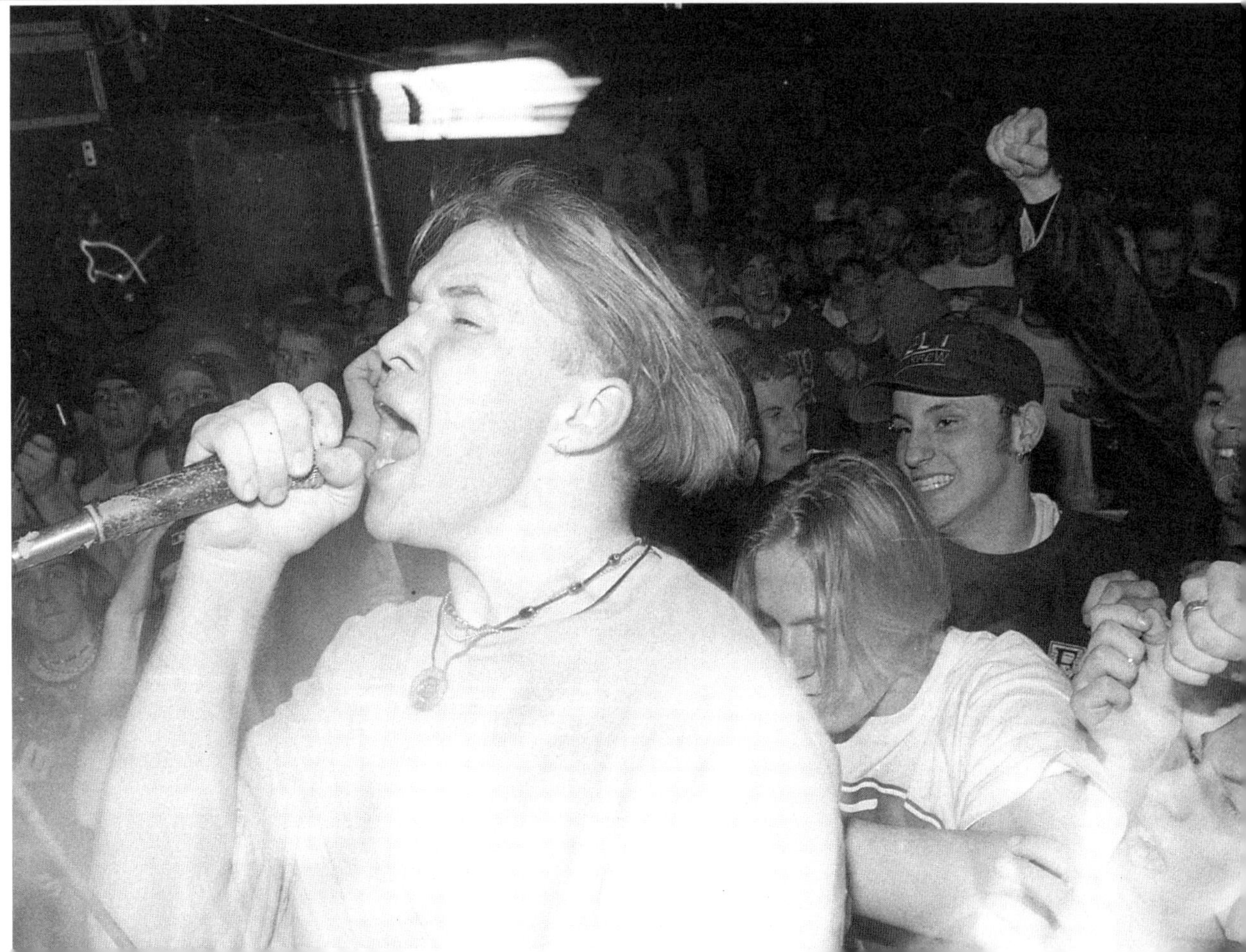

CHAPTER 5: FIRESTORM

MOE SHORTER: I think we (Junkyard Band) were actually the last ones to play the night before it burned down.

KURT POWERS: My band's second show was booked at the Safari Club. For us, growing up going to the Safari Club, we were so excited. This was going to be the shit! So we get to DC and something went drastically wrong. It was the day that the Safari Club burned down. Needless to say, we were like "FUCK." So technically, we were the last booked band at the Safari Club.

JAY MARTIN: Hearing many years later that the Safari Club burned down, it makes the fire extinguisher story that much more of a poignant memory for me.

SEAN DORSEY: Everyone now knows Safari ended up burning down. I heard it was over owner beef, but who knows.

DAVID BYRD: The last Battery show had to be moved. There was a fire. It happened the night before. There was speculation that it was for insurance money and stuff. You could definitely smell something burnt the next day. We looked inside and could see the ceiling caved in. It was kind of sad.

TRU PREY: Another fact about the last show is that Rain on the Parade played as well. In fact they made forty-four limited Bad Brains covers to commemorate Martin's returning home from prison. "Forty-four" was the number for John Riggins, the Redskins player's football jersey.

MARTIN CASTRO: We showed up. The place had caught on fire. We walked next door to the gay bar and looked at their "stage," and then moved the show there. Never did find out what caused the fire.

PHIL BAXLEY: I didn't get to go to the Battery reunion show. I stopped going to Safari around '96 or '97 because I went away to college.

MARK ADAMS: The last show we played there was November 2, 1990. We did a show with Abominog and Asylum. There were a lot of people at this show and it seemed like the Safari Club was here to stay. The next thing we heard was that it was closed down and nobody could get in touch with Haile.

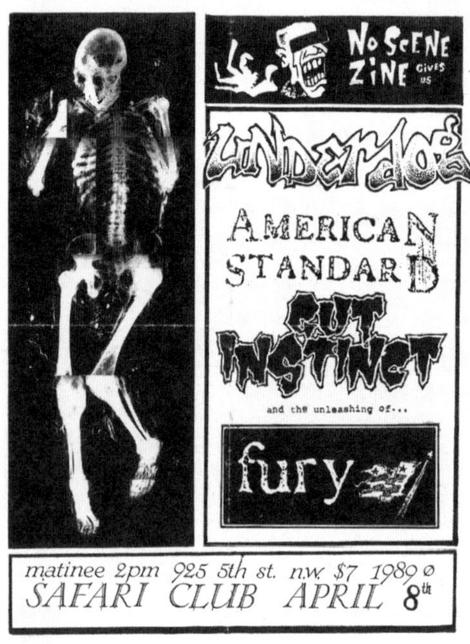

JASON FARRELL: What's funny about the Safari Club is in a lot of ways it further pushed Swiz to more hardcore, or at least "fuck anybody that won't accept what we're doing. Whatever's annoying about us, let's do more of *that*." That basically inspired Fury—that mentality and that scene made it so a band like Fury could exist. The only two shows they ever played were at the Safari Club. And that's it—that's all we ever did, then we recorded and then we were done. That was when we embraced it.

...that mentality and that scene made it so a band like Fury could exist. The only two shows they ever played were at the Safari Club.
—Jason Farrell

Facing page: Shawn Brown in Fury, 1989. Following page: Chris Thomson and Jason Farrell of Fury. Photos by Joe Wongananda.

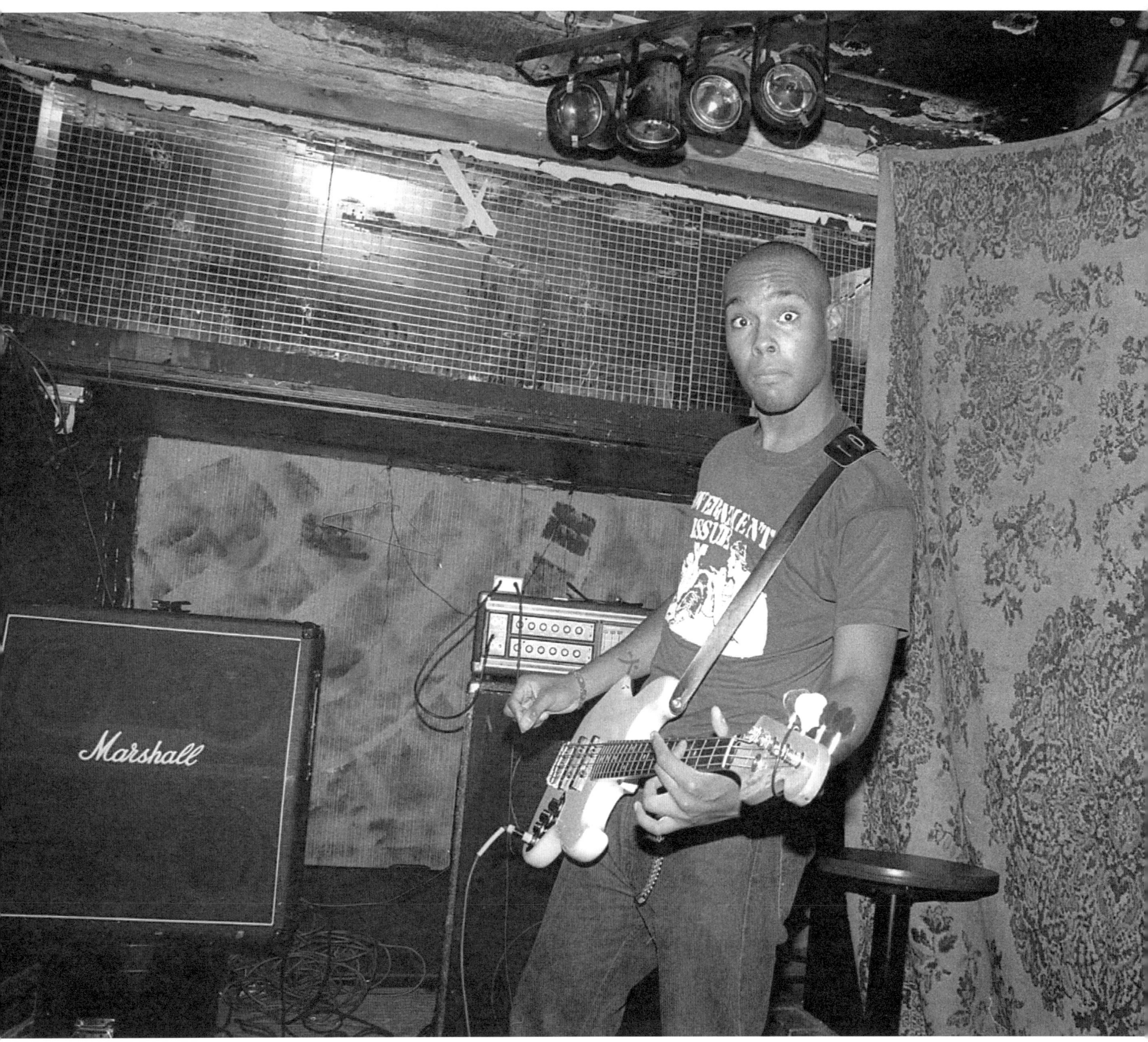
Marshall

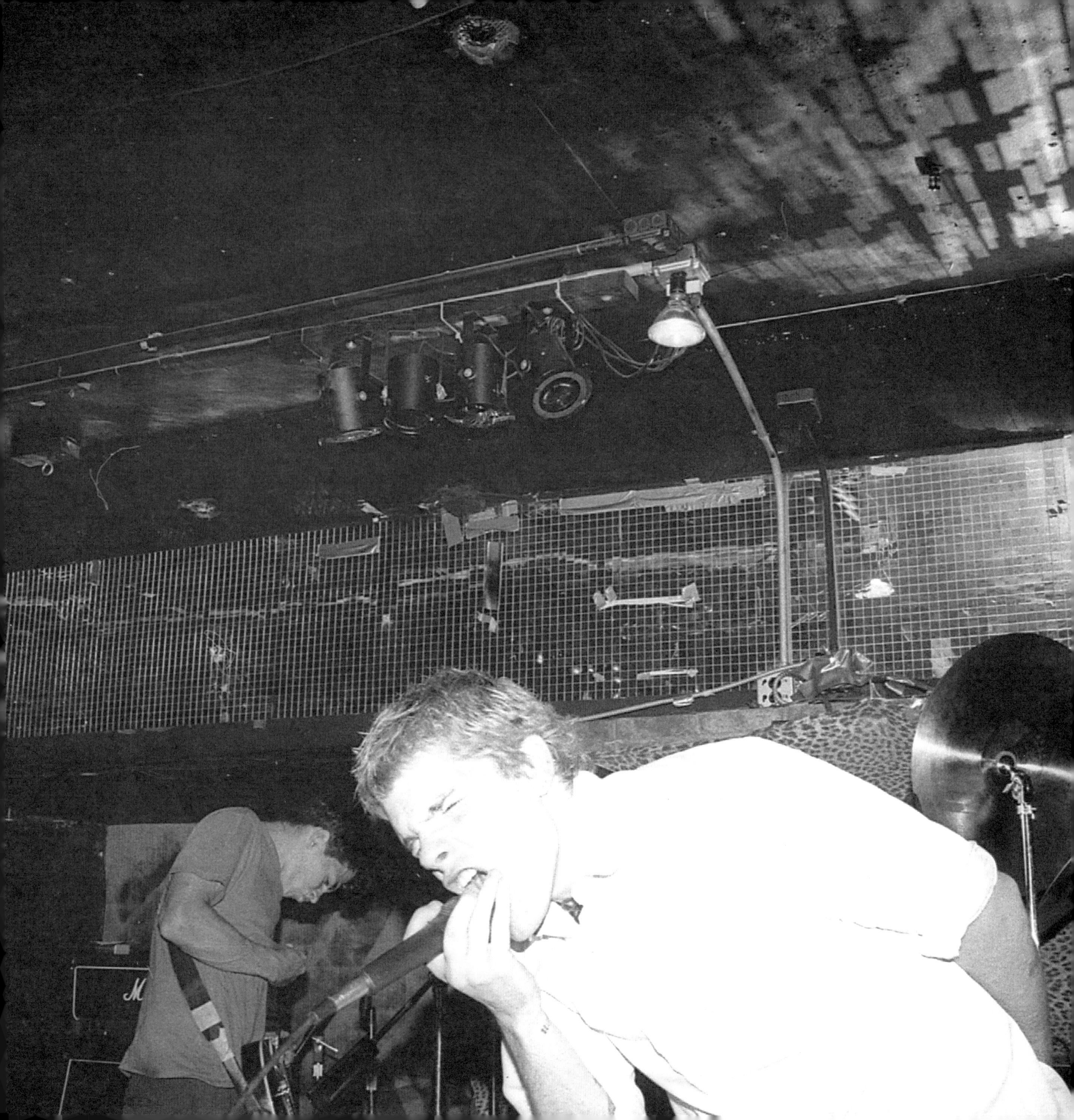

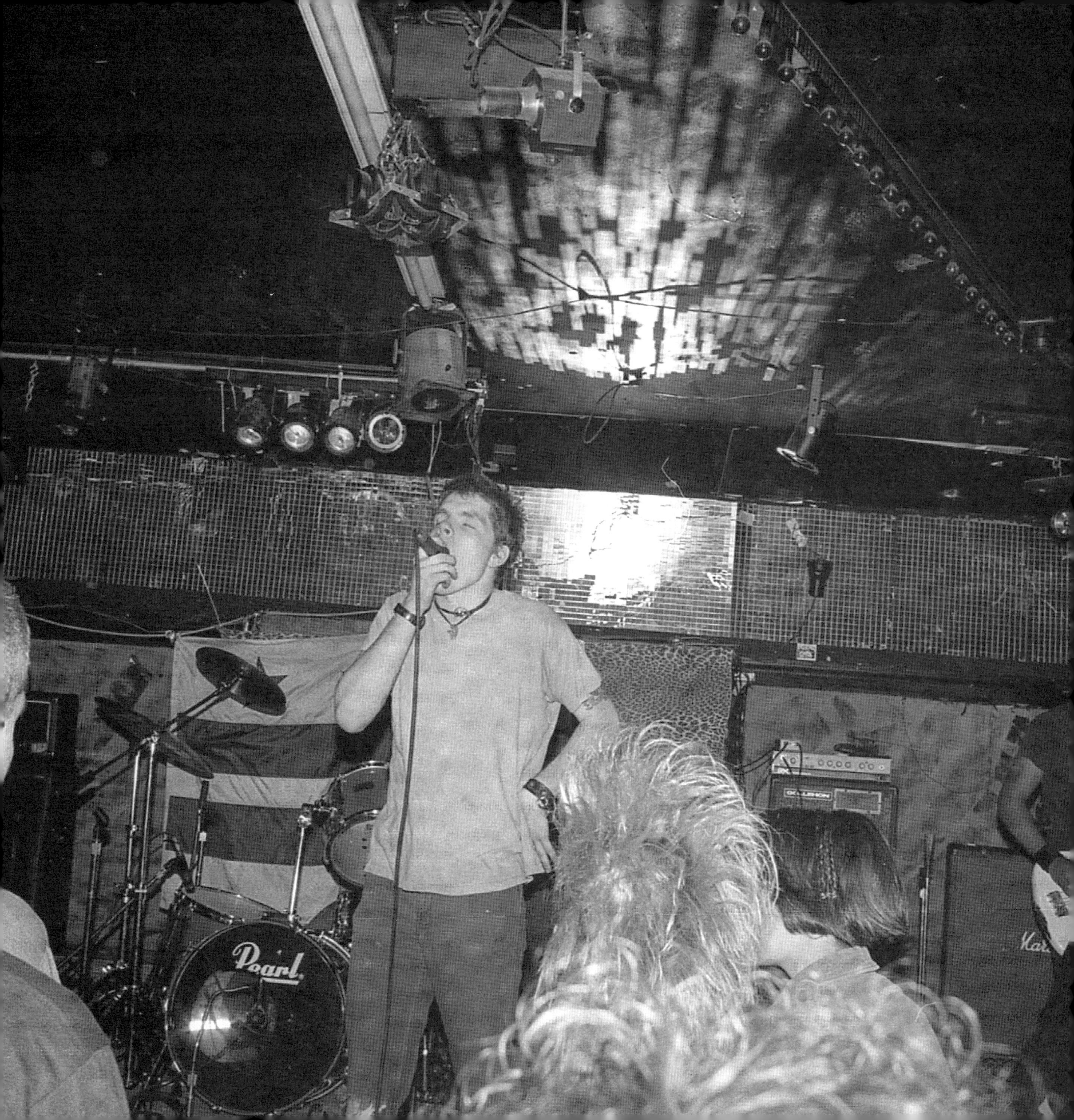
Pearl

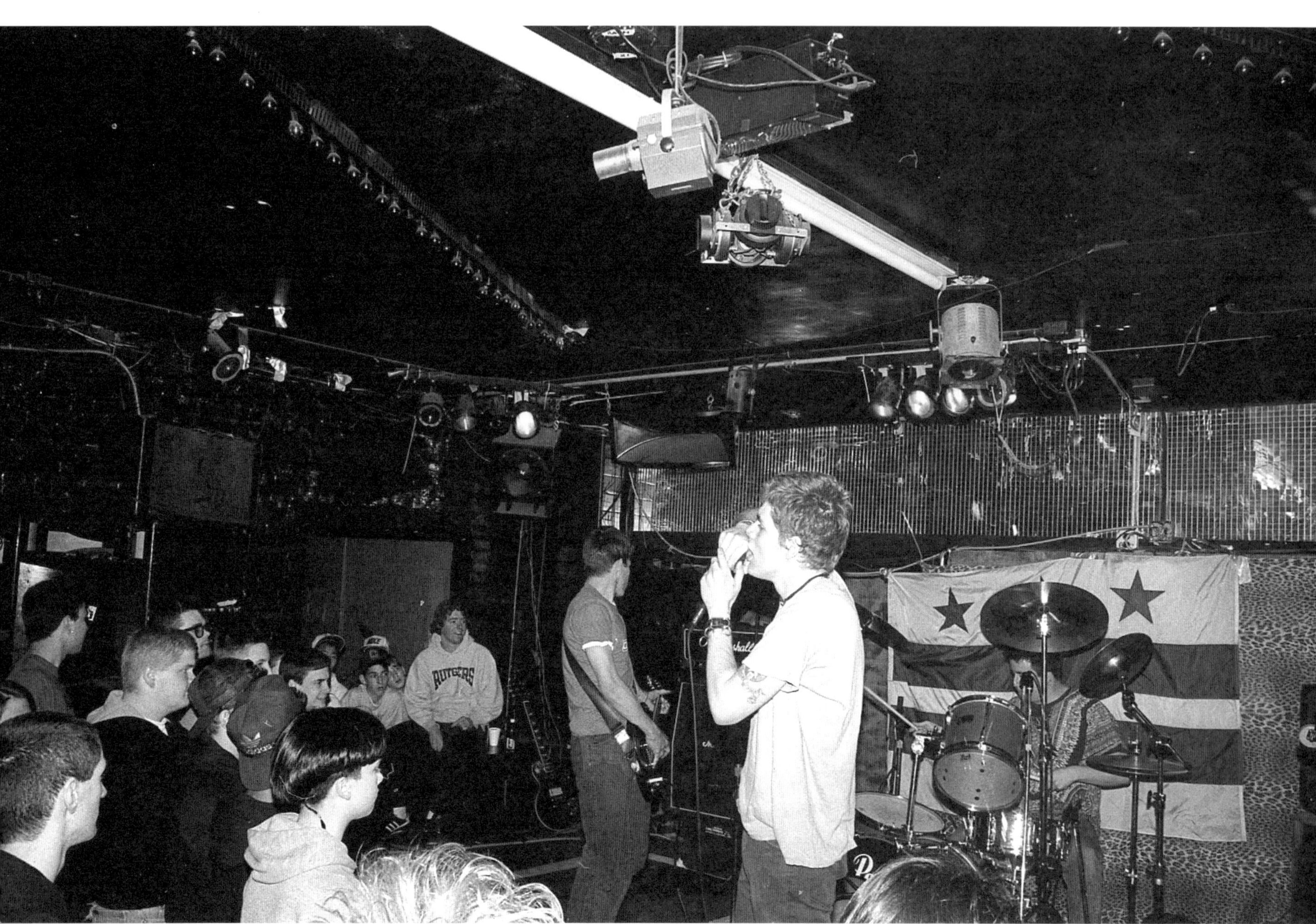

Fury: Chris Thomson, Jason Farrell, Alex Daniels, 1989. Photo by Joe Wongananda.

JORDAN COOPER: DC's Safari Club was one of those legendary places that you'd hear about that was part of the scene there. NY had A7 and CBs, Connecticut had Pogos and the Anthrax, LA, SF, Detroit and on and on, every place where punk took root had venues spring up out of necessity to give kids a place to hang out and hear, play, and see live music.

DEBORAH GOLDBERG: It was a healthy outlet. Nobody was using drugs or drinking. The kids were trying to understand their world through music. We had it so good. It was positive.

NATHAN ANDERSON: That was probably one of the best times of my life. My wife and I have been in the same scene for twenty-five years. We've known each other for nineteen years. I used to go to shows with her at the Safari Club.

STEVE ZEITZOFF: I think I went to almost every show for the next couple of years until someone shut the lights off on hardcore. Once it turned to the Victory stuff, I was done with it. I moved to Boston a year after high school.

TIM OWEN: It just stood out from all the other clubs that I've been to. It wasn't jaded. Shawna obviously stumbled onto something that created this whole social structure. It reinforced some of the things you hated about DC, that all the bands are snobby. There wasn't any of that with the Safari Club. Being that I got into punk when I did and that was my first exposure, and seeing that environment had such an effect on me. Where it probably would have been different if I'd grown up going to City Gardens and there were big bouncers and worrying about getting your head kicked in by skinheads.

MICHAEL STRAIGHT: I had ALL booked and Offspring, and I was starting to deal with contracts even though I was seventeen at the time. I had booked Citizens Arrest for a Sunday and Haile, the owner, said the show had to be on a Saturday and I was like "the band is already on tour." He had moved another show on me before. ALL and Avail was supposed to be the next week but I was done.

ADAM HELFER: I stopped going when I went on tour with Shelter, Inside Out, and Quicksand—then I joined the ashram. I guess that was in '90. I went back here and there in subsequent years and even bounced a few shows.

CF BEST: The last Safari show I went to was the Shelter show in 1990 that never happened, where everyone was waiting for hours and then they brought out the Gita bus and took us to the Krishna compound to see it out there.

·shelter·

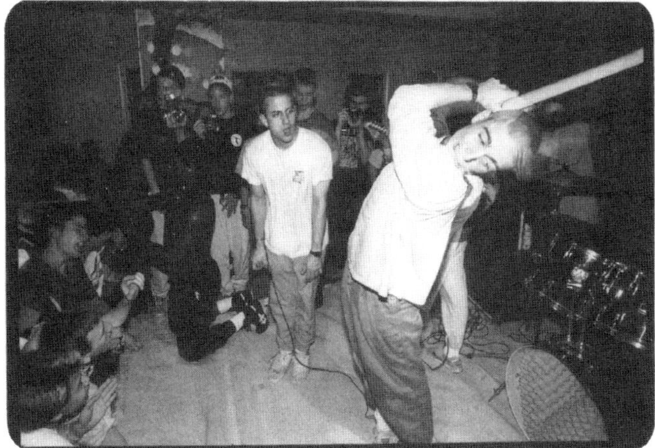

in defense of reality

TAYLOR STEELE: The only show I saw at Safari Club after '92 was when Better Than a Thousand played. I was going to support Jeff playing with them. We played at that Hare Krishna Temple, the Wilson Center, the Sanctuary, the BBQ Iguana, Asylum.

RICH DOLINGER: Some of the flyers for the Asylum shows on Ninth and U say *Safari Club 2* like someone was trying to bring it back. I was so glad when the real Safari Club reopened as Chamber of Sound.

TAYLOR STEELE: It was so small, though, they wouldn't have been able to fit all those people. I hated playing BBQ Iguana—that high stage. You could see on our 7-inch I'm trying to get people to sing and I'm doubled over.

RODNEY BUTINELLI: I heard about it when it reopened as Chamber of Sound but never got over there. There were more good points than negative points about the Safari Club, so I didn't want to go and be disappointed.

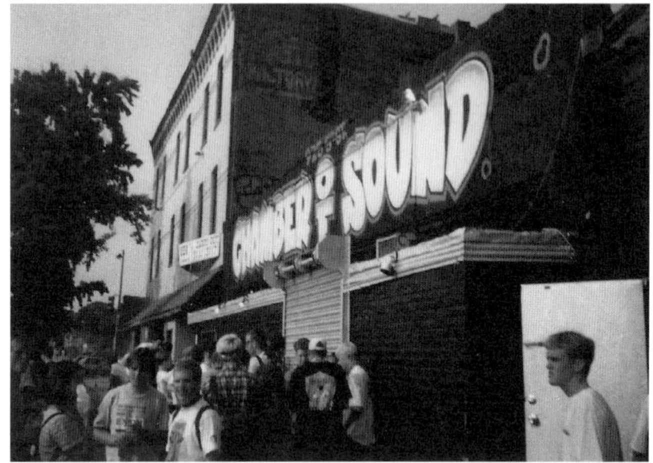

SHAWNA KENNEY: We had a lot of problems with the owner. We had to keep our eye on the door, but Pam and I never worked the door because otherwise we would have let everyone in for free. We hired friends who weren't so into hardcore. The owner would leave with the money in the middle of the show. We didn't know if he was gambling or what he was doing. Sometimes he'd come back and the bands would be waiting to get paid.

MICHAEL STRAIGHT: He'd have one of his guys do the clicker and at the end of the night the numbers would be off.

SHAWNA KENNEY: It got stressful. We moved our last two shows to the BBQ Iguana.

COLIN KELLY: From the parking lot watching the fellas cook chickens in burning barrels across the street to the bondage shop around the corner, to seeing Underdog, Token Entry, Gorilla Biscuits, Youth of Today so close you were part of the show. It just felt like having a show in your own home. I want it back again.

JOHN DUGAN: In retrospect, I wish I'd gone to a few more shows there—ALL, Moving Targets, Swiz are bands that still hold up, but you can't see them all.

CHRIS HARTNETT: You were the CBGB of DC. After that it all fell apart—the BBQ Iguana? Give me a break. Black Cat—go fuck yourself. And the 9:30 Club, you would get thrown out for doing a stage dive. Oh and those rickety old churches in Adams Morgan, I thought I was going to die sitting in the balcony.

KEN OLDEN: For many years we could actually say "the scene in DC is the top." That kept us motivated. We understood what that was.

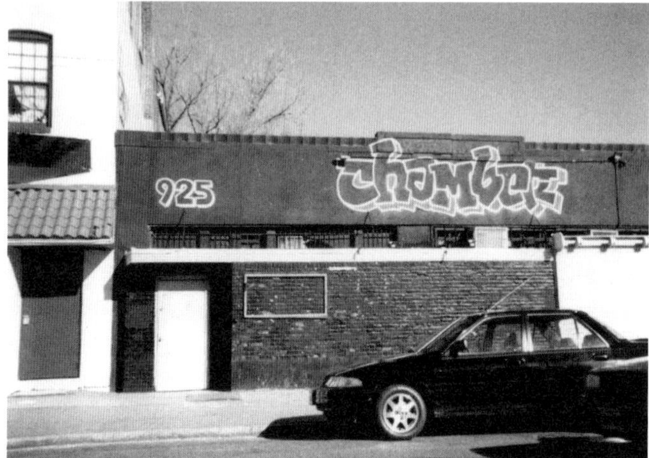

GABE ONRUBIA: I went out west in the early nineties, so I'd bring that element out there. When people asked me "what do you listen to?" I'd be like "Outburst, Judge, Initial Reaction, Gut Instinct" and all these people were like "what are you talking about?" Because when you say "DC" people were like "oh—9:30 Club and Minor Threat" but Safari Club was like a hidden thing, where if you said it and someone was receptive to those words you were like, "oh, you were there, too!" It was almost a binary code or something. I spent my entire teenage years there.

Photos of Safari Club after name change to Chamber of Sound. Photos by Gabe Banner.

JOHN GALBRAITH: Later the big agencies got involved. You couldn't do things the way we did them then. I did sign a couple of contracts, but they were for hip-hop, like we moved A Tribe Called Quest from Safari Club to WUST. Later on when SOIA was on In Effect I remember doing a contract for them. Rare Essence was there every other Friday.

Most of it was trust and it seemed to actually work.

SHAWNA KENNEY: I met Martin Castro and Gabe Banner in 1995 when I was working at Up Against the Wall—a hip-hop clothing store in Georgetown. They asked, "Did you used to book Safari shows?" I was like "um yeah, wow I haven't heard that name in a while." Martin told me he was doing shows there, and later that year he introduced me to Rich. We all went to a Slayer show together and then Rich invited me to come down to Safari.

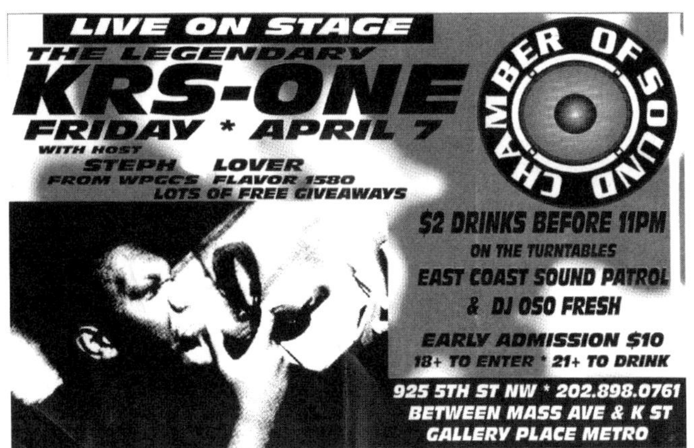

RICH DOLINGER: After the Slayer show, Shawna left her hat in my car. I asked Martin for her number. He said, "Just give me the hat. I'll get it back to her." I said, "I'm not only interested in getting her hat back to her (if you know what I mean)." Martin hooked me up, and I called her. We met at a Shelter, Earth Crisis, Baby Gopal show for the "hat exchange." I thought it was full circle bringing Shawna back to her old playground. I wanted her to feel the awe that I felt the first time I walked in there after being away for so many years.

SHAWNA KENNEY: It had been renamed Chamber of Sound. The sign was like bubbled graffiti letters. Shelter and Baby Gopal were playing. I was blown away by two things: how many girls were there compared to how it had been in the eighties, and how many people had cameras.

MARK ANDERSEN: Overall, I was pleased to see Safari Club flourish, even if a fair amount of music or attitudes didn't really speak to me. Like our own earlier scenes, it didn't have to be perfect as long as there was something real happening… The Safari scene was a way to learn, express yourself, to grow…no doubt to challenge some of the contradictions at the heart of the scene.

PHIL BAXLEY: I was brought up in a very conservative family. The hardcore scene exposed me to a lot of different points of view I wouldn't have encountered at such a young age. That was a big piece of what I got from it, all centered around the Safari Club—the PETA flyers, meeting Hare Krishnas, singing straight edge songs, and going home to drink beer, or whatever it was. It either helped you to become a huge hypocrite or helped see things from all points of view.

MARTIN CASTRO: At the end of my run was the beginning of booking agents, dealing with shitty people, and contracts. The last show was Battery for sure. That was their "welcome home" show. I did the rest of my shows at the Capital Ballroom.

SHAWNA KENNEY: I saw Haile driving a cab outside of WUST years later. I was going to a Weezer show at WUST, before it became the new 9:30 Club. He yelled to me and called me "Pam." Just like the old days, because he never seemed to be able to tell us two blonde chicks apart though we looked nothing alike.

I went alone to that first show. From that point on I've always had a community. —Zac Eller

RICH DOLINGER: I missed the final era of the Safari Club as my wife and I relocated to California in 1995. I missed Better Than A Thousand's debut show there, which also happens to be the location of the first Shelter show. I missed Chamberlain and Ashes selling the club out. But I'm grateful for the time I had. I love looking at the Start Today liner notes and seeing *Shawna and Pam Safari Club* in the "thank you list" and remembering how special that place was for all involved.

TOBY MORSE: A lot of history went down there—a lot of stuff that will never happen again.

ZAC ELLER: Every band that I was in started there. I went to every matinée to see the New York bands—this was the late eighties, early nineties. We all know what punk rock and hardcore means. It was a place for people to gather where we otherwise wouldn't have had anybody. That's what it was for me. I went alone to that first show. From that point on I've always had a community.

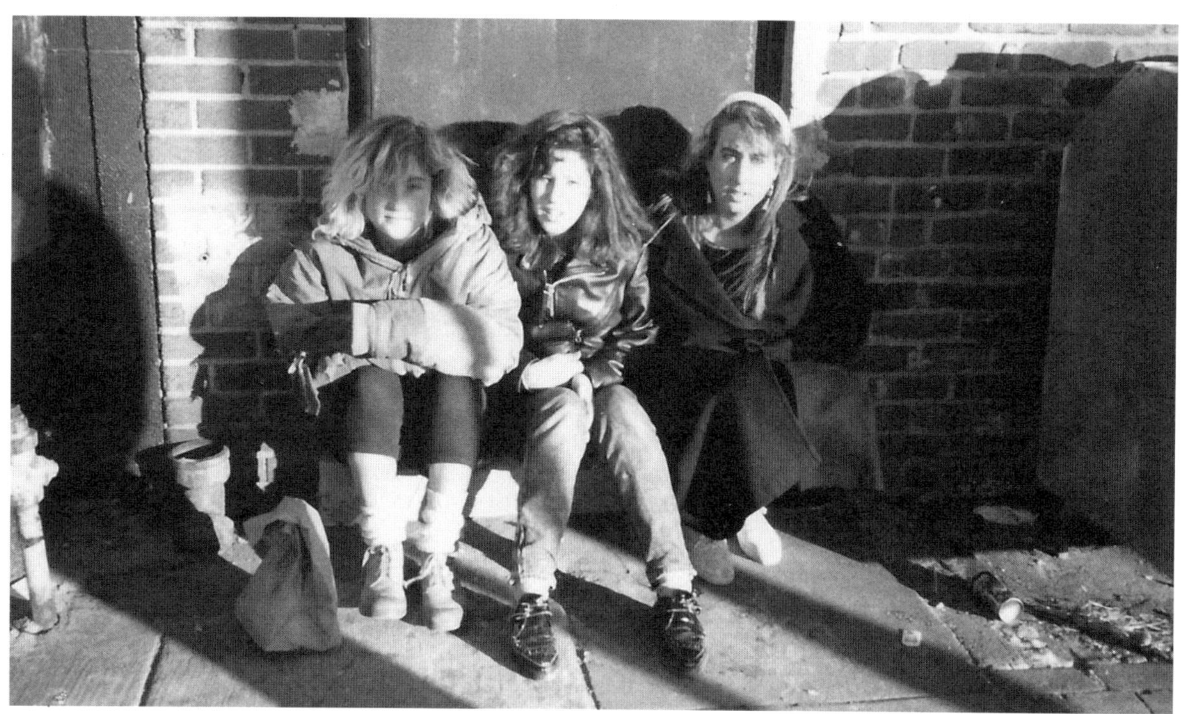

Raquel Safir, Eva Kritt, and Jen hanging outside of the club. Photo by Nathalie Sheinbein.

Cast of Characters:

Mark Adams: Deceased (guitar)

Billy Anderson: bouncer (9:30 Club)

Nathan Anderson: perpetual hardcore kid

Mark Andersen: Positive Force founder

Tommy Anthony: Four Walls Falling, Admiral (drums)

Gabe Banner: show promoter, Gauge (drums)

Chris Battista: known as "Cheesesteak"

Phil Baxley: hardcore fan

CF Best: Youth Without Hair

Pat Best: Indian Summer (vocals)

Dave Brown: Vicious Circle Records, Vinyl Ink (employee)

Cara Bruce: scenester

Matt Burger: Marathon, Worlds Collide (vocals)

Glenn Burns: hardcore fan

Rodney Butinelli: Parasite, Scooter Trash (drums)

David Byrd: Set to Explode (vocals)

Martin Castro: show promoter, 18th Amendment (creator)

Dan Cav: Resurrection, Absolution (bass)

Dave Chelsea-Siefert: retired punk rocker

Anthony Communale: Killing Time/Raw Deal (vocals)

Jordan Cooper: Revelation Records (owner)

Chuck Copeand: OG hardcore kid

Pat Crean: Goons, Musicband (vocals, guitar)

Gini Crowder-Marshall: doorperson/support staff

Alex Daniels: Swiz (drums)

Matt Dolan: American Standard (guitar)

Rich Dolinger: No Excuse, Product, Benchmark (guitar)

Sean Dorsey: Government Issue (drums)

Nam Dong: Teamster (guitar), No Excuse (vocals)

Meredith Wright-Dowell: scenester

Richi (Krakdown) Dowling: Krakdown (guitar)

John Dugan: Indian Summer, Chisel (drums)

Zac Eller: Worlds Collide, Bluetip (drums)

John Engle: hardcore kid

Jason Farrell: Swiz, Fury, Red Hare, Bluetip (guitar/vocals)

Seth Ford-Young: Initial Reaction (vocals), Tom Waits (bass)

Steve Francis: Indian Summer (vocals)

Lars Frederiksen: Rancid, UK Subs, Lars & the Bastards (vocals/guitar)

John (Cornerstone) Galbraith: show promoter, Cornerstone Records

Grant Garrettson: LD Kids, HR Band (drums)

Pam Gendell: show promoter

JR Glass: Next Step Up (vocals), promoter

Deborah Goldberg: photographer

Bradford Reid Goodwin: Askance (drums)

Andy Guida: Supertouch, Absolution (drums)

Steve Hart: Day of Suffering (guitar)

Chris Harnett: Elegant Mess (manager)

Karl "Hard Karl" Hedgepath: promoter, Hi Impact Records

Adam "Big Adam" Helfer: OG Krishna Kid, bouncer

Jon Hennessee: For the Living (vocals), promoter

Dave Hooser: hardcore kid

Russell Iglay: Underdog (bass)

Kenny Innouye: Marginal Man (guitar), promoter (9:30 Club)

Colin Kelly: hardcore kid

Shawna Kenney: promoter

Jason Kooken: hardcore kid

Mike Lars: Gut Instinct (guitar)

Nathan Larson: Swiz, Shudder to Think (bass), composer

Shane Legano: Press Your Luck, Hate-O-Four (guitar)

Ed Linton: soundman

Christopher "Chriscipline" Long: Discipline (drums)

Tom Lyle: Government Issue (bass)

Chris Lyman: Color Blind, Step Aside, Mayday (drums)

Alec MacKaye: Faith, Ignition (vocals)

Jay Martin: doorman (Safari Club)

Joseph P. McRedmond: Admiral, Hoover, The Crownhate Ruin (vocals/guitar)

Mike McTernan: Damnation AD (vocals)

Michelle Mennona: filmmaker/zinester

Heidi Minx: Franky & Minx (designer), Punk Rock Domestics (author)

Randy Moler: Step Aside (guitar)

Michael Moe: fan

Rob Moran: Unbroken, Over My Dead Body (bass)

Toby Morse: H2O (vocals)

Dan Mullahey: photographer

Ingrid Newkirk: PETA (founder/director)

Katyia Oddio: former DC printer, singer, scene supporter

Ken Olden: Damnation AD, Worlds Collide (guitar)

Anthony Olney: Barfight, scenester, doorman (9:30 Club)

Gabe Onrubia: hardcore kid

Jay Orr: Hate-O-Four, Benchmark (guitar)

Tim Owen: Jade Tree Records, Axtion Packed Records

Jason Powell: Fury for Another (vocals/guitar) artist

Sharie Powell: Fury for Another (bass)

Kurt Powers: Time Flies (vocals)

Tru Prey: Malfunction Records (owner), show promoter

Dave Saulnier: local shitbird

Miky Scheer: Four Walls Falling (bass)

Walter Schreifels: Quicksand, GB, YOT, Rival Schools, (guitar/bass/vocals)

Grant Sheehan: Gut Instinct (drums)

Sammy Siegler: GB, YOT, Rival Schools, Shelter, Judge (drums)

Moe Shorter: Junkyard Band (manager)

Ben Sizemore: Econochrist (vocals)

Arthur Smilios: GB, Token Entry, Judge (bass)

Joe Songco: Outburst (drums)

Steve Squint: scenester/Bad Brains (roadie)

Taylor Steele: Four Walls Falling (vocals)

Brien Stewart: Ruin By Design, Lickity Split, Product, Avail (vocals)

Michael Straight: punk

Kyle Style: flyer art, cover logo

Adam "A.C." Thompson: Elizabeth Herz, Device (vocals), journalist

Pete Tsouras: Fairweather (guitar)

Chuck Treece: McRad, Underdog (guitar)

Kurt Ubersax: Just Cause

Darren Walters: Jade Tree Records, Hi Impact Records

Rich Warwick: Barfight

Bryan Wassom: Sunspot Records, Two-Faced Judy (guitar)

Joe Wongananda: photographer

Steve Zeitzoff: photographer

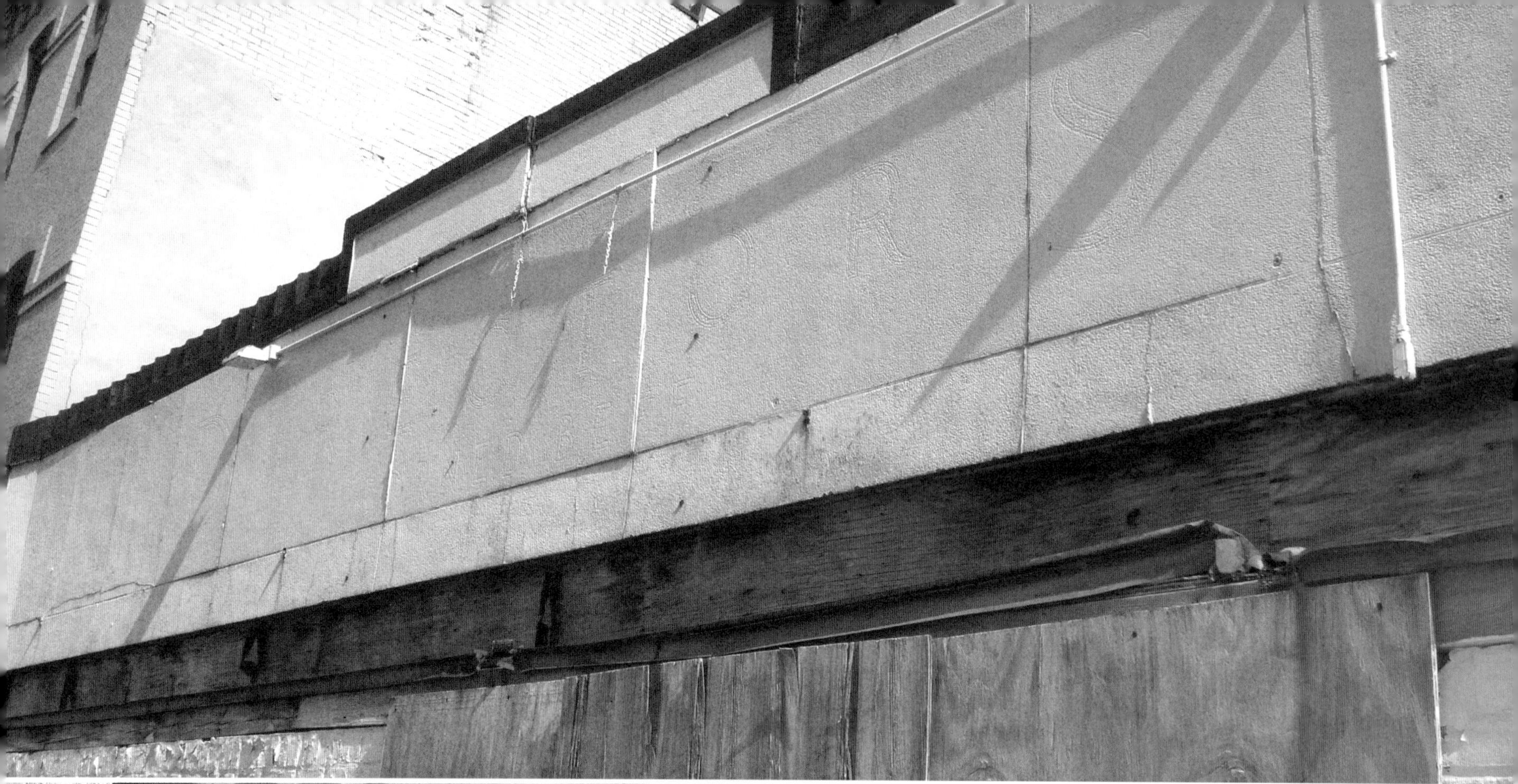

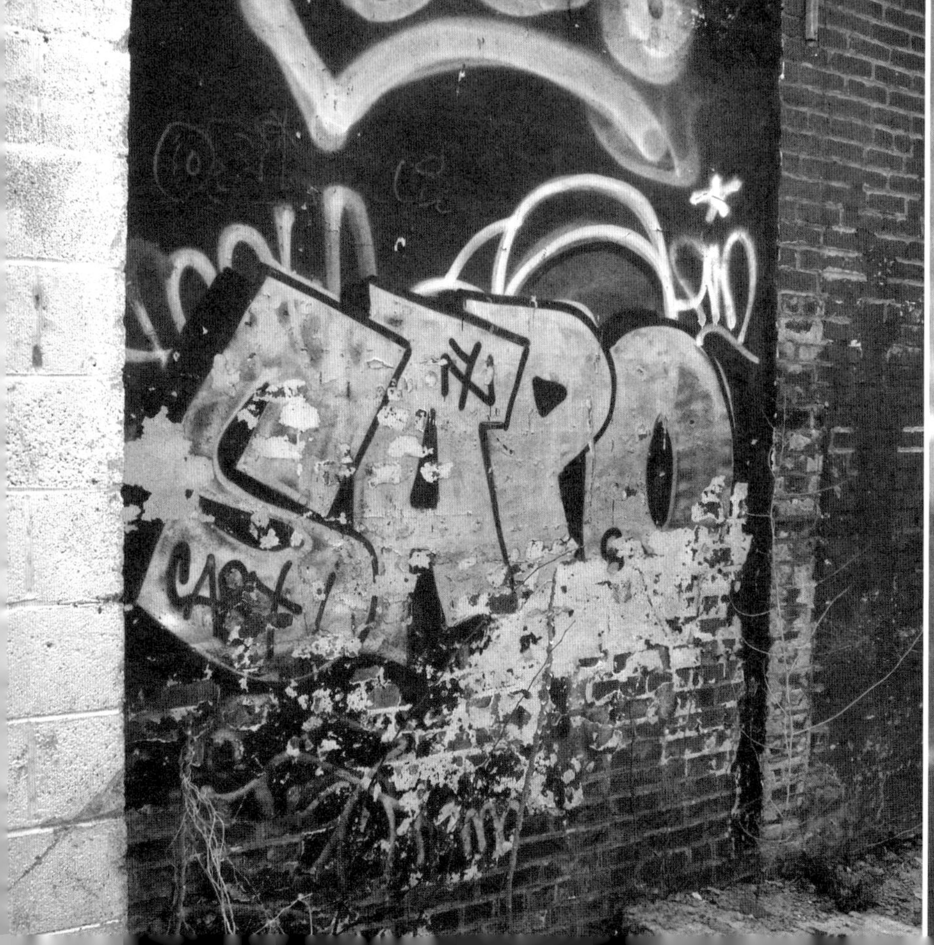

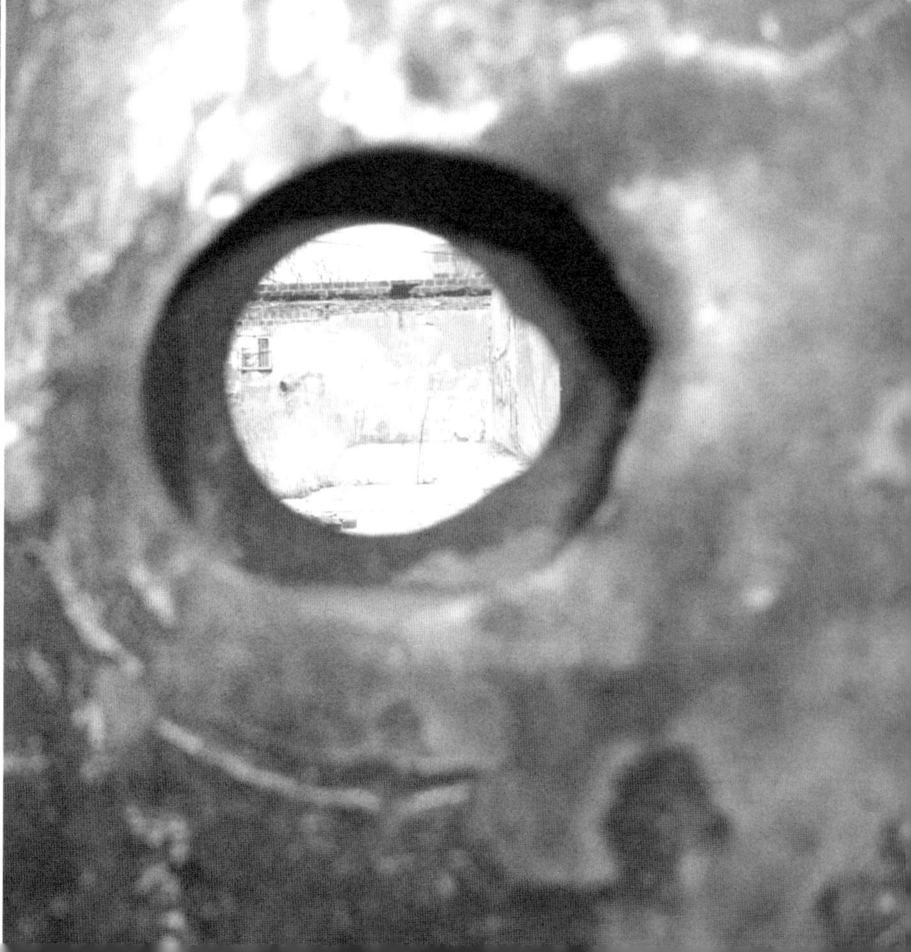

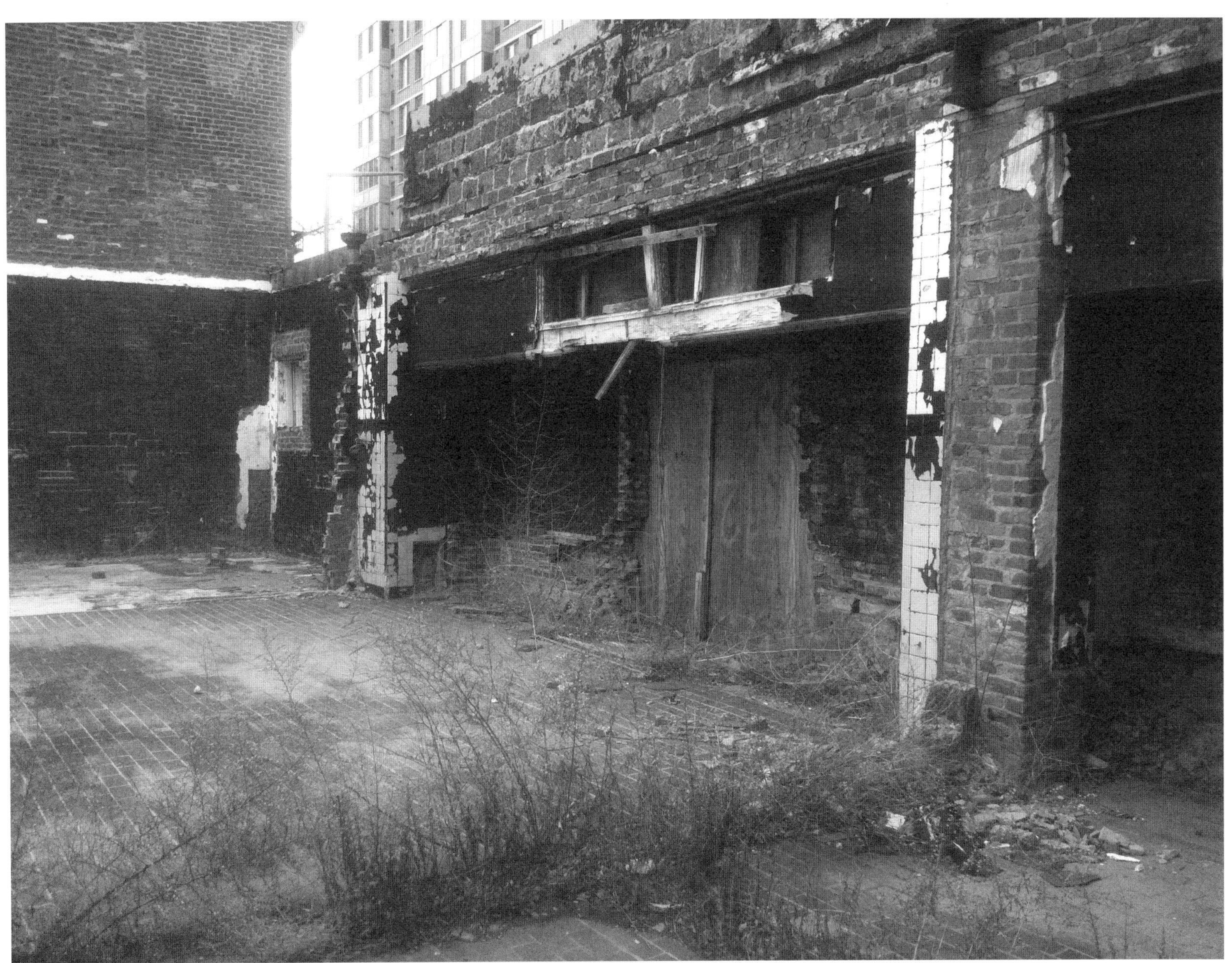

In Memorium:

Eric Allen

Andrea Ginsberg Anderson

Amy Baker

Carlos Batts

Santiago Benitez

Vance Bockis

Nate Camfiord

Skip Candelori

Randy Childs

Bob Dotolo

Todd Eckhardt

Dave Franklin

Joe Gary (Crunch)

Carlos Gordillo

Joe Graziano

Gene Hawkins

Miggy Jones

Ian Keeler

Big Bill Lanehardt

Big Rob

Adam Rutland

John Stabb

Kit Thomas

Kenny Wagner

Andy Wells

Elkin Yuen

THIS IS A GENUINE RARE BIRD BOOK

A Rare Bird Book | Rare Bird Books
453 South Spring Street, Suite 302
Los Angeles, CA 90013
rarebirdbooks.com

FIRST HARDCOVER EDITION

Set in Minion
Printed in Canada

10 9 8 7 6 5 4 3 2 1

Author photo by Kym Ghee

Book design by STARLING

Publisher's Cataloging-in-Publication data
Names: Kenney, Shawna, author. | Dolinger, Rich, author. | Thompson, A. C. (Adam Clay), foreword author.
Title: Live at the Safari Club , a history of hardcore punk in the nation's capital : 1988-1998 / Shawna Kenney with Rich Dolinger ; foreword by A. C. Thompson.
Description: First Hardcover Edition | A Barnacle Book | New York, NY; Los Angeles, CA: Rare Bird Books, 2017.
Identifiers: ISBN 9781945572456
Subjects: LCSH Punk rock music—Washington (D.C.) | Punk rock musicians. | Punk culture—History. | BISAC MUSIC / Genres & Styles / Punk
Classification: LCC ML3534.3 .K46 2017 | DDC 781.66—dc23

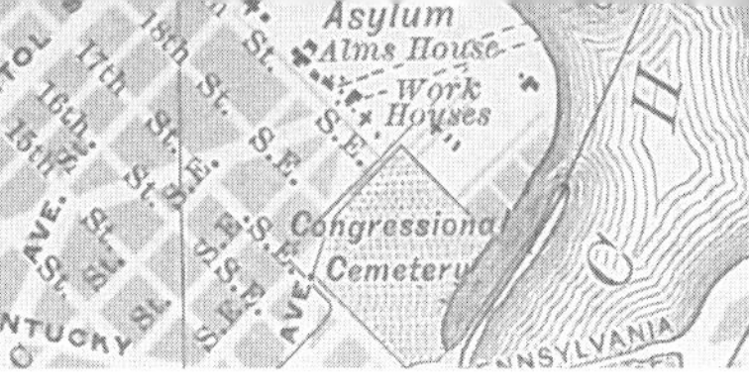

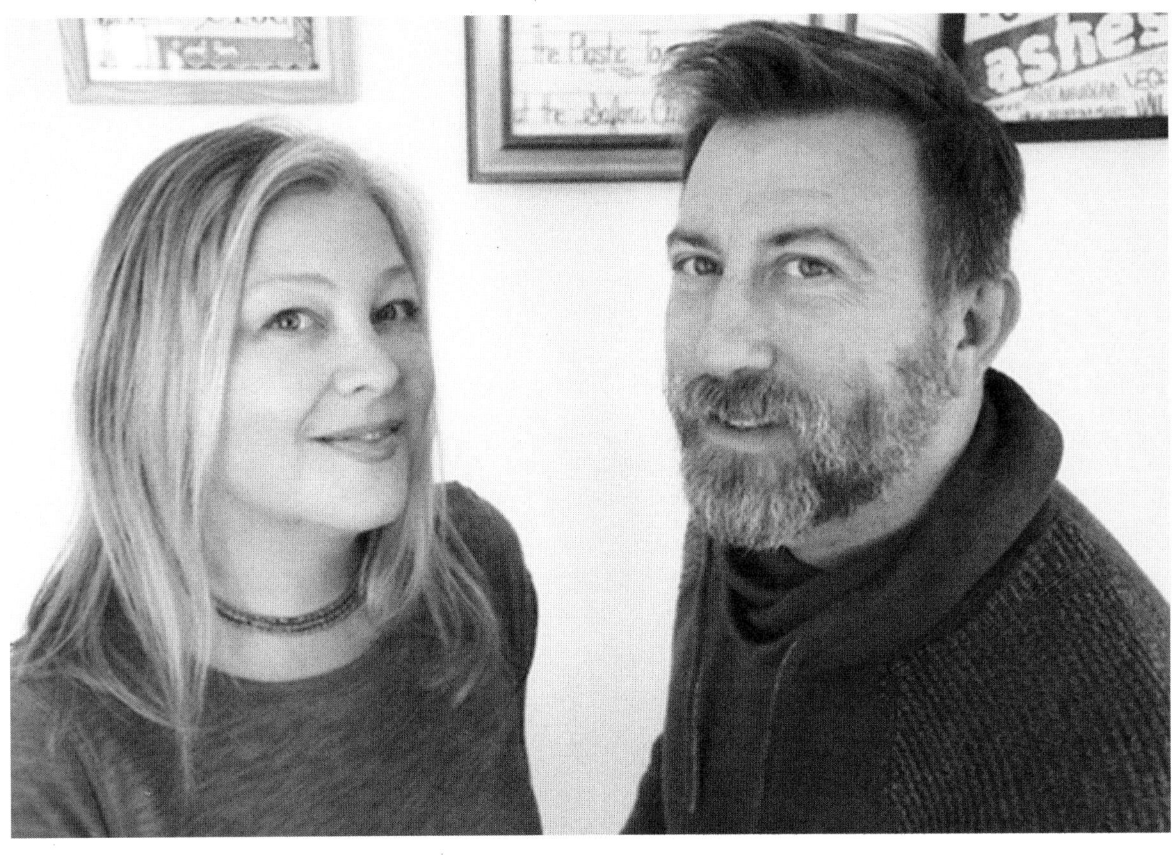

Rich Dolinger and Shawna Kenney met in Washington, DC through Safari Club promoter Martin Castro in 1995. They married in 2002 and now live in Los Angeles.

Acknowledgments

Thank you: Mark Adams, Mark Andersen, Tommy Anthony, Mark Beemer, Gabe Banner, Dave Brown, Martin Castro, Bryan Christner, Cynthia Connolly, Jordan Cooper, John Galbraith, Roger Gastman, Justin Goodman, Maggie Holliday, Eric Hochberg, Russell Iglay, Lisa Johnson, Jean Kenney, Jay Martin, Ian MacKaye, Alec MacKaye, Joseph McRedmond, Katya Oddio, Tru Prey, Steve Salardino and Skylight Books, Nathalie Sheinbein, Joe Songco, Kyle Talbott, A. C. Thompson, Chuck Treece, Kurt Ubersax, Chris Yormick, Kevin Young, Jim Wilson, Joe Wongananda, Chris Wolford and the Dethkills crew; Vacation Vinyl, Bruce Yarnall at the DC Historic Preservation Office, John Davis at the University of Maryland Michelle Smith Performing Arts Library, Michele Casto at the DC Public Library, and to every single person who took time to speak with us via phone, email, Skype, backstage, in alleys, in the backseats of cars, in diners, on front porches, on road trips or wherever. Thanks to those who went digging through personal memorabilia to help us tell this story.

Special thanks to Tyson Cornell and the whole Rare Bird Books crew for believing in us!

"LIVE AT THE SAFARI CLUB"